PySpark Cookbook

Over 60 recipes for implementing big data processing and analytics using Apache Spark and Python

Denny Lee
Tomasz Drabas

BIRMINGHAM - MUMBAI

PySpark Cookbook

Commissioning Editor: Amey Varangaonkar
Acquisition Editor: Aman Singh
Content Development Editor: Mayur Pawanikar
Technical Editor: Dinesh Pawar
Copy Editor: Safis Editing
Project Coordinator: Nidhi Joshi
Proofreader: Safis Editing
Indexer: Mariammal Chettiyar
Graphics: Tania Dutta
Production Coordinator: Shantanu Zagade

First published: June 2018

Production reference: 1280618

Published by Packt Publishing Ltd.
Livery Place
35 Livery Street
Birmingham
B3 2PB, UK.

ISBN 978-1-78883-536-7

www.packtpub.com

`mapt.io`

Mapt is an online digital library that gives you full access to over 5,000 books and videos, as well as industry leading tools to help you plan your personal development and advance your career. For more information, please visit our website.

Why subscribe?

- Spend less time learning and more time coding with practical eBooks and Videos from over 4,000 industry professionals

- Improve your learning with Skill Plans built especially for you

- Get a free eBook or video every month

- Mapt is fully searchable

- Copy and paste, print, and bookmark content

PacktPub.com

Did you know that Packt offers eBook versions of every book published, with PDF and ePub files available? You can upgrade to the eBook version at `www.PacktPub.com` and as a print book customer, you are entitled to a discount on the eBook copy. Get in touch with us at `service@packtpub.com` for more details.

At `www.PacktPub.com`, you can also read a collection of free technical articles, sign up for a range of free newsletters, and receive exclusive discounts and offers on Packt books and eBooks.

Contributors

About the authors

Denny Lee is a technology evangelist at Databricks. He is a hands-on data science engineer with 15+ years of experience. His key focuses are solving complex large-scale data problems—providing not only architectural direction but hands-on implementation of such systems. He has extensive experience of building greenfield teams as well as being a turnaround/change catalyst. Prior to joining Databricks, he was a senior director of data science engineering at Concur and was part of the incubation team that built Hadoop on Windows and Azure (currently known as HDInsight).

Tomasz Drabas is a data scientist specializing in data mining, deep learning, machine learning, choice modeling, natural language processing, and operations research. He is the author of *Learning PySpark* and *Practical Data Analysis Cookbook*. He has a PhD from University of New South Wales, School of Aviation. His research areas are machine learning and choice modeling for airline revenue management.

About the reviewer

Sridhar Alla is a big data practitioner helping companies solve complex problems in distributed computing and implement large-scale data science and analytics practice. He presents regularly at several prestigious conferences and provides training and consulting to companies. He loves writing code in Python, Scala, and Java. He has extensive hands-on knowledge of several Hadoop-based technologies, Spark, machine learning, deep learning and blockchain.

Packt is searching for authors like you

If you're interested in becoming an author for Packt, please visit `authors.packtpub.com` and apply today. We have worked with thousands of developers and tech professionals, just like you, to help them share their insight with the global tech community. You can make a general application, apply for a specific hot topic that we are recruiting an author for, or submit your own idea.

Table of Contents

Preface

Apache Spark is an open source framework for efficient cluster computing with a strong interface for data parallelism and fault tolerance. This book presents effective and time-saving recipes for leveraging the power of Python and putting it to use in the Spark ecosystem.

You'll start by learning about the Apache Spark architecture and seeing how to set up a Python environment for Spark. You'll then get familiar with the modules available in PySpark and start using them effortlessly. In addition to this, you'll discover how to abstract data with RDDs and DataFrames, and understand the streaming capabilities of PySpark. You'll then move on to using ML and MLlib in order to solve any problems related to the machine learning capabilities of PySpark, and you'll use GraphFrames to solve graph-processing problems. Finally, you will explore how to deploy your applications to the cloud using the spark-submit command.

By the end of this book, you will be able to use the Python API for Apache Spark to solve any problems associated with building data-intensive applications.

Who this book is for

This book is for you if you are a Python developer looking for hands-on recipes for using the Apache Spark 2.x ecosystem in the best possible way. A thorough understanding of Python (and some familiarity with Spark) will help you get the best out of the book.

What this book covers

Chapter 1, *Installing and Configuring Spark*, shows us how to install and configure Spark, either as a local instance, as a multi-node cluster, or in a virtual environment.

Chapter 2, *Abstracting Data with RDDs*, covers how to work with Apache Spark Resilient Distributed Datasets (RDDs).

Chapter 3, *Abstracting Data with DataFrames*, explores the current fundamental data structure—DataFrames.

Chapter 4, *Preparing Data for Modeling*, covers how to clean up your data and prepare it for modeling.

Chapter 5, *Machine Learning with MLlib*, shows how to build machine learning models with PySpark's MLlib module.

Chapter 6, *Machine Learning with the ML Module*, moves on to the currently supported machine learning module of PySpark—the ML module.

Chapter 7, *Structured Streaming with PySpark*, covers how to work with Apache Spark structured streaming within PySpark.

Chapter 8, *GraphFrames – Graph Theory with PySpark*, shows how to work with GraphFrames for Apache Spark.

To get the most out of this book

You need the following to smoothly work through the chapters:

- Apache Spark (downloadable from `http://spark.apache.org/downloads.html`)
- Python

Download the example code files

You can download the example code files for this book from your account at `www.packtpub.com`. If you purchased this book elsewhere, you can visit `www.packtpub.com/support` and register to have the files emailed directly to you.

You can download the code files by following these steps:

1. Log in or register at `www.packtpub.com`.
2. Select the **SUPPORT** tab.
3. Click on **Code Downloads & Errata**.
4. Enter the name of the book in the **Search** box and follow the onscreen instructions.

Once the file is downloaded, please make sure that you unzip or extract the folder using the latest version of:

- WinRAR/7-Zip for Windows
- Zipeg/iZip/UnRarX for Mac
- 7-Zip/PeaZip for Linux

The code bundle for the book is also hosted on GitHub at https://github.com/ PacktPublishing/PySpark-Cookbook. In case there's an update to the code, it will be updated on the existing GitHub repository.

We also have other code bundles from our rich catalog of books and videos available at https://github.com/PacktPublishing/. Check them out!

Download the color images

We also provide a PDF file that has color images of the screenshots/diagrams used in this book. You can download it here: https://www.packtpub.com/sites/default/files/ downloads/PySparkCookbook_ColorImages.pdf.

Conventions used

There are a number of text conventions used throughout this book.

CodeInText: Indicates code words in text, database table names, folder names, filenames, file extensions, pathnames, dummy URLs, user input, and Twitter handles. Here is an example: "Next, we call three functions: printHeader, checkJava, and checkPython."

A block of code is set as follows:

```
if [ "${_check_R_req}" = "true" ]; then
 checkR
fi
```

When we wish to draw your attention to a particular part of a code block, the relevant lines or items are set in bold:

```
if [ "$_machine" = "Mac" ]; then
    curl -O $_spark_source
elif [ "$_machine" = "Linux"]; then
    wget $_spark_source
```

Any command-line input or output is written as follows:

```
tar -xvf sbt-1.0.4.tgz
sudo mv sbt-1.0.4/ /opt/scala/
```

Bold: Indicates a new term, an important word, or words that you see onscreen. For example, words in menus or dialog boxes appear in the text like this. Here is an example: "Go to **File** | **Import appliance**; click on the button next to the path selection."

 Warnings or important notes appear like this.

 Tips and tricks appear like this.

Sections

In this book, you will find several headings that appear frequently (*Getting ready*, *How to do it...*, *How it works...*, *There's more...*, and *See also*).

To give clear instructions on how to complete a recipe, use these sections as follows:

Getting ready

This section tells you what to expect in the recipe and describes how to set up any software or any preliminary settings required for the recipe.

How to do it...

This section contains the steps required to follow the recipe.

How it works...

This section usually consists of a detailed explanation of what happened in the previous section.

There's more...

This section consists of additional information about the recipe in order to make you more knowledgeable about the recipe.

See also

This section provides helpful links to other useful information for the recipe.

Get in touch

Feedback from our readers is always welcome.

General feedback: Email `feedback@packtpub.com` and mention the book title in the subject of your message. If you have questions about any aspect of this book, please email us at `questions@packtpub.com`.

Errata: Although we have taken every care to ensure the accuracy of our content, mistakes do happen. If you have found a mistake in this book, we would be grateful if you would report this to us. Please visit `www.packtpub.com/submit-errata`, selecting your book, clicking on the Errata Submission Form link, and entering the details.

Piracy: If you come across any illegal copies of our works in any form on the internet, we would be grateful if you would provide us with the location address or website name. Please contact us at `copyright@packtpub.com` with a link to the material.

If you are interested in becoming an author: If there is a topic that you have expertise in and you are interested in either writing or contributing to a book, please visit `authors.packtpub.com`.

Reviews

Please leave a review. Once you have read and used this book, why not leave a review on the site that you purchased it from? Potential readers can then see and use your unbiased opinion to make purchase decisions, we at Packt can understand what you think about our products, and our authors can see your feedback on their book. Thank you!

For more information about Packt, please visit `packtpub.com`.

Installing and Configuring Spark

1

In this chapter, we will cover how to install and configure Spark, either as a local instance, a multi-node cluster, or in a virtual environment. You will learn the following recipes:

- Installing Spark requirements
- Installing Spark from sources
- Installing Spark from binaries
- Configuring a local instance of Spark
- Configuring a multi-node instance of Spark
- Installing Jupyter
- Configuring a session in Jupyter
- Working with Cloudera Spark images

Introduction

We cannot begin a book on Spark (well, on PySpark) without first specifying what Spark is. Spark is a powerful, flexible, open source, data processing and querying engine. It is extremely easy to use and provides the means to solve a huge variety of problems, ranging from processing unstructured, semi-structured, or structured data, through streaming, up to machine learning. With over 1,000 contributors from over 250 organizations (not to mention over 3,000 Spark Meetup community members worldwide), Spark is now one of the largest open source projects in the portfolio of the Apache Software Foundation.

The origins of Spark can be found in 2012 when it was first released; Matei Zacharia developed the first versions of the Spark processing engine at UC Berkeley as part of his PhD thesis. Since then, Spark has become extremely popular, and its popularity stems from a number of reasons:

- **It is fast**: It is estimated that Spark is 100 times faster than Hadoop when working purely in memory, and around 10 times faster when reading or writing data to a disk.
- **It is flexible**: You can leverage the power of Spark from a number of programming languages; Spark natively supports interfaces in Scala, Java, Python, and R.
- **It is extendible**: As Spark is an open source package, you can easily extend it by introducing your own classes or extending the existing ones.
- **It is powerful**: Many machine learning algorithms are already implemented in Spark so you do not need to add more tools to your stack—most of the data engineering and data science tasks can be accomplished while working in a single environment.
- **It is familiar**: Data scientists and data engineers, who are accustomed to using Python's `pandas`, or R's `data.frames` or `data.tables`, should have a much gentler learning curve (although the differences between these data types exist). Moreover, if you know SQL, you can also use it to wrangle data in Spark!
- **It is scalable**: Spark can run locally on your machine (with all the limitations such a solution entails). However, the same code that runs locally can be deployed to a cluster of thousands of machines with little-to-no changes.

For the remainder of this book, we will assume that you are working in a Unix-like environment such as Linux (throughout this book, we will use Ubuntu Server 16.04 LTS) or macOS (running macOS High Sierra); all the code provided has been tested in these two environments. For this chapter (and some other ones, too), an internet connection is also required as we will be downloading a bunch of binaries and sources from the internet.

 We will not be focusing on installing Spark in a Windows environment as it is not truly supported by the Spark developers. However, if you are inclined to try, you can follow some of the instructions you will find online, such as from the following link: `http://bit.ly/2Ar75ld`.

Knowing how to use the command line and how to set some environment variables on your system is useful, but not really required—we will guide you through the steps.

Installing Spark requirements

Spark requires a handful of environments to be present on your machine before you can install and use it. In this recipe, we will focus on getting your machine ready for Spark installation.

Getting ready

To execute this recipe, you will need a bash Terminal and an internet connection.

Also, before we start any work, you should clone the GitHub repository for this book. The repository contains all the codes (in the form of notebooks) and all the data you will need to follow the examples in this book. To clone the repository, go to `http://bit.ly/2ArlBck`, click on the **Clone or download** button, and copy the URL that shows up by clicking on the icon next to it:

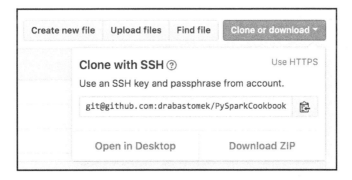

Next, go to your Terminal and issue the following command:

```
git clone git@github.com:drabastomek/PySparkCookbook.git
```

If your `git` environment is set up properly, the whole GitHub repository should clone to your disk. No other prerequisites are required.

How to do it...

There are just truly two main requirements for installing PySpark: Java and Python. Additionally, you can also install Scala and R if you want to use those languages, and we will also check for Maven, which we will use to compile the Spark sources.

To do this, we will use the `checkRequirements.sh` script to check for all the requirements: the script is located in the `Chapter01` folder from the GitHub repository.

The following code block shows the high-level portions of the script found in the `Chapter01/checkRequirements.sh` file. Note that some portions of the code were omitted here for brevity:

```bash
#!/bin/bash

# Shell script for checking the dependencies
#
# PySpark Cookbook
# Author: Tomasz Drabas, Denny Lee
# Version: 0.1
# Date: 12/2/2017

_java_required=1.8
_python_required=3.4
_r_required=3.1
_scala_required=2.11
_mvn_required=3.3.9

# parse command line arguments
_args_len="$#"
...

printHeader
checkJava
checkPython

if [ "${_check_R_req}" = "true" ]; then
  checkR
fi

if [ "${_check_Scala_req}" = "true" ]; then
  checkScala
fi

if [ "${_check_Maven_req}" = "true" ]; then
  checkMaven
fi
```

How it works...

First, we will specify all the required packages and their required minimum versions; looking at the preceding code, you can see that Spark 2.3.1 requires Java 1.8+ and Python 3.4 or higher (and we will always be checking for these two environments). Additionally, if you want to use R or Scala, the minimal requirements for these two packages are 3.1 and 2.11, respectively. Maven, as mentioned earlier, will be used to compile the Spark sources, and for doing that, Spark requires at least the 3.3.9 version of Maven.

 You can check the Spark requirements here: https://spark.apache.org/docs/latest/index.html
You can check the requirements for building Spark here: https://spark.apache.org/docs/latest/building-spark.html.

Next, we parse the command-line arguments:

```
if [ "$_args_len" -ge 0 ]; then
  while [[ "$#" -gt 0 ]]
  do
   key="$1"
   case $key in
    -m|--Maven)
    _check_Maven_req="true"
    shift # past argument
    ;;
    -r|--R)
    _check_R_req="true"
    shift # past argument
    ;;
    -s|--Scala)
    _check_Scala_req="true"
    shift # past argument
    ;;
    *)
    shift # past argument
   esac
  done
 fi
```

You, as a user, can specify whether you want to check additionally for R, Scala, and Maven dependencies. To do so, run the following code from your command line (the following code will check for all of them):

```
./checkRequirements.sh -s -m -r
```

The following is also a perfectly valid usage:

```
./checkRequirements.sh --Scala --Maven --R
```

Next, we call three functions: `printHeader`, `checkJava`, and `checkPython`. The `printHeader` function is nothing more than just a simple way for the script to state what it does and it really is not that interesting, so we will skip it here; it is, however, fairly self-explanatory, so you are welcome to peruse the relevant portions of the `checkRequirements.sh` script yourself.

Next, we will check whether Java is installed. First, we just print to the Terminal that we are performing checks on Java (this is common across all of our functions, so we will only mention it here):

```
function checkJava() {
  echo
  echo "##########################"
  echo
  echo "Checking Java"
  echo
```

Following this, we will check if the Java environment is installed on your machine:

```
if type -p java; then
  echo "Java executable found in PATH"
  _java=java
elif [[ -n "$JAVA_HOME" ]] && [[ -x "$JAVA_HOME/bin/java" ]]; then
  echo "Found Java executable in JAVA_HOME"
  _java="$JAVA_HOME/bin/java"
else
  echo "No Java found. Install Java version $_java_required or higher first
or specify JAVA_HOME variable that will point to your Java binaries."
  exit
fi
```

First, we use the `type` command to check if the `java` command is available; the `type -p` command returns the location of the `java` binary if it exists. This also implies that the `bin` folder containing Java binaries has been added to the `PATH`.

> If you are certain you have the binaries installed (be it Java, Python, R, Scala, or Maven), you can jump to the *Updating PATH* section in this recipe to see how to let your computer know where these binaries live.

If this fails, we will revert to checking if the JAVA_HOME environment variable is set, and if it is, we will try to see if it contains the required java binary: [[-x "$JAVA_HOME/bin/java"]]. Should this fail, the program will print the message that no Java environment could be found and will exit (without checking for other required packages, like Python).

If, however, the Java binary is found, then we can check its version:

```
_java_version=$("$_java" -version 2>&1 | awk -F '"' '/version/ {print $2}')
echo "Java version: $_java_version (min.: $_java_required)"

if [[ "$_java_version" < "$_java_required" ]]; then
 echo "Java version required is $_java_required. Install the required
version first."
 exit
fi
 echo
```

We first execute the java -version command in the Terminal, which would normally produce an output similar to the following screenshot:

```
endeavor:Chapter01 drabast$ java -version
java version "1.8.0_25"
Java(TM) SE Runtime Environment (build 1.8.0_25-b17)
Java HotSpot(TM) 64-Bit Server VM (build 25.25-b02, mixed mode)
```

We then pipe the previous output to awk to split (the -F switch) the rows at the quote '"' character (and will only use the first line of the output as we filter the rows down to those that contain /version/) and take the second (the $2) element as the version of the Java binaries installed on our machine. We will store it in the _java_version variable, which we also print to the screen using the echo command.

> If you do not know what awk is or how to use it, we recommend this book from Packt: http://bit.ly/2BtTcBV.

Finally, we check if the _java_version we just obtained is lower than _java_required. If this evaluates to true, we will stop the execution, instead telling you to install the required version of Java.

The logic implemented in the `checkPython`, `checkR`, `checkScala`, and `checkMaven` functions follows in a very similar way. The only differences are in what binary we call and in the way we check the versions:

- For Python, we run `"$_python" --version 2>&1 | awk -F ' ' '{print $2}'`, as checking the Python version (for Anaconda distribution) would print out the following to the screen: **Python 3.5.2 :: Anaconda 2.4.1 (x86_64)**
- For R, we use `"$_r" --version 2>&1 | awk -F ' ' '/R version/ {print $3}'`, as checking the R's version would write (a lot) to the screen; we only use the line that starts with `R version`: **R version 3.4.2 (2017-09-28) -- "Short Summer"**
- For Scala, we utilize `"$_scala" -version 2>&1 | awk F ' ' '{print $5}'`, given that checking Scala's version prints the following: **Scala code runner version 2.11.8 -- Copyright 2002-2016, LAMP/EPFL**
- For Maven, we check `"$_mvn" --version 2>&1 | awk -F ' ' '/Apache Maven/ {print $3}'`, as Maven prints out the following (and more!) when asked for its version: **Apache Maven 3.5.2 (138edd61fd100ec658bfa2d307c43b76940a5d7d; 2017-10-18T00:58:13-07:00)**

If you want to learn more, you should now be able to read the other functions with ease.

There's more...

If any of your dependencies are not installed, you need to install them before continuing with the next recipe. It goes beyond the scope of this book to guide you step-by-step through the installation process of all of these, but here are some helpful links to show you how to do it.

Installing Java

Installing Java is pretty straightforward.

On macOS, go to `https://www.java.com/en/download/mac_download.jsp` and download the version appropriate for your system. Once downloaded, follow the instructions to install it on your machine. If you require more detailed instructions, check this link: `http://bit.ly/2idEozX`.

On Linux, check the following link `http://bit.ly/2jGwuz1` for Linux Java installation instructions.

Installing Python

We have been using (and highly recommend) the Anaconda version of Python as it comes with the most commonly used packages included with the installer. It also comes built-in with the `conda` package management tool that makes installing other packages a breeze.

You can download Anaconda from `http://www.continuum.io/downloads`; select the appropriate version that will fulfill Spark's requirements. For macOS installation instructions, you can go to `http://bit.ly/2zZPuUf` and for a Linux installation manual check, you can go to `http://bit.ly/2ASLUvg`.

Installing R

R is distributed via **Comprehensive R Archive Network (CRAN)**. The macOS version can be downloaded from here, `https://cran.r-project.org/bin/macosx/`, whereas the Linux one is available here: `https://cran.r-project.org/bin/linux/`.

Download the version appropriate for your machine and follow the installation instructions on the screen. For the macOS version, you can choose to install just the R core packages without the GUI and everything else as Spark does not require those.

Installing Scala

Installing Scala is even simpler.

Go to `http://bit.ly/2Am757R` and download the `sbt-*.*.*.tgz` archive (at the time of writing this book, the latest version is `sbt-1.0.4.tgz`). Next, in your Terminal, navigate to the folder you have just downloaded Scala to and issue the following commands:

```
tar -xvf sbt-1.0.4.tgz
sudo mv sbt-1.0.4/ /opt/scala/
```

That's it. Now, you can skip to the *Updating PATH* section in this recipe to update your `PATH`.

Installing Maven

Maven's installation is quite similar to that of Scala. Go to `https://maven.apache.org/download.cgi` and download the `apache-maven-*.*.*-bin.tar.gz` archive. At the time of writing this book, the newest version was 3.5.2. Similarly to Scala, open the Terminal, navigate to the folder you have just downloaded the archive to, and type:

```
tar -xvf apache-maven-3.5.2-bin.tar.gz

sudo mv apache-maven-3.5.2-bin/ /opt/apache-maven/
```

Once again, that is it for what you need to do with regards to installing Maven. Check the next subsection for instructions on how to update your PATH.

Updating PATH

Unix-like operating systems (Windows, too) use the concept of a PATH to search for binaries (or executables, in the case of Windows). The PATH is nothing more than a list of folders separated by the colon character ' : ' that tells the operating system where to look for binaries.

To add something to your PATH (and make it a permanent change), you need to edit either the `.bash_profile` (macOS) or `.bashrc` (Linux) files; these are located in the root folder for your user. Thus, to add both Scala and Maven binaries to the PATH, you can do the following (on macOS):

```
cp ~/.bash_profile ~/.bash_profile_old   # make a copy just in case

echo export SCALA_HOME=/opt/scala >> ~/.bash_profile

echo export MAVEN_HOME=/opt/apache-maven >> ~/.bash_profile

echo PATH=$SCALA_HOME/bin:$MAVEN_HOME/bin:$PATH >> ~/.bash_profile
```

On Linux, the equivalent looks as follows:

```
cp ~/.bashrc ~/.bashrc_old   # make a copy just in case

echo export SCALA_HOME=/opt/scala >> ~/.bashrc

echo export MAVEN_HOME=/opt/apache-maven >> ~/.bashrc

echo PATH=$SCALA_HOME/bin:$MAVEN_HOME/bin:$PATH >> ~/.bashrc
```

The preceding commands simply append to the end of either of the `.bash_profile` or `.bashrc` files using the redirection operator `>>`.

Once you execute the preceding commands, restart your Terminal, and:

```
echo $PATH
```

It should now include paths to both the Scala and Maven binaries.

Installing Spark from sources

Spark is distributed in two ways: either as precompiled binaries or as a source code that gives you the flexibility to choose, for example, whether you need support for Hive or not. In this recipe, we will focus on the latter.

Getting ready

To execute this recipe, you will need a bash Terminal and an internet connection. Also, to follow through with this recipe, you will have to have already checked and/or installed all the required environments we went through in the previous recipe. In addition, you need to have administrative privileges (via the `sudo` command) which will be necessary to move the compiled binaries to the destination folder.

If you are not an administrator on your machine, you can call the script with the `-ns` (or `--nosudo`) parameter. The destination folder will then switch to your home directory and will create a `spark` folder within it. By default, the binaries will be moved to the `/opt/spark` folder and that's why you need administrative rights.

No other prerequisites are required.

How to do it...

There are five major steps we will undertake to install Spark from sources (check the highlighted portions of the code):

1. Download the sources from Spark's website
2. Unpack the archive

3. Build
4. Move to the final destination
5. Create the necessary environmental variables

The skeleton for our code looks as follows (see the `Chapter01/installFromSource.sh` file):

```bash
#!/bin/bash

# Shell script for installing Spark from sources
#
# PySpark Cookbook
# Author: Tomasz Drabas, Denny Lee
# Version: 0.1
# Date: 12/2/2017

_spark_source="http://mirrors.ocf.berkeley.edu/apache/spark/spark-2.3.1/spark-2.3.1.tgz"
_spark_archive=$( echo "$_spark_source" | awk -F '/' '{print $NF}' )
_spark_dir=$( echo "${_spark_archive%.*}" )
_spark_destination="/opt/spark"

...

checkOS
printHeader
downloadThePackage
unpack
build
moveTheBinaries
setSparkEnvironmentVariables
cleanUp
```

How it works...

First, we specify the location of Spark's source code. The `_spark_archive` contains the name of the archive; we use `awk` to extract the last element (here, it is specified by the `$NF` flag) from the `_spark_source`. The `_spark_dir` contains the name of the directory our archive will unpack into; in our current case, this will be `spark-2.3.1`. Finally, we specify our destination folder where we will be going to move the binaries to: it will either be `/opt/spark` (default) or your home directory if you use the `-ns` (or `--nosudo`) switch when calling the `./installFromSource.sh` script.

Next, we check the OS name we are using:

```
function checkOS(){
  _uname_out="$(uname -s)"
  case "$_uname_out" in
    Linux*) _machine="Linux";;
    Darwin*) _machine="Mac";;
    *) _machine="UNKNOWN:${_uname_out}"
  esac

  if [ "$_machine" = "UNKNOWN:${_uname_out}" ]; then
    echo "Machine $_machine. Stopping."
    exit
  fi
}
```

First, we get the short name of the operating system using the `uname` command; the `-s` switch returns a shortened version of the OS name. As mentioned earlier, we only focus on two operating systems: macOS and Linux, so if you try to run this script on Windows or any other system, it will stop. This portion of the code is necessary to set the `_machine` flag properly: macOS and Linux use different methods to download the Spark source codes and different bash profile files to set the environment variables.

Next, we print out the header (we will skip the code for this part here, but you are welcome to check the `Chapter01/installFromSource.sh` script). Following this, we download the necessary source codes:

```
function downloadThePackage() {
  ...
  if [ -d _temp ]; then
     sudo rm -rf _temp
  fi

  mkdir _temp
  cd _temp

  if [ "$_machine" = "Mac" ]; then
     curl -O $_spark_source
  elif [ "$_machine" = "Linux"]; then
     wget $_spark_source
  else
     echo "System: $_machine not supported."
     exit
  fi

}
```

First, we check whether a `_temp` folder exists and, if it does, we delete it. Next, we recreate an empty `_temp` folder and download the sources into it; on macOS, we use the `curl` method while on Linux, we use `wget` to download the sources.

 Did you notice the ellipsis '...' character in our code? Whenever we use such a character, we omit some less relevant or purely informational portions of the code. They are still present, though, in the sources checked into the GitHub repository.

Once the sources land on our machine, we unpack them using the `tar` tool, `tar -xf $_spark_archive`. This happens inside the `unpack` function.

Finally, we can start building the sources into binaries:

```
function build(){
  ...

  cd "$_spark_dir"
  ./dev/make-distribution.sh --name pyspark-cookbook -Phadoop-2.7 -Phive -
Phive-thriftserver -Pyarn

}
```

We use the `make-distribution.sh` script (distributed with Spark) to create our own Spark distribution, named `pyspark-cookbook`. The previous command will build the Spark distribution for Hadoop 2.7 and with Hive support. We will also be able to deploy it over YARN. Underneath the hood, the `make-distribution.sh` script is using Maven to compile the sources.

Once the compilation finishes, we need to move the binaries to the `_spark_destination` folder:

```
function moveTheBinaries() {

  ...
  if [ -d "$_spark_destination" ]; then
     sudo rm -rf "$_spark_destination"
  fi

  cd ..
  sudo mv $_spark_dir/ $_spark_destination/

}
```

First, we check if the folder in the destination exists and, if it does, we remove it. Next, we simply move (mv) the `$_spark_dir` folder to its new home.

> This is when you will need to type in the password if you did not use the `-ns` (or `--nosudo`) flag when invoking the `installFromSource.sh` script.

One of the last steps is to add new environment variables to your bash profile file:

```
function setSparkEnvironmentVariables() {
...

if [ "$_machine" = "Mac" ]; then
    _bash=~/.bash_profile
else
    _bash=~/.bashrc
fi
_today=$( date +%Y-%m-%d )

# make a copy just in case
if ! [ -f "$_bash.spark_copy" ]; then
        cp "$_bash" "$_bash.spark_copy"
fi

echo >> $_bash
echo "##################################################" >> $_bash
echo "# SPARK environment variables" >> $_bash
echo "#" >> $_bash
echo "# Script: installFromSource.sh" >> $_bash
echo "# Added on: $_today" >>$_bash
echo >> $_bash

echo "export SPARK_HOME=$_spark_destination" >> $_bash
echo "export PYSPARK_SUBMIT_ARGS=\"--master local[4]\"" >> $_bash
echo "export PYSPARK_PYTHON=$(type -p python)" >> $_bash
echo "export PYSPARK_DRIVER_PYTHON=jupyter" >> $_bash

 echo "export PYSPARK_DRIVER_PYTHON_OPTS=\"notebook --
NotebookApp.open_browser=False --NotebookApp.port=6661\"" >> $_bash

 echo "export PATH=$SPARK_HOME/bin:\$PATH" >> $_bash
}
```

First, we check what OS system we're on and select the appropriate bash profile file. We also grab the current date (the `_today` variable) so that we can include that information in our bash profile file, and create its safe copy (just in case, and if one does not already exist). Next, we start to append new lines to the bash profile file:

- We first set the `SPARK_HOME` variable to the `_spark_destination`; this is either going to be the `/opt/spark` or `~/spark` location.
- The `PYSPARK_SUBMIT_ARGS` variable is used when you invoke `pyspark`. It instructs Spark to use four cores of your CPU; changing it to `--master local[*]` will use all the available cores.
- We specify the `PYSPARK_PYTHON` variable so, in case of multiple Python installations present on the machine, `pyspark` will use the one that we checked for in the first recipe.
- Setting the `PYSPARK_DRIVER_PYTHON` to `jupyter` will start a Jupyter session (instead of the PySpark interactive shell).
- The `PYSPARK_DRIVER_PYTHON_OPS` instructs Jupyter to:
  - Start a `notebook`
  - Do not open the browser by default: use the `--NotebookApp.open_browser=False` flag
  - Change the default port (`8888`) to `6661` (because we are big fans of not having things at default for safety reasons)

Finally, we add the `bin` folder from `SPARK_HOME` to the `PATH`.

The last step is to `cleanUp` after ourselves; we simply remove the `_temp` folder with everything in it.

Now that we have installed Spark, let's test if everything works. First, in order to make all the environment variables accessible in the Terminal's session, we need to refresh the `bash` session: you can either close and reopen the Terminal, or execute the following command (on macOS):

```
source ~/.bash_profile
```

On Linux, execute the following command:

```
source ~/.bashrc
```

Next, you should be able to execute the following:

```
pyspark --version
```

If all goes well, you should see a response similar to the one shown in the following screenshot:

```
[endeavor:Chapter03 drabast$ pyspark --version
Welcome to

      ____              __
     / __/__  ___ _____/ /__
    _\ \/ _ \/ _ `/ __/  '_/
   /__ / .__/\_,_/_/ /_/\_\   version 2.3.0
      /_/

Using Scala version 2.11.8, Java HotSpot(TM) 64-Bit Server VM, 1.8.0_25
Branch master
Compiled by user sameera on 2018-02-22T19:24:29Z
Revision a0d7949896e70f427e7f3942ff340c9484ff0aab
Url git@github.com:sameeragarwal/spark.git
Type --help for more information.
```

There's more...

Instead of using the `make-distribution.sh` script from Spark, you can use Maven directly to compile the sources. For instance, if you wanted to build the default version of Spark, you could simply type (from the `_spark_dir` folder):

```
./build/mvn clean package
```

This would default to Hadoop 2.6. If your version of Hadoop was 2.7.2 and was deployed over YARN, you can do the following:

```
./build/mvn -Pyarn -Phadoop-2.7 -Dhadoop.version=2.7.2 -DskipTests clean
package
```

You can also use Scala to build Spark:

```
./build/sbt package
```

See also

- If you want to study more on how to build and/or enable certain features of Spark, check Spark's website: http://spark.apache.org/docs/latest/building-spark.html

Installing Spark from binaries

Installing Spark from already precompiled binaries is even easier than doing the same from the sources. In this recipe, we will show you how to do this by downloading the binaries from the web or by using `pip`.

Getting ready

To execute this recipe, you will need a bash Terminal and an internet connection. Also, to follow through with this recipe, you will need to have already checked and/or installed all the required environments we went through in the *Installing Spark requirements* recipe. In addition, you need to have administrative privileges (via the `sudo` command), as these will be necessary to move the compiled binaries to the destination folder.

 If you are not an administrator on your machine, you can call the script with the `-ns` (or `--nosudo`) parameter. The destination folder will then switch to your home directory and will create a `spark` folder within it; by default, the binaries will be moved to the `/opt/spark` folder and that's why you need administrative rights.

No other prerequisites are required.

How to do it...

To install from the binaries, we only need four steps (see the following source code) as we do not need to compile the sources:

1. Download the precompiled binaries from Spark's website.
2. Unpack the archive.
3. Move to the final destination.
4. Create the necessary environmental variables.

The skeleton for our code looks as follows (see the `Chapter01/installFromBinary.sh` file):

```bash
#!/bin/bash

# Shell script for installing Spark from binaries
```

```
#
# PySpark Cookbook
# Author: Tomasz Drabas, Denny Lee
# Version: 0.1
# Date: 12/2/2017

_spark_binary="http://mirrors.ocf.berkeley.edu/apache/spark/spark-2.3.1/spa
rk-2.3.1-bin-hadoop2.7.tgz"
_spark_archive=$( echo "$_spark_binary" | awk -F '/' '{print $NF}' )
_spark_dir=$( echo "${_spark_archive%.*}" )
_spark_destination="/opt/spark"

...

checkOS
printHeader
downloadThePackage
unpack
moveTheBinaries
setSparkEnvironmentVariables
cleanUp
```

How it works...

The code is exactly the same as with the previous recipe so we will not be repeating it here; the only major difference is that we do not have the build stage in this script, and the _spark_source variable is different.

As in the previous recipe, we start by specifying the location of Spark's source code, which is in _spark_source. The _spark_archive contains the name of the archive; we use awk to extract the last element. The _spark_dir contains the name of the directory our archive will unpack into; in our current case, this will be spark-2.3.1. Finally, we specify our destination folder where we will be moving the binaries to: it will either be /opt/spark (default) or your home directory if you use the -ns (or --nosudo) switch when calling the ./installFromBinary.sh script.

Next, we check the OS name. Depending on whether you work in a Linux or macOS environment, we will use different tools to download the archive from the internet (check the downloadThePackage function). Also, when setting up the environment variables, we will output to different bash profile files: the .bash_profile on macOS and the .bashrc on Linux (check the setEnvironmentVariables function).

Following the OS check, we download the package: on macOS, we use `curl` and on Linux, we use `wget` tools to attain this goal. Once the package is downloaded, we unpack it using the `tar` tool, and then move it to its destination folder. If you are running with `sudo` privileges (without the `-ns` or `--nosudo` parameters), the binaries will be moved to the `/opt/spark` folder; if not—they will end up in the `~/spark` folder.

Finally, we add environment variables to the appropriate bash profile files: check the previous recipe for an explanation of what is being added and for what reason. Also, follow the steps at the end of the previous recipe to test if your environment is working properly.

There's more...

Nowadays, there is an even simpler way to install PySpark on your machine, that is, by using pip.

 `pip` is Python's package manager. If you installed Python 2.7.9 or Python 3.4 from `http://python.org`, then `pip` is already present on your machine (the same goes for our recommended Python distribution—Anaconda). If you do not have `pip`, you can easily install it from here: `https://pip.pypa.io/en/stable/installing/`.

To install PySpark via `pip`, just issue the following command in the Terminal:

```
pip install pyspark
```

Or, if you use Python 3.4+, you may also try:

```
pip3 install pyspark
```

You should see the following screen in your Terminal:

```
endeavor:learningPySpark drabast$ pip install pyspark
Collecting pyspark
  Downloading pyspark-2.2.0.post0.tar.gz (188.3MB)
    100% |████████████████████████████████| 188.3MB 3.7kB/s
Requirement already satisfied: py4j==0.10.4 in /Users/drabast/anaconda/lib/python3.5/site-packages (from pyspark)
Building wheels for collected packages: pyspark
  Running setup.py bdist_wheel for pyspark ... done
  Stored in directory: /Users/drabast/Library/Caches/pip/wheels/5f/0b/b3/5cb16b15d28dcc32f8e7ec91a044829642874bb7586f6e6cbe
Successfully built pyspark
Installing collected packages: pyspark
Successfully installed pyspark-2.2.0
```

Configuring a local instance of Spark

There is actually not much you need to do to configure a local instance of Spark. The beauty of Spark is that all you need to do to get started is to follow either of the previous two recipes (installing from sources or from binaries) and you can begin using it. In this recipe, however, we will walk you through the most useful `SparkSession` configuration options.

Getting ready

In order to follow this recipe, a working Spark environment is required. This means that you will have to have gone through the previous three recipes and have successfully installed and tested your environment, or had a working Spark environment already set up.

No other prerequisites are necessary.

How to do it...

To configure your session, in a Spark version which is lower that version 2.0, you would normally have to create a `SparkConf` object, set all your options to the right values, and then build the `SparkContext` (`SqlContext` if you wanted to use `DataFrames`, and `HiveContext` if you wanted access to Hive tables). Starting from Spark 2.0, you just need to create a `SparkSession`, just like in the following snippet:

```
spark = SparkSession.builder \
    .master("local[2]") \
    .appName("Your-app-name") \
    .config("spark.some.config.option", "some-value") \
    .getOrCreate()
```

How it works...

To create a `SparkSession`, we will use the `Builder` class (accessed via the `.builder` property of the `SparkSession` class). You can specify some basic properties of the `SparkSession` here:

- The `.master(...)` allows you to specify the driver node (in our preceding example, we would be running a local session with two cores)

- The `.appName(...)` gives you means to specify a friendly name for your app

- The `.config(...)` method allows you to refine your session's behavior further; the list of the most important `SparkSession` parameters is outlined in the following table

- The `.getOrCreate()` method returns either a new `SparkSession` if one has not been created yet, or returns a pointer to an already existing `SparkSession`

The following table gives an example list of the most useful configuration parameters for a local instance of Spark:

 Some of these parameters are also applicable if you are working in a cluster environment with multiple worker nodes. In the next recipe, we will explain how to set up and administer a multi-node Spark cluster deployed over YARN.

Parameter	Function	Default
spark.app.name	Specifies a friendly name for your application	(none)
spark.driver.cores	Number of cores for the driver node to use. This is only applicable for app deployments in a cluster mode (see the following spark.submit.deployMode parameter).	1
spark.driver.memory	Specifies the amount of memory for the driver process. If using spark-submit in client mode, you should specify this in a command line using --driver-memory switch rather than configuring your session using this parameter as JVM would have already started at this point.	1g
spark.executor.cores	Number of cores for an executor to use. Setting this parameter while running locally allows you to use all the available cores on your machine.	1 in YARN deployment, all available cores on the worker in standalone and Mesos deployments
spark.executor.memory	Specifies the amount of memory per each executor process.	1g
spark.submit.pyFiles	List of .zip, .egg, or .py files, separated by commas. These will be added to the PYTHONPATH so that they are accessible for Python apps.	(none)

`spark.submit.deployMode`	Deploy mode of the Spark driver program. Specifying `'client'` will launch the driver program locally on the machine (it can be the driver node), while specifying `'cluster'` will utilize one of the nodes on a remote cluster.	(none)
`spark.pyspark.python`	Python binary that should be used by the driver and all the executors.	(none)

There are some environment variables that also allow you to further fine-tune your Spark environment. Specifically, we are talking about the PYSPARK_DRIVER_PYTHON and PYSPARK_DRIVER_PYTHON_OPTS variables. We have already covered these in the *Installing Spark from sources* recipe.

See also

- Check the full list of all available configuration options here: `https://spark.apache.org/docs/latest/configuration.html`

Configuring a multi-node instance of Spark

Setting up a multi-node Spark cluster requires quite a few more steps to get it ready. In this recipe, we will go step-by-step through the script that will help you with this process; the script needs to run on the driver node and all the executors to set up the environment.

Getting ready

In this recipe, we are solely focusing on a Linux environment (we are using Ubuntu Server 16.04 LTS). The following prerequisites are required before you can follow with the rest of the recipe:

- A clean installation of a Linux distribution; in our case, we have installed Ubuntu Server 16.04 LTS on each machine in our cluster of three Dell R710s.
- Each machine needs to be connected to the internet and accessible from your local machine. You will need the machines' IPs and their hostnames; on Linux, you can check the IP by issuing the `ifconfig` command and reading the `inet addr`. To check your hostname, type at `cat/etc/hostname`.

- On each server, we added a user group called `hadoop`. Following this, we have created a user called `hduser` and added it to the `hadoop` group. Also, make sure that the `hduser` has `sudo` rights. If you do not know how to do this, check the *See also* section of this recipe.
- Make sure you have added the ability to reach your servers via SSH. If you cannot do this, run `sudo apt-get install openssh-server openssh-client` on each server to install the necessary environments.
- If you want to read and write to Hadoop and Hive, you need to have these two environments installed and configured on your cluster. Check `https://data-flair.training/blogs/install-hadoop-2-x-on-ubuntu/` for Hadoop installation and configuration and `http://www.bogotobogo.com/Hadoop/BigData_hadoop_Hive_Install_On_Ubuntu_16_04.php` for Hive.

 If you have these two environments set up, some of the steps from our script would be obsolete. However, we will present all of the steps as follows, assuming you only want the Spark environment.

No other prerequisites are required.

For the purpose of automating the deployment of the Spark environment in a cluster setup, you will also have to:

1. Create a `hosts.txt` file. Each entry on the list is the IP address of one of the servers followed by two spaces and a hostname. **Do not delete the** `driver:` **nor** `executors:` **lines**. Also, note that we only allow one driver in our cluster (some clusters support redundant drivers). An example of the content of this file is as follows:

```
driver:
192.168.17.160  pathfinder

executors:
192.168.17.161  discovery1
192.168.17.162  discovery2
```

2. On your local machine, add the IPs and hostnames to your `/etc/hosts` file so you can access the servers via hostnames instead of IPs (once again, we are assuming you are running a Unix-like system such as macOS or Linux). For example, the following command will add `pathfinder` to our `/etc/hosts` file: `sudo echo 192.168.1.160  pathfinder >> /etc/hosts`. Repeat this for all machines from your server.

3. Copy the `hosts.txt` file to each machine in your cluster; we assume the file will be placed in the root folder for the `hduser`. You can attain this easily with the `scp hosts.txt hduser@<your-server-name>:~` command, where `<your-server-name>` is the hostname of the machine.

4. To run the `installOnRemote.sh` script (see the `Chapter01/installOnRemote.sh` file) from your local machine, do the following: `ssh -tq hduser@<your-server-name> "echo $(base64 -i installOnRemote.sh) | base64 -d | sudo bash"`. We will go through these steps in detail in the `installOnRemote.sh` script in the next section.

5. Follow the prompts on the screen to finalize the installation and configuration steps. Repeat step 4 for each machine in your cluster.

How to do it...

The `installOnRemote.sh` script for this recipe can be found in the `Chapter01` folder in the GitHub repository: `http://bit.ly/2ArlBck`. Some portions of the script are very similar to the ones we have outlined in the previous recipes, so we will skip those; you can refer to previous recipes for more information (especially the *Installing Spark requirements* and the *Installing Spark from binaries* recipes).

The top-level structure of the script is as follows:

```bash
#!/bin/bash

# Shell script for installing Spark from binaries
# on remote servers
#
# PySpark Cookbook
# Author: Tomasz Drabas, Denny Lee
# Version: 0.1
# Date: 12/9/2017

_spark_binary="http://mirrors.ocf.berkeley.edu/apache/spark/spark-2.3.1/spark-2.3.1-bin-hadoop2.7.tgz"
_spark_archive=$( echo "$_spark_binary" | awk -F '/' '{print $NF}' )
_spark_dir=$( echo "${_spark_archive%.*}" )
_spark_destination="/opt/spark"
_java_destination="/usr/lib/jvm/java-8-oracle"

_python_binary="https://repo.continuum.io/archive/Anaconda3-5.0.1-Linux-x86_64.sh"
```

```
_python_archive=$( echo "$_python_binary" | awk -F '/' '{print $NF}' )
_python_destination="/opt/python"

_machine=$(cat /etc/hostname)
_today=$( date +%Y-%m-%d )

_current_dir=$(pwd) # store current working directory

...

printHeader
readIPs
checkJava
installScala
installPython
updateHosts
configureSSH
downloadThePackage
unpack
moveTheBinaries
setSparkEnvironmentVariables
updateSparkConfig
cleanUp
```

We have highlighted the portions of the script that are more relevant to this recipe in bold font.

How it works...

As with the previous recipes, we will first specify where we are going to download the Spark binaries from and create all the relevant global variables we are going to use later.

Next, we read in the hosts.txt file:

```
function readIPs() {
 input="./hosts.txt"

 driver=0
 executors=0
 _executors=""

 IFS=''
 while read line
 do
```

```
if [[ "$master" = "1" ]]; then
    _driverNode="$line"
    driver=0
fi

if [[ "$slaves" = "1" ]]; then
  _executors=$_executors"$line\n"
fi

if [[ "$line" = "driver:" ]]; then
    driver=1
    executors=0
fi

if [[ "$line" = "executors:" ]]; then
    executors=1
    driver=0
fi

if [[ -z "${line}" ]]; then
    continue
fi
done < "$input"
}
```

We store the path to the file in the input variable. The driver and the executors variables are flags we use to skip the "driver:" and the "executors:" lines from the input file. The _executors empty string will store the list of executors, which are delimited by a newline "\n".

IFS stands for **internal field separator**. Whenever bash reads a line from a file, it will split it on that character. Here, we will set it to an empty character ' ' so that we preserve the double spaces between the IP address and the hostname.

Next, we start reading the file, line-by-line. Let's see how the logic works inside the loop; we'll start a bit out of order so that the logic is easier to understand:

- If the line we just read equals to "driver:" (the if [["$line" = "driver:"]]; conditional), we set the driver flag to 1 so that when the next line is read, we store it as a _driverNode (this is done inside the if [["$driver" = "1"]]; conditional). Inside that conditional, we also reset the executors flag to 0. The latter is done in case you start with executors first, followed by a single driver in the hosts.txt. Once the line with the driver node information is read, we reset the driver flag to 0.

- On the other hand, if the `line` we just read equals to `"executors:"` (the `if [[ "$line" = "executors:" ]];` conditional), we set the `executors` flag to 1 (and reset the `driver` flag to 0). This guarantees that the next line read will be appended to the _executors string, separated by the `"\n"` newline character (this happens inside the `if [[ "$executors" = "1" ]];` conditional). Note that we do not set the `executor` flag to 0 as we allow for more than one executor.
- If we encounter an empty line—which we can check for in bash with the `if [[ -z "${line}" ]];` conditional—we skip it.

You might notice that we use the `"<"` redirection pipe to read in the data (indicated here by the input variable).

You can read more about the redirection pipes here: `http://www.tldp. org/LDP/abs/html/io-redirection.html.`

Since Spark requires Java and Scala to work, next we have to check if Java is installed, and we will install Scala (as it normally isn't present while Java might be). This is achieved with the following functions:

```
function checkJava() {
  if type -p java; then
     echo "Java executable found in PATH"
     _java=java
  elif [[ -n "$JAVA_HOME" ]] && [[ -x "$JAVA_HOME/bin/java" ]]; then
     echo "Found Java executable in JAVA_HOME"
     _java="$JAVA_HOME/bin/java"
  else
     echo "No Java found. Install Java version $_java_required or higher
first or specify JAVA_HOME    variable that will point to your Java
binaries."
     installJava
  fi
}

function installJava() {
  sudo apt-get install python-software-properties
  sudo add-apt-repository ppa:webupd8team/java
  sudo apt-get update
  sudo apt-get install oracle-java8-installer
}
```

```
function installScala() {
 sudo apt-get install scala
}

function installPython() {
 curl -O "$_python_binary"
 chmod 0755 ./"$_python_archive"
 sudo bash ./"$_python_archive" -b -u -p "$_python_destination"
}
```

The logic here doesn't differ much from what we presented in the *Installing Spark requirements* recipe. The only notable difference in the checkJava function is that if we do not find Java on the PATH variable or inside the JAVA_HOME folder, we do not exit but run installJava, instead.

There are many ways to install Java; we have already presented you with one of them earlier in this book—check the *Installing Java* section in the *Installing Spark requirements* recipe. Here, we used the built-in apt-get tool.

The apt-get tool is a convenient, fast, and efficient utility for installing packages on your Linux machine. **APT** stands for **Advanced Packaging Tool**.

First, we install the python-software-properties. This set of tools provides an abstraction of the used apt repositories. It enables easy management of distribution as well as independent software vendor software sources. We need this as in the next line we add the add-apt-repository; we add a new repository as we want the Oracle Java distribution. The sudo apt-get update command refreshes the contents of the repositories and, in our current case, fetches all the packages available in ppa:webupd8team/java. Finally, we install the Java package: just follow the prompts on the screen. We will install Scala the same way.

The default location where the package should install is /usr/lib/jvm/java-8-oracle. If this is not the case or you want to install it in a different folder, you will have to alter the _java_destination variable inside the script to reflect the new destination.

The advantage of using this tool is this: if there are already Java and Scala environments installed on a machine, using `apt-get` will either skip the installation (if the environment is up-to-date with the one available on the server) or ask you to update to the newest version.

We will also install the Anaconda distribution of Python (as mentioned many times previously, since we highly recommend this distribution). To achieve this goal, we must download the `Anaconda3-5.0.1-Linux-x86_64.sh` script first and then follow the prompts on the screen. The `-b` parameter to the script will not update the `.bashrc` file (we will do that later), the `-u` switch will update the Python environment in case `/usr/local/python` already exists, and `-p` will force the installation to that folder.

Having passed the required installation steps, we will now update the `/etc/hosts` files on the remote machines:

```
function updateHosts() {

  _hostsFile="/etc/hosts"

  # make a copy (if one already doesn't exist)
  if ! [ -f "/etc/hosts.old" ]; then
      sudo cp "$_hostsFile" /etc/hosts.old
  fi

  t="####################################################\n"
  t=$t"#\n"
  t=$t"# IPs of the Spark cluster machines\n"
  t=$t"#\n"
  t=$t"# Script: installOnRemote.sh\n"
  t=$t"# Added on: $_today\n"
  t=$t"#\n"
  t=$t"$_driverNode\n"
  t=$t"$_executors\n"

  sudo printf "$t" >> $_hostsFile

}
```

This is a simple function that, first, creates a copy of the `/etc/hosts` file, and then appends the IPs and hostnames of the machines in our cluster. Note that the format required by the `/etc/hosts` file is the same as in the `hosts.txt` file we use: per row, an IP address of the machine followed by two spaces followed by the hostname.

We use two spaces for readability purposes—one space separating an IP and the hostname would also work.

Also, note that we do not use the echo command here, but printf; the reason behind this is that the printf command prints out a formatted version of the string, properly handling the newline "\n" characters.

Next, we configure the passwordless SSH sessions (check the following *See also* subsection) to aid communication between the driver node and the executors:

```
function configureSSH() {
    # check if driver node
    IFS=" "
    read -ra temp <<< "$_driverNode"
    _driver_machine=( ${temp[1]} )
    _all_machines="$_driver_machine\n"

    if [ "$_driver_machine" = "$_machine" ]; then
        # generate key pairs (passwordless)
        sudo -u hduser rm -f ~/.ssh/id_rsa
        sudo -u hduser ssh-keygen -t rsa -P "" -f ~/.ssh/id_rsa

        IFS="\n"
        read -ra temp <<< "$_executors"
        for executor in ${temp[@]}; do
            # skip if empty line
            if [[ -z "${executor}" ]]; then
                continue
            fi
            # split on space
            IFS=" "
            read -ra temp_inner <<< "$executor"
            echo
            echo "Trying to connect to ${temp_inner[1]}"

            cat ~/.ssh/id_rsa.pub | ssh "hduser"@"${temp_inner[1]}" 'mkdir
-p .ssh && cat >> .ssh/authorized_keys'

            _all_machines=$_all_machines"${temp_inner[1]}\n"
        done
    fi

    echo "Finishing up the SSH configuration"
}
```

Inside this function, we first check if we are on the driver node, as defined in the `hosts.txt` file, as we only need to perform these tasks on the driver. The `read -ra temp <<< "$_driverNode"` command reads the `_driverNode` (in our case, it is `192.168.1.160 pathfinder`), and splits it at the space character (remember what `IFS` stands for?). The `-a` switch instructs the `read` method to store the split `_driverNode` string in the `temp` array and the `-r` parameter makes sure that the backslash does not act as an escape character. We store the name of the driver in the `_driver_machine` variable and append it to the `_all_machines` string (we will use this later).

If we are executing this script on the driver machine, the first thing we must do is remove the old SSH key (using the `rm` function with the `-f`, force switch) and create a new one. The `sudo -u hduser` switch allows us to perform these actions as the `hduser` (instead of the `root` user).

 When we submit the script to run from our local machine, we start an SSH session as a root on the remote machine. You will see how this is done shortly, so take our word on that for now.

We will use the `ssh-keygen` method to create the SSH key pair. The `-t` switch allows us to select the encryption algorithm (we are using RSA encryption), the `-P` switch determines the password to use (we want this passwordless, so we choose `""`), and the `-f` parameter specifies the filename for storing the keys.

Next, we loop through all the executors: we need to append the contents of `~/.ssh/id_rsa.pub` to their `~/.ssh/authorized_keys` files. We split the `_executors` at the `"\n"` character and loop through all of them. To deliver the contents of the `id_rsa.pub` file to the executors, we use the `cat` tool to print out the contents of the `id_rsa.pub` file and then pipe it to the `ssh` tool. The first parameter we pass to the `ssh` is the username and the hostname we want to connect to. Next, we pass the commands we want to execute on the remote machine. First, we attempt to create the `.ssh` folder if one does not exist. This is followed by outputting the `id_rsa.pub` file to `.ssh/authorized_keys`.

Following the SSH session's configurations on the cluster, we download the Spark binaries, unpack them, and move them to `_spark_destination`.

 We have outlined these steps in the *Installing Spark from sources* and *Installing Spark from binaries* sections, so we recommend that you check them out.

Finally, we need to set two Spark configuration files: the `spark-env.sh` and the `slaves` files:

```
function updateSparkConfig() {
    cd $_spark_destination/conf

    sudo -u hduser cp spark-env.sh.template spark-env.sh
    echo "export JAVA_HOME=$_java_destination" >> spark-env.sh
    echo "export SPARK_WORKER_CORES=12" >> spark-env.sh

    sudo -u hduser cp slaves.template slaves
    printf "$_all_machines" >> slaves
}
```

We need to append the `JAVA_HOME` variable to `spark-env.sh` so that Spark can find the necessary libraries. We must also specify the number of cores per worker to be `12`; this goal is attained by setting the `SPARK_WORKER_CORES` variable.

> You might want to tune the `SPARK_WORKER_CORES` value to your needs. Check this spreadsheet for help: `http://c2fo.io/img/apache-spark-config-cheatsheet/C2FO-Spark-Config-Cheatsheet.xlsx` (which is available from here: `http://c2fo.io/c2fo/spark/aws/emr/2016/07/06/apache-spark-config-cheatsheet/`).

Next, we have to output the hostnames of all the machines in our cluster to the `slaves` file.

In order to execute the script on the remote machine, and since we need to run it in an elevated mode (as `root` using `sudo`), we need to encrypt the script before we send it over the wire. An example of how this is done is as follows (from macOS to remote Linux):

```
ssh -tq hduser@pathfinder "echo $(base64 -i installOnRemote.sh) | base64 -d | sudo bash"
```

Or from Linux to remote Linux:

```
ssh -tq hduser@pathfinder "echo $(base64 -w0 installOnRemote.sh) | base64 -d | sudo bash"
```

The preceding script uses the `base64` encryption tool to encrypt the `installOnRemote.sh` script before pushing it over to the remote. Once on the remote, we once again use `base64` to decrypt the script (the `-d` switch) and run it as `root` (via `sudo`). Note that in order to run this type of script, we also pass the `-tq` switch to the `ssh` tool; the `-t` option forces a pseudo Terminal allocation so that we can execute arbitrary screen-based scripts on the remote machine, and the `-q` option quiets all the messages but those from our script.

Assuming all goes well, once the script finishes executing on all your machines, Spark has been successfully installed and configured on your cluster. However, before you can use Spark, you need either to close the connection to your driver and SSH to it again, or type:

```
source ~/.bashrc
```

This is so that the newly created environment variables are available, and your PATH is updated.

To start your cluster, you can type:

```
start-all.sh
```

And all the machines in the cluster should be coming to life and be recognized by Spark.

In order to check if everything started properly, type:

```
jps
```

And it should return something similar to the following (in our case, we had three machines in our cluster):

```
40334 Master
41297 Worker
41058 Worker
```

See also

Here's a list of useful links that might help you to go through with this recipe:

- If you do not know how to add a user group, check this link: https://www.techonthenet.com/linux/sysadmin/ubuntu/create_group_14_04.php
- To add a sudo user, check this link: https://www.digitalocean.com/community/tutorials/how-to-add-and-delete-users-on-ubuntu-16-04
- Here are step-by-step manual instructions on how to install Spark: https://data-flair.training/blogs/install-apache-spark-multi-node-cluster/.
- Here is how to set a passwordless SSH communication between machines: https://www.tecmint.com/ssh-passwordless-login-using-ssh-keygen-in-5-easy-steps/

Installing Jupyter

Jupyter provides a means to conveniently cooperate with your Spark environment. In this recipe, we will guide you in how to install Jupyter on your local machine.

Getting ready

We require a working installation of Spark. This means that you will have followed the steps outlined in the first, and either the second or third recipes. In addition, a working Python environment is also required.

No other prerequisites are required.

How to do it...

If you do not have `pip` installed on your machine, you will need to install it before proceeding.

1. To do this, open your Terminal and type (on macOS):

   ```
   curl -O https://bootstrap.pypa.io/get-pip.py
   ```

   Or the following on Linux:

   ```
   wget https://bootstrap.pypa.io/get-pip.py
   ```

2. Next, type (applies to both operating systems):

   ```
   python get-pip.py
   ```

   This will install `pip` on your machine.

3. All you have to do now is install Jupyter with the following command:

   ```
   pip install jupyter
   ```

How it works...

`pip` is a management tool for installing Python packages for **PyPI**, the **Python Package Index**. This service hosts a wide range of Python packages and is the easiest and quickest way to distribute your Python packages.

However, calling `pip install` does not only search for the packages on PyPI: in addition, VCS project URLs, local project directories, and local or remote source archives are also scanned.

Jupyter is one of the most popular interactive shells that supports developing code in a wide variety of environments: Python is not the only one that's supported.

Directly from `http://jupyter.org`:

> *"The Jupyter Notebook is an open-source web application that allows you to create and share documents that contain live code, equations, visualizations, and narrative text. Uses include: data cleaning and transformation, numerical simulation, statistical modeling, data visualization, machine learning, and much more."*

Another way to install Jupyter, if you are using Anaconda distribution for Python, is to use its package management tool, the `conda`. Here's how:

```
conda install jupyter
```

Note that `pip install` will also work in Anaconda.

There's more...

Now that you have Jupyter on your machine, and assuming you followed the steps of either the *Installing Spark from sources* or the *Installing Spark from binaries* recipes, you should be able to start using Jupyter to interact with PySpark.

To refresh your memory, as part of installing Spark scripts, we have appended two environment variables to the bash profile file: `PYSPARK_DRIVER_PYTHON` and `PYSPARK_DRIVER_PYTHON_OPTS`. Using these two environment variables, we set the former to use `jupyter` and the latter to start a `notebook` service.

If you now open your Terminal and type:

```
pyspark
```

When you open your browser and navigate to `http://localhost:6661`, you should see a window not that different from the one in the following screenshot:

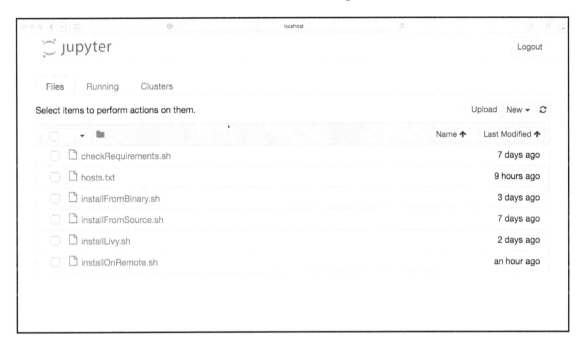

See also

- Check out `https://pypi.python.org/pypi`, as the number of really cool projects available for Python is mind-boggling

Configuring a session in Jupyter

Working in Jupyter is great as it allows you to develop your code interactively, and document and share your notebooks with colleagues. The problem, however, with running Jupyter against a local Spark instance is that the `SparkSession` gets created automatically and by the time the notebook is running, you cannot change much in that session's configuration.

In this recipe, we will learn how to install Livy, a REST service to interact with Spark, and `sparkmagic`, a package that will allow us to configure sessions interactively as well:

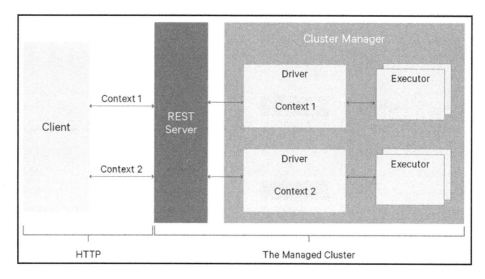

Source: http://bit.ly/2iO3EwC

Getting ready

We assume that you either have installed Spark via binaries or compiled the sources as we have shown you in the previous recipes. In other words, by now, you should have a working Spark environment. You will also need Jupyter: if you do not have it, follow the steps from the previous recipe to install it.

No other prerequisites are required.

How to do it...

To install Livy and `sparkmagic`, we have created a script that will do this automatically with minimal interaction from you. You can find it in the `Chapter01/installLivy.sh` folder. You should be familiar with most of the functions that we're going to use here by now, so we will focus only on those that are different (highlighted in bold in the following code). Here is the high-level view of the script's structure:

```bash
#!/bin/bash

# Shell script for installing Spark from binaries
#
# PySpark Cookbook
# Author: Tomasz Drabas, Denny Lee
# Version: 0.1
# Date: 12/2/2017

_livy_binary="http://mirrors.ocf.berkeley.edu/apache/incubator/livy/0.4.0-i
ncubating/livy-0.4.0-incubating-bin.zip"
_livy_archive=$( echo "$_livy_binary" | awk -F '/' '{print $NF}' )
_livy_dir=$( echo "${_livy_archive%.*}" )
_livy_destination="/opt/livy"
_hadoop_destination="/opt/hadoop"
...
checkOS
printHeader
createTempDir
downloadThePackage $( echo "${_livy_binary}" )
unpack $( echo "${_livy_archive}" )
moveTheBinaries $( echo "${_livy_dir}" ) $( echo "${_livy_destination}" )

# create log directory inside the folder
mkdir -p "$_livy_destination/logs"

checkHadoop
installJupyterKernels
setSparkEnvironmentVariables
cleanUp
```

How it works...

As with all other scripts we have presented so far, we will begin by setting some global variables.

If you do not know what these mean, check the *Installing Spark from sources* recipe.

Livy requires some configuration files from Hadoop. Thus, as part of this script, we allow you to install Hadoop should it not be present on your machine. That is why we now allow you to pass arguments to the downloadThePackage, unpack, and moveTheBinaries functions.

The changes to the functions are fairly self-explanatory, so for the sake of space, we will not be pasting the code here. You are more than welcome, though, to peruse the relevant portions of the installLivy.sh script.

Installing Livy drills down literally to downloading the package, unpacking it, and moving it to its final destination (in our case, this is /opt/livy).

Checking if Hadoop is installed is the next thing on our to-do list. To run Livy with local sessions, we require two environment variables: SPARK_HOME and HADOOP_CONF_DIR; the SPARK_HOME is definitely set but if you do not have Hadoop installed, you most likely will not have the latter environment variable set:

```
function checkHadoop() {
    if type -p hadoop; then
        echo "Hadoop executable found in PATH"
        _hadoop=hadoop
    elif [[ -n "$HADOOP_HOME" ]] && [[ -x "$HADOOP_HOME/bin/hadoop" ]];
then
        echo "Found Hadoop executable in HADOOP_HOME"
        _hadoop="$HADOOP_HOME/bin/hadoop"
    else
        echo "No Hadoop found. You should install Hadoop first. You can
still continue but some functionality might not be available. "
        echo
        echo -n "Do you want to install the latest version of Hadoop?
[y/n]: "
        read _install_hadoop

        case "$_install_hadoop" in
            y*) installHadoop ;;
            n*) echo "Will not install Hadoop" ;;
            *)  echo "Will not install Hadoop" ;;
        esac
    fi
}

function installHadoop() {
_hadoop_binary="http://mirrors.ocf.berkeley.edu/apache/hadoop/common/hadoop
-2.9.0/hadoop-2.9.0.tar.gz"
    _hadoop_archive=$( echo "$_hadoop_binary" | awk -F '/' '{print $NF}' )
    _hadoop_dir=$( echo "${_hadoop_archive%.*}" )
    _hadoop_dir=$( echo "${_hadoop_dir%.*}" )

    downloadThePackage $( echo "${_hadoop_binary}" )
```

```
    unpack $( echo "${_hadoop_archive}" )
    moveTheBinaries $( echo "${_hadoop_dir}" ) $( echo
"${_hadoop_destination}" )
}
```

The `checkHadoop` function first checks if the `hadoop` binary is present on the `PATH`; if not, it will check if the `HADOOP_HOME` variable is set and, if it is, it will check if the `hadoop` binary can be found inside the `$HADOOP_HOME/bin` folder. If both attempts fail, the script will ask you if you want to install the latest version of Hadoop; the default answer is `n` but if you answer `y`, the installation will begin.

Once the installation finishes, we will begin installing the additional kernels for the Jupyter Notebooks.

A kernel is a piece of software that translates the commands from the frontend notebook to the backend environment (like Python). For a list of available Jupyter kernels check out the following link: `https://github.com/jupyter/jupyter/wiki/Jupyter-kernels`. Here are some instructions on how to develop a kernel yourself: `http://jupyter-client.readthedocs.io/en/latest/kernels.html`.

Here's the function that handles the kernel's installation:

```
function installJupyterKernels() {
    # install the library
    pip install sparkmagic
    echo

    # ipywidgets should work properly
    jupyter nbextension enable --py --sys-prefix widgetsnbextension
    echo

    # install kernels
    # get the location of sparkmagic
    _sparkmagic_location=$(pip show sparkmagic | awk -F ':' '/Location/
{print $2}')

    _temp_dir=$(pwd) # store current working directory

    cd $_sparkmagic_location # move to the sparkmagic folder
    jupyter-kernelspec install sparkmagic/kernels/sparkkernel
    jupyter-kernelspec install sparkmagic/kernels/pysparkkernel
    jupyter-kernelspec install sparkmagic/kernels/pyspark3kernel

    echo
```

```
    # enable the ability to change clusters programmatically
    jupyter serverextension enable --py sparkmagic
    echo

    # install autowizwidget
    pip install autovizwidget

    cd $_temp_dir
}
```

First, we install the `sparkmagic` package for Python. Quoting directly from `https://github.com/jupyter-incubator/sparkmagic`:

> *"Sparkmagic is a set of tools for interactively working with remote Spark clusters through Livy, a Spark REST server, in Jupyter Notebooks. The Sparkmagic project includes a set of magics for interactively running Spark code in multiple languages, as well as some kernels that you can use to turn Jupyter into an integrated Spark environment."*

The following command enables the Javascript extensions in Jupyter Notebooks so that `ipywidgets` can work properly; if you have an Anaconda distribution of Python, this package will be installed automatically.

Following this, we install the kernels. We need to switch to the folder where `sparkmagic` was installed into. The `pip show <package>` command displays all relevant information about the installed packages; from the output, we only extract the `Location` using `awk`.

To install the kernels, we use the `jupyter-kernelspec install <kernel>` command. For example, the command will install the `sparkmagic` kernel for the Scala API of Spark:

```
jupyter-kernelspec install sparkmagic/kernels/sparkkernel
```

Once all the kernels are installed, we enable Jupyter to use `sparkmagic` so that we can change clusters programmatically. Finally, we will install the `autovizwidget`, an auto-visualization library for `pandas dataframes`.

This concludes the Livy and `sparkmagic` installation part.

There's more...

Now that we have everything in place, let's see what this can do.

First, start Jupyter (note that we do not use the `pyspark` command):

```
jupyter notebook
```

You should now be able to see the following options if you want to add a new notebook:

If you click on PySpark, it will open a notebook and connect to a kernel.

There are a number of available *magics* to interact with the notebooks; type `%%help` to list them all. Here's the list of the most important ones:

Magic	Example	Explanation
info	`%%info`	Outputs session information from Livy.
cleanup	`%%cleanup -f`	Delete all sessions running on the current Livy endpoint. The −f switch forces the cleanup.
delete	`%%delete -f -s 0`	Deletes the session specified by the −s switch; the −f switch forces the deletion.
configure	`%%configure -f {"executorMemory": "1000M", "executorCores": 4}`	Arguably the most useful magic. Allows you to configure your session. Check http://bit.ly/2kSKlXr for the full list of available configuration parameters.
sql	`%%sql -o tables -q` `SHOW TABLES`	Executes an SQL query against the current `SparkSession`.
local	`%%local` `a=1`	All the code in the notebook cell with this magic will be executed locally against the Python environment.

Once you have configured your session, you will get information back from Livy about the active sessions that are currently running:

```
In [1]: %%configure
        {
            "executorCores" : 3
        }

        Current session configs: {'kind': 'pyspark', 'executorCores': 3}

        No active sessions.
```

Let's try to create a simple data frame using the following code:

```python
from pyspark.sql.types import *

# Generate our data
ListRDD = sc.parallelize([
    (123, 'Skye', 19, 'brown'),
    (223, 'Rachel', 22, 'green'),
    (333, 'Albert', 23, 'blue')
])

# The schema is encoded using StructType
schema = StructType([
    StructField("id", LongType(), True),
    StructField("name", StringType(), True),
    StructField("age", LongType(), True),
    StructField("eyeColor", StringType(), True)
])

# Apply the schema to the RDD and create DataFrame
drivers = spark.createDataFrame(ListRDD, schema)

# Creates a temporary view using the data frame
drivers.createOrReplaceTempView("drivers")
```

Once you execute the preceding code in a cell inside the notebook, only then will the SparkSession be created:

```
Starting Spark application
```

ID	YARN Application ID	Kind	State	Spark UI	Driver log	Current session?
1	None	pyspark	idle			✔

```
SparkSession available as 'spark'.
```

If you execute `%%sql` magic, you will get the following:

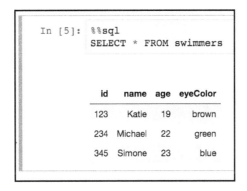

See also

- Check the Livy REST API in case you want to submit jobs programmatically: `https://livy.incubator.apache.org/docs/latest/rest-api.html`. Also, for a list of configurable parameters available in `sparkmagic`, go to: `https://github.com/jupyter-incubator/sparkmagic/blob/master/examples/Pyspark%20Kernel.ipynb`.

Working with Cloudera Spark images

Cloudera is a company that was founded in 2008 by ex-employees of Google, Yahoo!, Oracle, and Facebook. It was an early adopter of open source technologies like Apache Hadoop when it was still fresh from the oven; as a matter of a fact, the author of Hadoop itself joined the company shortly thereafter. Today, Cloudera sells licenses for a broad array of open source products, mostly from the Apache Software Foundation, and also provides consulting services.

In this recipe, we will look at a free virtual image from Cloudera that we can use to learn how to use the newest technologies supported by the company.

Getting ready

To go through this recipe, you will need a working installation of a VirtualBox, a free virtualization tool from Oracle.

Here are the instructions for installing VirtualBox:
On Windows: `https://www.htpcbeginner.com/install-virtualbox-on-windows/`
On Linux:
`https://www.packtpub.com/books/content/installing-virtualbox-linux`
On Mac: `https://www.youtube.com/watch?v=lEvM-No4eQo`.

To run the VMs, you will need:

- A 64-bit host; Windows 10, macOS, and most of the Linux distributions are 64-bit systems
- A minimum 4 GB of RAM dedicated for the VM, thus a system with a minimum of 8 GB of RAM is required

No other prerequisites are required.

How to do it...

To begin with, in order to download the Cloudera QuickStart VM:

1. Go to `https://www.cloudera.com/downloads/quickstart_vms/5-12.html`.
2. Select VirtualBox as your platform from the dropdown on the right, and click on the **Get it now** button.
3. A window to register will show up; fill it in as appropriate and follow the instructions on the screen:

Chapter 1

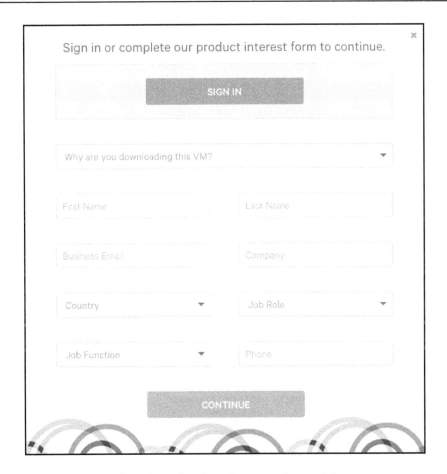

Note, that it is a 6 GB+ download, so it may take a while.

4. Once downloaded, open the VirtualBox.
5. Go to **File | Import appliance**, click on the button next to the path selection, and find the `.ovf` file (it should be accompanied by the `.vmdk` file, which is appropriate for the version you just downloaded).

On macOS, the image is automatically decompressed upon downloading. On Windows and Linux, you might need to unzip the archive first.

You should see a progress bar that is similar to this one:

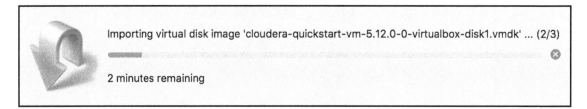

Once imported, you should see a window like this:

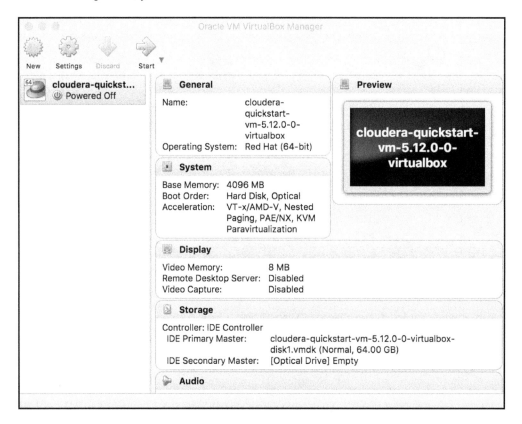

6. If you now click on **Start**, you should see a new window pop up, and Cloudera VM (that is built on CentOS) should start booting up. Once done, a window similar to the following one should show up on your screen:

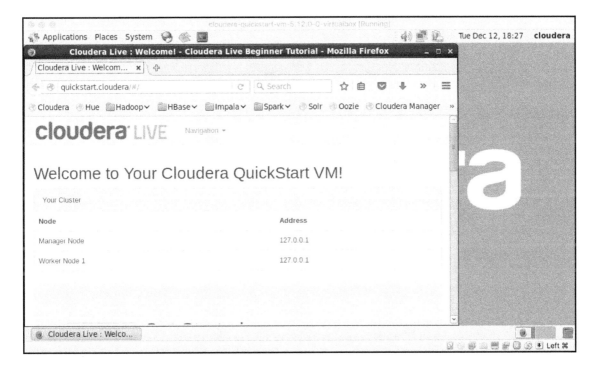

How it works...

There is really not much to configure: Cloudera QuickStart VM has everything you need to get going. As a matter of fact, this is a much simpler solution for Windows users than installing all the necessary environments. However, at the time of writing this book, it only comes with Spark 1.6.0:

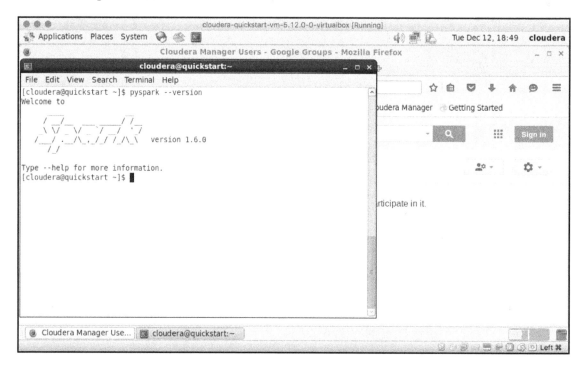

Nothing, however, can stop you from upgrading to Spark 2.3.1 by following either the *Installing Spark from sources* or *Installing Spark from binaries* recipes we presented earlier in this book.

Abstracting Data with RDDs

2

In this chapter, we will cover how to work with Apache Spark Resilient Distributed Datasets. You will learn the following recipes:

- Creating RDDs
- Reading data from files
- Overview of RDD transformations
- Overview of RDD actions
- Pitfalls of using RDDs

Introduction

Resilient Distributed Datasets (**RDDs**) are collections of immutable JVM objects that are distributed across an Apache Spark cluster. Please note that if you are new to Apache Spark, you may want to initially skip this chapter as Spark DataFrames/Datasets are both significantly easier to develop and typically have faster performance. More information on Spark DataFrames can be found in the next chapter.

An RDD is the most fundamental dataset type of Apache Spark; any action on a Spark DataFrame eventually gets *translated* into a highly optimized execution of transformations and actions on RDDs (see the paragraph on catalyst optimizer in `Chapter 3`, *Abstracting Data with DataFrames*, in the *Introduction* section).

Data in an RDD is split into chunks based on a key and then dispersed across all the executor nodes. RDDs are highly resilient, that is, there are able to recover quickly from any issues as the same data chunks are replicated across multiple executor nodes. Thus, even if one executor fails, another will still process the data. This allows you to perform your functional calculations against your dataset very quickly by harnessing the power of multiple nodes. RDDs keep a log of all the execution steps applied to each chunk. This, on top of the data replication, speeds up the computations and, if anything goes wrong, RDDs can still recover the portion of the data lost due to an executor error.

While it is common to lose a node in distributed environments (for example, due to connectivity issues, hardware problems), distribution and replication of the data defends against data loss, while data lineage allows the system to recover quickly.

Creating RDDs

For this recipe, we will start creating an RDD by generating the data within the PySpark. To create RDDs in Apache Spark, you will need to first install Spark as shown in the previous chapter. You can use the PySpark shell and/or Jupyter notebook to run these code samples.

Getting ready

We require a working installation of Spark. This means that you would have followed the steps outlined in the previous chapter. As a reminder, to start PySpark shell for your local Spark cluster, you can run this command:

```
./bin/pyspark --master local[n]
```

Where n is the number of cores.

How to do it...

To quickly create an RDD, run PySpark on your machine via the bash terminal, or you can run the same query in a Jupyter notebook. There are two ways to create an RDD in PySpark: you can either use the parallelize() method—a collection (list or an array of some elements) or reference a file (or files) located either locally or through an external source, as noted in subsequent recipes.

The following code snippet creates your RDD (myRDD) using the sc.parallelize() method:

```
myRDD = sc.parallelize([('Mike', 19), ('June', 18), ('Rachel',16), ('Rob',
18), ('Scott', 17)])
```

To view what is inside your RDD, you can run the following code snippet:

```
myRDD.take(5)
```

The output is as follows:

```
Out[10]: [('Mike', 19), ('June', 18), ('Rachel',16), ('Rob', 18), ('Scott', 17)]
```

How it works...

Let's break down the two methods in the preceding code snippet: `sc.parallelize()` and `take()`.

Spark context parallelize method

Under the covers, there are quite a few actions that happened when you created your RDD. Let's start with the RDD creation and break down this code snippet:

```
myRDD = sc.parallelize(
  [('Mike', 19), ('June', 18), ('Rachel',16), ('Rob', 18), ('Scott', 17)]
  )
```

Focusing first on the statement in the `sc.parallelize()` method, we first created a Python list (that is, `[A, B, ..., E]`) composed of a list of arrays (that is, `('Mike', 19)`, `('June', 19)`, `...`, `('Scott', 17)`). The `sc.parallelize()` method is the SparkContext's `parallelize` method to create a parallelized collection. This allows Spark to distribute the data across multiple nodes, instead of depending on a single node to process the data:

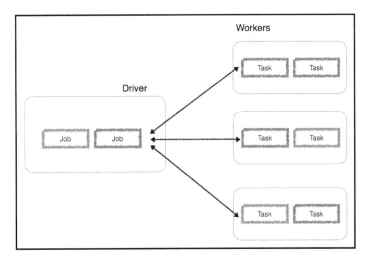

Now that we have created myRDD as a parallelized collection, Spark can operate against this data in parallel. Once created, the distributed dataset (distData) can be operated on in parallel. For example, we can call myRDD.reduceByKey(add) to add up the grouped by keys of the list; we have recipes for RDD operations in subsequent sections of this chapter.

.take(...) method

Now that you have created your RDD (myRDD), we will use the take() method to return the values to the console (or notebook cell). We will now execute an RDD action (more information on this in subsequent recipes), take(). Note that a common approach in PySpark is to use collect(), which returns all values in your RDD from the Spark worker nodes to the driver. There are performance implications when working with a large amount of data as this translates to large volumes of data being transferred from the Spark worker nodes to the driver. For small amounts of data (such as this recipe), this is perfectly fine, but, as a matter of habit, you should pretty much always use the take(n) method instead; it returns the first n elements of the RDD instead of the whole dataset. It is a more efficient method because it first scans one partition and uses those statistics to determine the number of partitions required to return the results.

Reading data from files

For this recipe, we will create an RDD by reading a local file in PySpark. To create RDDs in Apache Spark, you will need to first install Spark as noted in the previous chapter. You can use the PySpark shell and/or Jupyter notebook to run these code samples. Note that while this recipe is specific to reading local files, a similar syntax can be applied for Hadoop, AWS S3, Azure WASBs, and/or Google Cloud Storage:

Storage type	Example
Local files	`sc.textFile('/local folder/filename.csv')`
Hadoop HDFS	`sc.textFile('hdfs://folder/filename.csv')`
AWS S3 (https://docs.aws.amazon.com/emr/latest/ReleaseGuide/emr-spark-configure.html)	`sc.textFile('s3://bucket/folder/filename.csv')`
Azure WASBs (https://docs.microsoft.com/en-us/azure/hdinsight/hdinsight-hadoop-use-blob-storage)	`sc.textFile('wasb://bucket/folder/filename.csv')`

Google Cloud Storage (`https:/`
`/cloud.google.com/`
`dataproc/docs/concepts/`
`connectors/cloud-`
`storage#other_`
`sparkhadoop_clusters`)
	`sc.textFile('gs://bucket/folder/filename.csv')`

Databricks DBFS (`https://`
`docs.databricks.com/`
`user-guide/dbfs-`
`databricks-file-system.`
`html`)
	`sc.textFile('dbfs://folder/filename.csv')`

Getting ready

In this recipe, we will be reading a tab-delimited (or comma-delimited) file, so please ensure that you have a text (or CSV) file available. For your convenience, you can download the `airport-codes-na.txt` and `departuredelays.csv` files from `https://github.com/drabastomek/learningPySpark/tree/master/Chapter03/flight-data`. Ensure your local Spark cluster can access this file (for example, `~/data/flights/airport-codes-na.txt`).

How to do it...

Once you start the PySpark shell via the bash terminal (or you can run the same query within Jupyter notebook), execute the following query:

```
myRDD = (
    sc
    .textFile(
        '~/data/flights/airport-codes-na.txt'
        , minPartitions=4
        , use_unicode=True
    ).map(lambda element: element.split("\t"))
)
```

If you are running Databricks, the same file is already included in the `/databricks-datasets` folder; the command is:

```
myRDD = sc.textFile('/databricks-
datasets/flights/airport-codes-na.txt').map(lambda
element: element.split("\t"))
```

When running the query:

```
myRDD.take(5)
```

The resulting output is:

```
Out[22]:   [[u'City', u'State', u'Country', u'IATA'], [u'Abbotsford', u'BC',
u'Canada', u'YXX'], [u'Aberdeen', u'SD', u'USA', u'ABR'], [u'Abilene',
u'TX', u'USA', u'ABI'], [u'Akron', u'OH', u'USA', u'CAK']]
```

Diving in a little deeper, let's determine the number of rows in this RDD. Note that more information on RDD actions such as `count()` is included in subsequent recipes:

```
myRDD.count()

# Output
# Out[37]: 527
```

Also, let's find out the number of partitions that support this RDD:

```
myRDD.getNumPartitions()

# Output
# Out[33]: 4
```

How it works...

The first code snippet to read the file and return values via `take` can be broken down into its two components: `sc.textFile()` and `map()`.

.textFile(...) method

To read the file, we are using SparkContext's `textFile()` method via this command:

```
(
    sc
    .textFile(
        '~/data/flights/airport-codes-na.txt'
        , minPartitions=4
        , use_unicode=True
    )
)
```

Only the first parameter is required, which indicates the location of the text file as per `~/data/flights/airport-codes-na.txt`. There are two optional parameters as well:

- `minPartitions`: Indicates the minimum number of partitions that make up the RDD. The Spark engine can often determine the best number of partitions based on the file size, but you may want to change the number of partitions for performance reasons and, hence, the ability to specify the minimum number.
- `use_unicode`: Engage this parameter if you are processing Unicode data.

Note that if you were to execute this statement without the subsequent `map()` function, the resulting RDD would not reference the tab-delimiter—basically a list of strings that is:

```
myRDD = sc.textFile('~/data/flights/airport-codes-na.txt')
myRDD.take(5)

# Out[35]:  [u'City\tState\tCountry\tIATA', u'Abbotsford\tBC\tCanada\tYXX',
u'Aberdeen\tSD\tUSA\tABR', u'Abilene\tTX\tUSA\tABI',
u'Akron\tOH\tUSA\tCAK']
```

.map(...) method

To make sense of the tab-delimiter with an RDD, we will use the `.map(...)` function to transform the data from a list of strings to a list of lists:

```
myRDD = (
    sc
    .textFile('~/data/flights/airport-codes-na.txt')
    .map(lambda element: element.split("\t"))
)
```

The key components of this map transformation are:

- `lambda`: An anonymous function (that is, a function defined without a name) composed of a single expression
- `split`: We're using PySpark's split function (within `pyspark.sql.functions`) to split a string around a regular expression pattern; in this case, our delimiter is a tab (that is, `\t`)

Putting the `sc.textFile()` and `map()` functions together allows us to read the text file and split by the tab-delimiter to produce an RDD composed of a parallelized list of lists collection:

```
Out[22]:  [[u'City', u'State', u'Country', u'IATA'], [u'Abbotsford', u'BC',
u'Canada', u'YXX'], [u'Aberdeen', u'SD', u'USA', u'ABR'], [u'Abilene',
u'TX', u'USA', u'ABI'], [u'Akron', u'OH', u'USA', u'CAK']]
```

Partitions and performance

Earlier in this recipe, if we had run `sc.textFile()` without specifying `minPartitions` for this dataset, we would only have two partitions:

```
myRDD = (
    sc
    .textFile('/databricks-datasets/flights/airport-codes-na.txt')
    .map(lambda element: element.split("\t"))
)

myRDD.getNumPartitions()

# Output
Out[2]: 2
```

But as noted, if the `minPartitions` flag is specified, then you would get the specified four partitions (or more):

```
myRDD = (
    sc
    .textFile(
        '/databricks-datasets/flights/airport-codes-na.txt'
        , minPartitions=4
    ).map(lambda element: element.split("\t"))
)

myRDD.getNumPartitions()
```

```
# Output
Out[6]: 4
```

A key aspect of partitions for your RDD is that the more partitions you have, the higher the parallelism. Potentially, having more partitions will improve your query performance. For this portion of the recipe, let's use a slightly larger file, `departuredelays.csv`:

```
# Read the `departuredelays.csv` file and count number of rows
myRDD = (
    sc
    .textFile('/data/flights/departuredelays.csv')
    .map(lambda element: element.split(","))
)

myRDD.count()

# Output Duration: 3.33s
Out[17]: 1391579

# Get the number of partitions
myRDD.getNumPartitions()

# Output:
Out[20]: 2
```

As noted in the preceding code snippet, by default, Spark will create two partitions and take 3.33 seconds (on my small cluster) to count the 1.39 million rows in the departure delays CSV file.

Executing the same command, but also specifying `minPartitions` (in this case, eight partitions), you will notice that the `count()` method completed in 2.96 seconds (instead of 3.33 seconds with eight partitions). Note that these values may be different based on your machine's configuration, but the key takeaway is that modifying the number of partitions may result in faster performance due to parallelization. Check out the following code:

```
# Read the `departuredelays.csv` file and count number of rows
myRDD = (
    sc
    .textFile('/data/flights/departuredelays.csv', minPartitions=8)
    .map(lambda element: element.split(","))
)

myRDD.count()

# Output Duration: 2.96s
Out[17]: 1391579
```

```
# Get the number of partitions
myRDD.getNumPartitions()

# Output:
Out[20]: 8
```

Overview of RDD transformations

As noted in preceding sections, there are two types of operation that can be used to shape data in an RDD: transformations and actions. A transformation, as the name suggests, *transforms* one RDD into another. In other words, it takes an existing RDD and transforms it into one or more output RDDs. In the preceding recipes, we had used a `map()` function, which is an example of a transformation to split the data by its tab-delimiter.

Transformations are lazy (unlike actions). They only get executed when an action is called on an RDD. For example, calling the `count()` function is an action; more information is available in the following section on actions.

Getting ready

This recipe will be reading a tab-delimited (or comma-delimited) file, so please ensure that you have a text (or CSV) file available. For your convenience, you can download the `airport-codes-na.txt` and `departuredelays.csv` files from `https://github.com/drabastomek/learningPySpark/tree/master/Chapter03/flight-data`. Ensure your local Spark cluster can access this file (for example, `~/data/flights/airport-codes-na.txt`).

> If you are running Databricks, the same file is already included in the `/databricks-datasets` folder; the command is
>
> ```
> myRDD = sc.textFile('/databricks-
> datasets/flights/airport-codes-na.txt').map(lambda line:
> line.split("\t"))
> ```

Many of the transformations in the next section will use the RDDs `airports` or `flights`; let's set them up using this code snippet:

```
# Setup the RDD: airports
airports = (
    sc
```

```
    .textFile('~/data/flights/airport-codes-na.txt')
    .map(lambda element: element.split("\t"))
)

airports.take(5)

# Output
Out[11]:
[[u'City', u'State', u'Country', u'IATA'],
 [u'Abbotsford', u'BC', u'Canada', u'YXX'],
 [u'Aberdeen', u'SD', u'USA', u'ABR'],
 [u'Abilene', u'TX', u'USA', u'ABI'],
 [u'Akron', u'OH', u'USA', u'CAK']]


# Setup the RDD: flights
flights = (
    sc
    .textFile('/databricks-datasets/flights/departuredelays.csv')
    .map(lambda element: element.split(","))
)

flights.take(5)

# Output
[[u'date', u'delay', u'distance', u'origin', u'destination'],
 [u'01011245', u'6', u'602', u'ABE', u'ATL'],
 [u'01020600', u'-8', u'369', u'ABE', u'DTW'],
 [u'01021245', u'-2', u'602', u'ABE', u'ATL'],
 [u'01020605', u'-4', u'602', u'ABE', u'ATL']]
```

How to do it...

In this section, we list common Apache Spark RDD transformations and code snippets. A more complete list can be found at `https://spark.apache.org/docs/latest/rdd-programming-guide.html#transformations`, `https://spark.apache.org/docs/latest/api/python/pyspark.html#pyspark.RDD` and `https://training.databricks.com/visualapi.pdf`.

The transformations include the following common tasks:

- Removing the header line from your text file: `zipWithIndex()`
- Selecting columns from your RDD: `map()`
- Running a WHERE (filter) clause: `filter()`

- Getting the distinct values: `distinct()`
- Getting the number of partitions: `getNumPartitions()`
- Determining the size of your partitions (that is, the number of elements within each partition): `mapPartitionsWithIndex()`

.map(...) transformation

The `map(f)` transformation returns a new RDD formed by passing each element through a function, `f`.

Look at the following code snippet:

```
# Use map() to extract out the first two columns
airports.map(lambda c: (c[0], c[1])).take(5)
```

This will produce the following output:

```
# Output
[(u'City', u'State'),
 (u'Abbotsford', u'BC'),
 (u'Aberdeen', u'SD'),

 (u'Abilene', u'TX'),
 (u'Akron', u'OH')]
```

.filter(...) transformation

The `filter(f)` transformation returns a new RDD based on selecting elements for which the `f` function returns true. Therefore, look at the following code snippet:

```
# User filter() to filter where second column == "WA"
(
    airports
    .map(lambda c: (c[0], c[1]))
    .filter(lambda c: c[1] == "WA")
    .take(5)
)
```

This will produce the following output:

```
# Output
[(u'Bellingham', u'WA'),
 (u'Moses Lake', u'WA'),
 (u'Pasco', u'WA'),
```

```
(u'Pullman', u'WA'),
(u'Seattle', u'WA')]
```

.flatMap(...) transformation

The flatMap(f) transformation is similar to map, but the new RDD flattens out all of the elements (that is, a sequence of events). Let's look at the following snippet:

```
# Filter only second column == "WA",
# select first two columns within the RDD,
# and flatten out all values
(
    airports
    .filter(lambda c: c[1] == "WA")
    .map(lambda c: (c[0], c[1]))
    .flatMap(lambda x: x)
    .take(10)
)
```

The preceding code will produce the following output:

```
# Output
[u'Bellingham',
 u'WA',
 u'Moses Lake',
 u'WA',
 u'Pasco',
 u'WA',
 u'Pullman',
 u'WA',
 u'Seattle',
 u'WA']
```

.distinct() transformation

The distinct() transformation returns a new RDD containing the distinct elements of the source RDD. So, look at the following code snippet:

```
# Provide the distinct elements for the
# third column of airports representing
# countries
(
    airports
    .map(lambda c: c[2])
    .distinct()
```

```
        .take(5)
    )
```

This will return the following output:

```
# Output
[u'Canada', u'USA', u'Country']
```

.sample(...) transformation

The `sample(withReplacement, fraction, seed)` transformation samples a fraction of the data, with or without replacement (the `withReplacement` parameter), based on a random seed.

Look at the following code snippet:

```
# Provide a sample based on 0.001% the
# flights RDD data specific to the fourth
# column (origin city of flight)
# without replacement (False) using random
# seed of 123
(
    flights
    .map(lambda c: c[3])
    .sample(False, 0.001, 123)
    .take(5)
)
```

We can expect the following result:

```
# Output
[u'ABQ', u'AEX', u'AGS', u'ANC', u'ATL']
```

.join(...) transformation

The `join(RDD')` transformation returns an RDD of *(key, (val_left, val_right))* when calling RDD *(key, val_left)* and RDD *(key, val_right)*. Outer joins are supported through left outer join, right outer join, and full outer join.

Look at the following code snippet:

```
# Flights data
#  e.g. (u'JFK', u'01010900')
flt = flights.map(lambda c: (c[3], c[0]))
```

```
# Airports data
# e.g. (u'JFK', u'NY')
air = airports.map(lambda c: (c[3], c[1]))

# Execute inner join between RDDs
flt.join(air).take(5)
```

This will give you the following result:

```
# Output
[(u'JFK', (u'01010900', u'NY')),
 (u'JFK', (u'01011200', u'NY')),
 (u'JFK', (u'01011900', u'NY')),
 (u'JFK', (u'01011700', u'NY')),
 (u'JFK', (u'01010800', u'NY'))]
```

.repartition(...) transformation

The `repartition(n)` transformation repartitions the RDD into n partitions by randomly reshuffling and uniformly distributing data across the network. As noted in the preceding recipes, this can improve performance by running more parallel threads concurrently. Here's a code snippet that does precisely that:

```
# The flights RDD originally generated has 2 partitions
flights.getNumPartitions()

# Output
2

# Let's re-partition this to 8 so we can have 8
# partitions
flights2 = flights.repartition(8)

# Checking the number of partitions for the flights2 RDD
flights2.getNumPartitions()

# Output
8
```

.zipWithIndex() transformation

The `zipWithIndex()` transformation appends (or ZIPs) the RDD with the element indices. This is very handy when wanting to remove the header row (first row) of a file.

Look at the following code snippet:

```
# View each row within RDD + the index
# i.e. output is in form ([row], idx)
ac = airports.map(lambda c: (c[0], c[3]))
ac.zipWithIndex().take(5)
```

This will generate this result:

```
# Output
[((u'City', u'IATA'), 0),
 ((u'Abbotsford', u'YXX'), 1),
 ((u'Aberdeen', u'ABR'), 2),
 ((u'Abilene', u'ABI'), 3),
 ((u'Akron', u'CAK'), 4)]
```

To remove the header from your data, you can use the following code:

```
# Using zipWithIndex to skip header row
# - filter out row 0
# - extract only row info
(
    ac
    .zipWithIndex()
    .filter(lambda (row, idx): idx > 0)
    .map(lambda (row, idx): row)
    .take(5)
)
```

The preceding code will skip the header, as shown as follows:

```
# Output
[(u'Abbotsford', u'YXX'),
 (u'Aberdeen', u'ABR'),
 (u'Abilene', u'ABI'),
 (u'Akron', u'CAK'),
 (u'Alamosa', u'ALS')]
```

.reduceByKey(...) transformation

The reduceByKey(f) transformation reduces the elements of the RDD using f by the key. The f function should be commutative and associative so that it can be computed correctly in parallel.

Look at the following code snippet:

```
# Determine delays by originating city
# - remove header row via zipWithIndex()
#   and map()
(
    flights
    .zipWithIndex()
    .filter(lambda (row, idx): idx > 0)
    .map(lambda (row, idx): row)
    .map(lambda c: (c[3], int(c[1])))
    .reduceByKey(lambda x, y: x + y)
    .take(5)
)
```

This will generate the following output:

```
# Output
[(u'JFK', 387929),
 (u'MIA', 169373),
 (u'LIH', -646),
 (u'LIT', 34489),
 (u'RDM', 3445)]
```

.sortByKey(...) transformation

The `sortByKey(asc)` transformation orders *(key, value)* RDD by *key* and returns an RDD in ascending or descending order. Look at the following code snippet:

```
# Takes the origin code and delays, remove header
# runs a group by origin code via reduceByKey()
# sorting by the key (origin code)
(
    flights
    .zipWithIndex()
    .filter(lambda (row, idx): idx > 0)
    .map(lambda (row, idx): row)
    .map(lambda c: (c[3], int(c[1])))
    .reduceByKey(lambda x, y: x + y)
    .sortByKey()
    .take(50)
)
```

This will produce this output:

```
# Output
[(u'ABE', 5113),
 (u'ABI', 5128),
 (u'ABQ', 64422),
 (u'ABY', 1554),
 (u'ACT', 392),
 ...]
```

.union(...) transformation

The union(RDD) transformation returns a new RDD that is the union of the source and argument RDDs. Look at the following code snippet:

```
# Create `a` RDD of Washington airports
a = (
    airports
    .zipWithIndex()
    .filter(lambda (row, idx): idx > 0)
    .map(lambda (row, idx): row)
    .filter(lambda c: c[1] == "WA")
)

# Create `b` RDD of British Columbia airports
b = (
    airports
    .zipWithIndex()
    .filter(lambda (row, idx): idx > 0)
    .map(lambda (row, idx): row)
    .filter(lambda c: c[1] == "BC")
)

# Union WA and BC airports
a.union(b).collect()
```

This will generate the following output:

```
# Output
[[u'Bellingham', u'WA', u'USA', u'BLI'],
 [u'Moses Lake', u'WA', u'USA', u'MWH'],
 [u'Pasco', u'WA', u'USA', u'PSC'],
 [u'Pullman', u'WA', u'USA', u'PUW'],
 [u'Seattle', u'WA', u'USA', u'SEA'],
 ...
 [u'Vancouver', u'BC', u'Canada', u'YVR'],
```

```
[u'Victoria', u'BC', u'Canada', u'YYJ'],
[u'Williams Lake', u'BC', u'Canada', u'YWL']]
```

.mapPartitionsWithIndex(...) transformation

The `mapPartitionsWithIndex(f)` is similar to map but runs the `f` function separately on each partition and provides an index of the partition. It is useful to determine the data skew within partitions (check the following snippet):

```
# Source: https://stackoverflow.com/a/38957067/1100699
def partitionElementCount(idx, iterator):
  count = 0
  for _ in iterator:
    count += 1
  return idx, count

# Use mapPartitionsWithIndex to determine
flights.mapPartitionsWithIndex(partitionElementCount).collect()
```

The preceding code will produce the following result:

```
# Output
[0,
 174293,
 1,
 174020,
 2,
 173849,
 3,
 174006,
 4,
 173864,
 5,
 174308,
 6,
 173620,
 7,
 173618]
```

How it works...

Recall that a transformation takes an existing RDD and transforms it into one or more output RDDs. It is also a lazy process that is not initiated until an action is executed. In the following join example, the action is the `take()` function:

```
# Flights data
#  e.g. (u'JFK', u'01010900')
flt = flights.map(lambda c: (c[3], c[0]))

# Airports data
# e.g. (u'JFK', u'NY')
air = airports.map(lambda c: (c[3], c[1]))

# Execute inner join between RDDs
flt.join(air).take(5)

# Output
[(u'JFK', (u'01010900', u'NY')),
 (u'JFK', (u'01011200', u'NY')),
 (u'JFK', (u'01011900', u'NY')),
 (u'JFK', (u'01011700', u'NY')),
 (u'JFK', (u'01010800', u'NY'))]
```

To better understand what is happening when running this join, let's review the Spark UI. Every Spark session launches a web-based UI, which is, by default, on port `4040`, for example, `http://localhost:4040`. It includes the following information:

- A list of scheduler stages and tasks
- A summary of RDD sizes and memory usage
- Environmental information
- Information about the running executors

For more information, please refer to the Apache Spark Monitoring documentation page at `https://spark.apache.org/docs/latest/monitoring.html`.

To dive deeper into Spark internals, a great video is Patrick Wendell's *Tuning and Debugging in Apache Spark* video, which is available at `https:/ /www.youtube.com/watch?v=kkOG_aJ9KjQ`.

As can be seen in the following DAG visualization, the join statement and two preceding map transformations have a single job (**Job 24**) that created two stages (**Stage 32** and **Stage 33**):

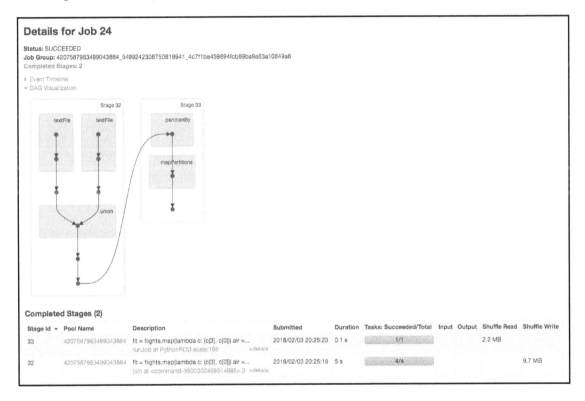

Details for Job 24

Let's dive deeper into these two stages:

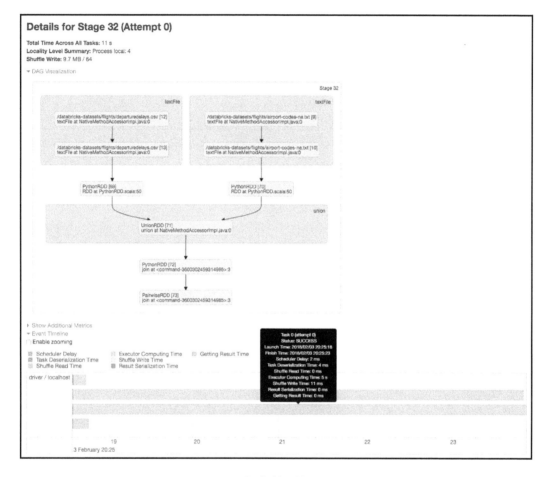

Details of Stage 32

To better understand the tasks executed in the first stage (**Stage 32**), we can dive deeper into the stage's **DAG Visualization** as well as the **Event Timeline**:

- The two `textFile` callouts are to extract the two different files (`departuredelays.csv` and `airport-codes-na.txt`)
- Once the `map` functions are complete, to support the `join`, Spark executes `UnionRDD` and `PairwiseRDD` to perform the basics behind the join as part of the `union` task

In the next stage, the `partitionBy` and `mapPartitions` tasks shuffle and re-map the partitions prior to providing the output via the `take()` function:

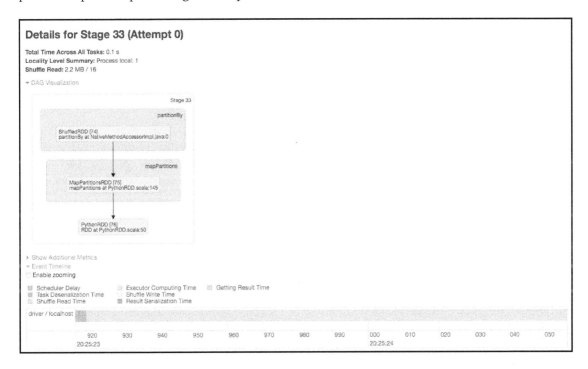

Details of Stage 33

 Note that that if you execute the same statements without the `take()` function (or some other *action*), only *transformation* operations will be executed with nothing showing up in the Spark UI denoting lazy processing.

For example, if you were to execute the following code snippet, note that the output is a pointer to a Python RDD:

```
# Same join statement as above but no action operation such as take()
flt = flights.map(lambda c: (c[3], c[0]))
air = airports.map(lambda c: (c[3], c[1]))
flt.join(air)

# Output
Out[32]: PythonRDD[101] at RDD at PythonRDD.scala:50
```

Overview of RDD actions

As noted in preceding sections, there are two types of Apache Spark RDD operations: transformations and actions. An *action* returns a value to the driver after running a computation on the dataset, typically on the workers. In the preceding recipes, the `take()` and `count()` RDD operations are examples of *actions*.

Getting ready

This recipe will be reading a tab-delimited (or comma-delimited) file, so please ensure that you have a text (or CSV) file available. For your convenience, you can download the `airport-codes-na.txt` and `departuredelays.csv` files from learning `http://bit.ly/2nroHbh`. Ensure your local Spark cluster can access this file (`~/data/flights/airport-codes-na.txt`).

> If you are running Databricks, the same file is already included in the `/databricks-datasets` folder; the command is
>
> ```
> myRDD = sc.textFile('/databricks-
> datasets/flights/airport-codes-na.txt').map(lambda line:
> line.split("\t"))
> ```

Many of the transformations in the next section will use the RDDs `airports` or `flights`; let's set them up by using the following code snippet:

```
# Setup the RDD: airports
airports = (
    sc
    .textFile('~/data/flights/airport-codes-na.txt')
    .map(lambda element: element.split("\t"))
)

airports.take(5)

# Output
Out[11]:
[[u'City', u'State', u'Country', u'IATA'],
 [u'Abbotsford', u'BC', u'Canada', u'YXX'],
 [u'Aberdeen', u'SD', u'USA', u'ABR'],
 [u'Abilene', u'TX', u'USA', u'ABI'],
 [u'Akron', u'OH', u'USA', u'CAK']]
```

```
# Setup the RDD: flights
flights = (
    sc
    .textFile('~/data/flights/departuredelays.csv', minPartitions=8)
    .map(lambda line: line.split(","))
)

flights.take(5)

# Output
[[u'date', u'delay', u'distance', u'origin', u'destination'],
 [u'01011245', u'6', u'602', u'ABE', u'ATL'],
 [u'01020600', u'-8', u'369', u'ABE', u'DTW'],
 [u'01021245', u'-2', u'602', u'ABE', u'ATL'],
 [u'01020605', u'-4', u'602', u'ABE', u'ATL']]
```

How to do it...

The following list outlines common Apache Spark RDD transformations and code snippets. A more complete list can be found in the Apache Spark documentation, **RDD Programing Guide | Transformations**, at https://spark.apache.org/docs/latest/rdd-programming-guide.html#transformations, the PySpark RDD API at https://spark.apache.org/docs/latest/api/python/pyspark.html#pyspark.RDD, and Essential Core and Intermediate Spark Operations at https://training.databricks.com/visualapi.pdf.

.take(...) action

We have already discussed this, but, for the sake of completeness, the take(n) action returns an array with the first n elements of the RDD. Look at the following code:

```
# Print to console the first 3 elements of
# the airports RDD
airports.take(3)
```

This will generate the following output:

```
# Output
[[u'City', u'State', u'Country', u'IATA'],
 [u'Abbotsford', u'BC', u'Canada', u'YXX'],
 [u'Aberdeen', u'SD', u'USA', u'ABR']]
```

.collect() action

We have also cautioned you about using this action; `collect()` returns all of the elements from the workers to the driver. Thus, look at the following code:

```
# Return all airports elements
# filtered by WA state
airports.filter(lambda c: c[1] == "WA").collect()
```

This will generate the following output:

```
# Output
[[u'Bellingham', u'WA', u'USA', u'BLI'],  [u'Moses Lake', u'WA', u'USA',
u'MWH'],  [u'Pasco', u'WA', u'USA', u'PSC'],  [u'Pullman', u'WA', u'USA',
u'PUW'],  [u'Seattle', u'WA', u'USA', u'SEA'],  [u'Spokane', u'WA', u'USA',
u'GEG'],  [u'Walla Walla', u'WA', u'USA', u'ALW'],  [u'Wenatchee', u'WA',
u'USA', u'EAT'],  [u'Yakima', u'WA', u'USA', u'YKM']]
```

.reduce(...) action

The `reduce(f)` action aggregates the elements of an RDD by `f`. The `f` function should be commutative and associative so that it can be computed correctly in parallel. Look at the following code:

```
# Calculate the total delays of flights
# between SEA (origin) and SFO (dest),
# convert delays column to int
# and summarize
flights\
  .filter(lambda c: c[3] == 'SEA' and c[4] == 'SFO')\
  .map(lambda c: int(c[1]))\
  .reduce(lambda x, y: x + y)
```

This will produce the following result:

```
# Output
22293
```

We need to make an important note here, however. When using `reduce()`, the reducer function needs to be associative and commutative; that is, a change in the order of elements and operands does not change the result.

Associativity rule: `(6 + 3) + 4 = 6 + (3 + 4)`
Commutative rule: `6 + 3 + 4 = 4 + 3 + 6`

Error can occur if you ignore the aforementioned rules.

As an example, see the following RDD (with one partition only!):

```
data_reduce = sc.parallelize([1, 2, .5, .1, 5, .2], 1)
```
Reducing data to divide the current result by the subsequent one, we would expect a value of 10:

```
works = data_reduce.reduce(lambda x, y: x / y)
```
Partitioning the data into three partitions will produce an incorrect result:

```
data_reduce = sc.parallelize([1, 2, .5, .1, 5, .2], 3)
data_reduce.reduce(lambda x, y: x / y)
```
It will produce `0.004`.

.count() action

The `count()` action returns the number of elements in the RDD. See the following code:

```
(
    flights
    .zipWithIndex()
    .filter(lambda (row, idx): idx > 0)
    .map(lambda (row, idx): row)
    .count()
)
```

This will produce the following result:

```
# Output
1391578
```

.saveAsTextFile(...) action

The `saveAsTextFile()` action saves your RDD into a text file; note that each partition is a separate file. See the following snippet:

```
# Saves airports as a text file
#   Note, each partition has their own file
```

```
# saveAsTextFile
airports.saveAsTextFile("/tmp/denny/airports")
```

This will actually save the following files:

```
# Review file structure
# Note that `airports` is a folder with two
# files (part-zzzzz) as the airports RDD is
# comprised of two partitions.
/tmp/denny/airports/_SUCCESS
/tmp/denny/airports/part-00000
/tmp/denny/airports/part-00001
```

How it works...

Recall that actions return a value to the driver after running a computation on the dataset, typically on the workers. Examples of some Spark actions include count() and take(); for this section, we will be focusing on reduceByKey():

```
# Determine delays by originating city
# - remove header row via zipWithIndex()
#   and map()
flights.zipWithIndex()\
  .filter(lambda (row, idx): idx > 0)\
  .map(lambda (row, idx): row)\
  .map(lambda c: (c[3], int(c[1])))\
  .reduceByKey(lambda x, y: x + y)\
  .take(5)

# Output
[(u'JFK', 387929),
 (u'MIA', 169373),
 (u'LIH', -646),
 (u'LIT', 34489),
 (u'RDM', 3445)]
```

To better understand what is happening when running this join, let's review the Spark UI. Every Spark Session launches a web-based UI, which is, by default, on port 4040, for example, http://localhost:4040. It includes the following information:

- A list of scheduler stages and tasks
- A summary of RDD sizes and memory usage
- Environmental information
- Information about the running executors

For more information, please refer to the Apache Spark Monitoring documentation page at `https://spark.apache.org/docs/latest/monitoring.html`.

To dive deeper into Spark internals, a great video is Patrick Wendell's *Tuning and Debugging in Apache Spark* video, which is available at `https://www.youtube.com/watch?v=kkOG_aJ9KjQ`.

Here is the DAG visualization of the preceding code snippet, which is executed when the `reduceByKey()` action is called; note that Job 14 represents only the `reduceByKey()` of part the DAG. A previous job had executed and returned the results based on the `zipWithIndex()` transformation, which is not included in **Job 14**:

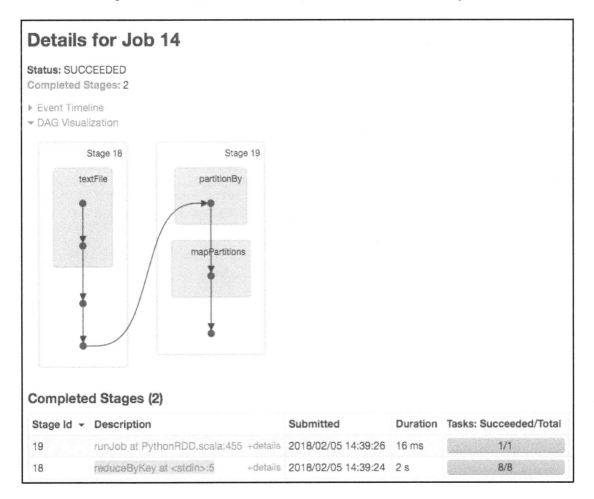

Digging further into the tasks that make up each stage, notice that the bulk of the work is done in **Stage 18**. Note the eight parallel tasks that end up processing data, from extracting it from the file (`/tmp/data/departuredelays.csv`) to executing `reduceByKey()` in parallel:

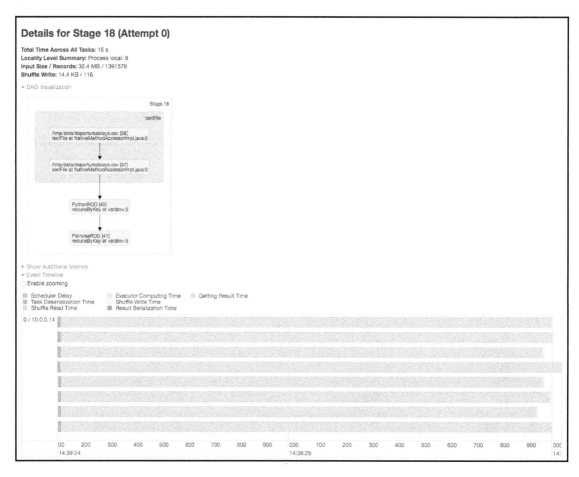

Details of Stage 18

A few important callouts are as follows:

- Spark's `reduceByKey(f)` assumes the `f` function is commutative and associative so that it can be computed correctly in parallel. As noted in the Spark UI, all eight tasks are processing the data extraction (`sc.textFile`) and `reduceByKey()` in parallel, providing faster performance.
- As noted in the *Getting ready* section of this recipe, we executed `sc.textFile($fileLocation, minPartitions=8)`... This forced the RDD to have eight partitions (at least eight partitions), which translated to eight tasks being executed in parallel:

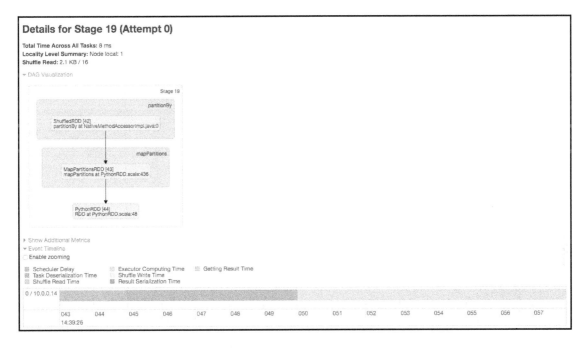

Now that you have executed `reduceByKey()`, we will run `take(5)`, which executes another stage that shuffles the eight partitions from the workers to the single driver node; that way, the data can be collected for viewing in the console.

Pitfalls of using RDDs

The key concern associated with using RDDs is that they can take a lot of time to master. The flexibility of running functional operators such as map, reduce, and shuffle allows you to perform a wide variety of transformations against your data. But with this power comes great responsibility, and it is potentially possible to write code that is inefficient, such as the use of GroupByKey; more information can be found in *Avoid GroupByKey* at https://databricks.gitbooks.io/databricks-spark-knowledge-base/content/best_practices/prefer_reducebykey_over_groupbykey.html.

Generally, you will typically have slower performance when using RDDs compared to Spark DataFrames, as noted in the following diagram:

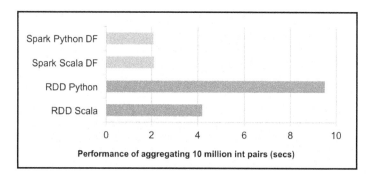

Source: Introducing DataFrames in Apache Spark for Large Scale Data Science
at https://databricks.com/blog/2015/02/17/introducing-dataframes-in-spark-for-large-scale-data-science.html

 It is also important to note that with Apache Spark 2.0+, datasets have functional operators (giving you flexibility similar to RDDs), yet also utilize the catalyst optimizer, providing faster performance. More information on datasets will be discussed in the next chapter.

The reason RDDs are slow—especially within the context of PySpark—is because whenever a PySpark program is executed using RDDs, there is a potentially large overhead to execute the job. As noted in the following diagram, in the PySpark driver, the Spark Context uses Py4j to launch a JVM using JavaSparkContext. Any RDD transformations are initially mapped to PythonRDD objects in Java.

Once these tasks are pushed out to the Spark worker(s), `PythonRDD` objects launch Python `subprocesses` using pipes to send both code and data to be processed in Python:

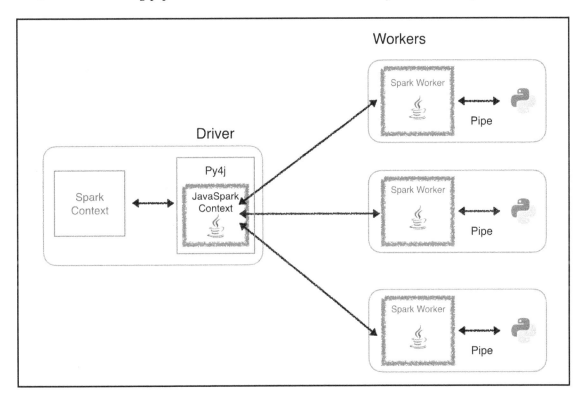

While this approach allows PySpark to distribute the processing of the data to multiple Python `subprocesses` on multiple workers, as you can see, there is a lot of context switching and communications overhead between Python and the JVM.

An excellent resource on PySpark performance is Holden Karau's *Improving PySpark Performance: Spark Performance Beyond the JVM* at `http:/ /bit.ly/2bx89bn`.

This is even more apparent when using Python UDFs, as the performance is significantly slower because all of the data will need to be transferred to the driver prior to using a Python UDF. Note that vectorized UDFs were introduced as part of Spark 2.3 and will improve PySpark UDF performance. For more information, please refer to *Introducing Vectorized UDFs for PySpark* at `https://databricks.com/blog/2017/10/30/introducing-vectorized-udfs-for-pyspark.html`.

Getting ready

As in the previous sections, let's make use of the `flights` dataset and create an RDD and a DataFrame against this dataset:

```
## Create flights RDD
flights = sc.textFile('/databricks-datasets/flights/departuredelays.csv')\
  .map(lambda line: line.split(","))\
  .zipWithIndex()\
  .filter(lambda (row, idx): idx > 0)\
  .map(lambda (row, idx): row)

# Create flightsDF DataFrame
flightsDF = spark.read\
  .options(header='true', inferSchema='true')
  .csv('~/data/flights/departuredelays.csv')
flightsDF.createOrReplaceTempView("flightsDF")
```

How to do it...

In this section, we will run the same `group by` statement—one via an RDD using `reduceByKey()`, and one via a DataFrame using Spark SQL `GROUP BY`. For this query, we will sum the time delays grouped by originating city and sort according to the originating city:

```
# RDD: Sum delays, group by and order by originating city
flights.map(lambda c: (c[3], int(c[1]))).reduceByKey(lambda x, y: x +
y).sortByKey().take(50)

# Output (truncated)
# Duration: 11.08 seconds
[(u'ABE', 5113),
 (u'ABI', 5128),
 (u'ABQ', 64422),
 (u'ABY', 1554),
 (u'ACT', 392),
 ... ]
```

For this particular configuration, it took 11.08 seconds to extract the columns, execute `reduceByKey()` to summarize the data, execute `sortByKey()` to order it, and then return the values to the driver:

```
# RDD: Sum delays, group by and order by originating city
spark.sql("select origin, sum(delay) as TotalDelay from flightsDF group by
origin order by origin").show(50)

# Output (truncated)
# Duration: 4.76s
+------+----------+
|origin|TotalDelay|
+------+----------+
|  ABE |      5113|
|  ABI |      5128|
|  ABQ |     64422|
|  ABY |      1554|
|  ACT |       392|
...
+------+----------+
```

There are many advantages of Spark DataFrames, including, but not limited to the following:

- You can execute Spark SQL statements (not just through the Spark DataFrame API)
- There is a schema associated with your data so you can specify the column name instead of position
- In this configuration and example, the query completes in 4.76 seconds, while RDDs complete in 11.08 seconds

It is impossible to improve your RDD query by specifying `minPartitions` within `sc.textFile()` when originally loading the data to increase the number of partitions:
```
flights = sc.textFile('/databricks-
datasets/flights/departuredelays.csv', minPartitions=8),
...
```

```
flights = sc.textFile('/databricks-datasets/flights/departuredelays.csv',
minPartitions=8), ...
```

For this configuration, the same query returned in 6.63 seconds. While this approach is faster, its still slower than DataFrames; in general, DataFrames are faster out of the box with the default configuration.

How it works...

To better understand the performance of the previous RDD and DataFrame, let's return to the Spark UI. For starters, when we run the `flights` RDD query, three separate jobs are executed, as can be seen in Databricks Community Edition in the following screenshot:

```
1  # How to do it
2  flights.map(lambda c: (c[3], int(c[1]))).reduceByKey(lambda x, y: x + y).sortByKey().take(50)

▼ (3) Spark Jobs
    ▶ Job 24   View (Stages: 2/2)
    ▶ Job 25   View (Stages: 1/1, 1 skipped)
    ▶ Job 26   View (Stages: 2/2, 1 skipped)
```

Each of these jobs spawn their own set of stages to initially read the text (or CSV) file, execute `reduceByKey()`, and execute the `sortByKey()` functions:

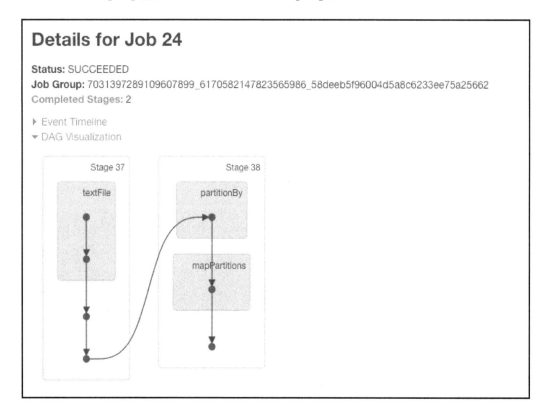

With two additional jobs to complete the `sortByKey()` execution:

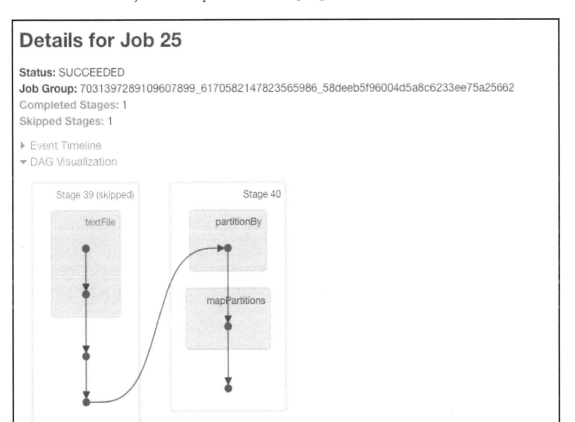

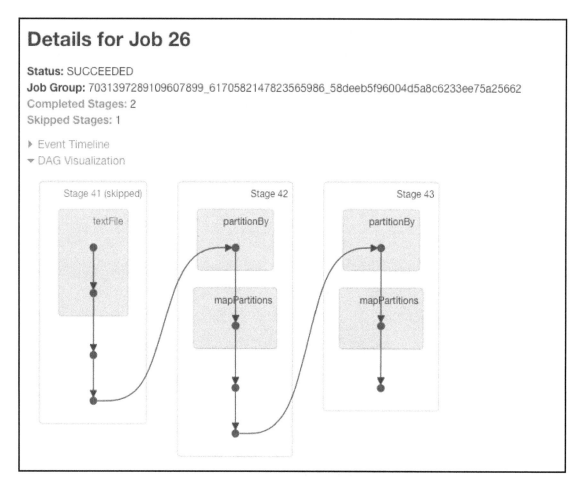

As can be observed, by using RDDs directly, there can potentially be a lot of overhead, generating multiple jobs and stages to complete a single query.

In the case of Spark DataFrames, for this query it is much simpler for it to consist of a single job with two stages. Note that the Spark UI has a number of DataFrame-specific set tasks, such as `WholeStageCodegen` and `Exchange`, that significantly improve the performance of Spark dataset and DataFrame queries. More information about the Spark SQL engine catalyst optimizer can be found in the next chapter:

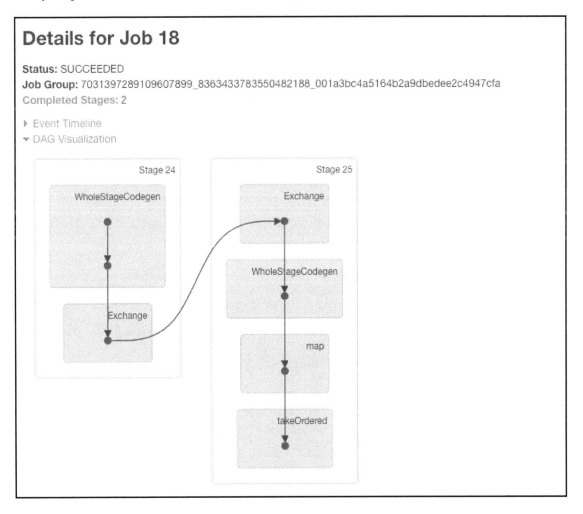

Abstracting Data with DataFrames

3

In this chapter, you will learn about the following recipes:

- Creating DataFrames
- Accessing underlying RDDs
- Performance optimizations
- Inferring the schema using reflection
- Specifying the schema programmatically
- Creating a temporary table
- Using SQL to interact with DataFrames
- Overview of DataFrame transformations
- Overview of DataFrame actions

Introduction

In this chapter, we will explore the current fundamental data structure—DataFrames. DataFrames take advantage of the developments in the tungsten project and the Catalyst Optimizer. These two improvements bring the performance of PySpark on par with that of either Scala or Java.

Project tungsten is a set of improvements to Spark Engine aimed at bringing its execution process closer to the *bare metal*. The main deliverables include:

- **Code generation at runtime**: This aims at leveraging the optimizations implemented in modern compilers
- **Taking advantage of the memory hierarchy**: The algorithms and data structures exploit memory hierarchy for fast execution

- **Direct-memory management**: Removes the overhead associated with Java garbage collection and JVM object creation and management
- **Low-level programming**: Speeds up memory access by loading immediate data to CPU registers
- **Virtual function dispatches elimination**: This eliminates the necessity of multiple CPU calls

 Check this blog from Databricks for more information: `https://www.databricks.com/blog/2015/04/28/project-tungsten-bringing-spark-closer-to-bare-metal.html`.

The Catalyst Optimizer sits at the core of Spark SQL and powers both the SQL queries executed against the data and DataFrames. The process starts with the query being issued to the engine. The logical plan of execution is first being optimized. Based on the optimized logical plan, multiple physical plans are derived and pushed through a cost optimizer. The selected, most cost-efficient plan is then translated (using code generation optimizations implemented as part of the tungsten project) into an optimized RDD-based execution code.

Creating DataFrames

A Spark DataFrame is an immutable collection of data distributed within a cluster. The data inside a DataFrame is organized into named columns that can be compared to tables in a relational database.

In this recipe, we will learn how to create Spark DataFrames.

Getting ready

To execute this recipe, you need to have a working Spark 2.3 environment. If you do not have one, you might want to go back to `Chapter 1`, *Installing and Configuring Spark*, and follow the recipes you find there.

All the code that you will need for this chapter can be found in the GitHub repository we set up for the book: `http://bit.ly/2ArlBck`; go to `Chapter 3` and open the `3. Abstracting data with DataFrames.ipynb` notebook.

There are no other requirements.

How to do it...

There are many ways to create a DataFrame, but the simplest way is to create an RDD and convert it into a DataFrame:

```
sample_data = sc.parallelize([
      (1, 'MacBook Pro', 2015, '15"', '16GB', '512GB SSD'
        , 13.75, 9.48, 0.61, 4.02)
    , (2, 'MacBook', 2016, '12"', '8GB', '256GB SSD'
        , 11.04, 7.74, 0.52, 2.03)
    , (3, 'MacBook Air', 2016, '13.3"', '8GB', '128GB SSD'
        , 12.8, 8.94, 0.68, 2.96)
    , (4, 'iMac', 2017, '27"', '64GB', '1TB SSD'
        , 25.6, 8.0, 20.3, 20.8)
])

sample_data_df = spark.createDataFrame(
    sample_data
    , [
        'Id'
        , 'Model'
        , 'Year'
        , 'ScreenSize'
        , 'RAM'
        , 'HDD'
        , 'W'
        , 'D'
        , 'H'
        , 'Weight'
    ]
)
```

How it works...

If you have read the previous chapter, you probably already know how to create RDDs. In this example, we simply call the `sc.parallelize(...)` method.

Our sample dataset contains just a handful of records of the relatively recent Apple computers. However, as with all RDDs, it is hard to figure out what each element of the tuple stands for since RDDs are schema-less structures.

Therefore, when using the `.createDataFrame(...)` method of `SparkSession`, we pass a list of column names as the second argument; the first argument is the RDD we wish to transform into a DataFrame.

Now, if we peek inside the `sample_data` RDD using `sample_data.take(1)`, we will retrieve the first record:

```
[(1, 'MacBook Pro', 2015, '15"', '16GB', '512GB SSD', 13.75, 9.48, 0.61, 4.02)]
```

To compare the content of a DataFrame, we can run `sample_data_df.take(1)` to get the following:

```
[Row(Id=1, Model='MacBook Pro', Year=2015, ScreenSize='15"', RAM='16GB', HDD='512GB SSD', W=13.75, D=9.48, H=0.61, Weight=4.02)]
```

As you can now see, a DataFrame is a collection of `Row(...)` objects. A `Row(...)` object consists of data that is named, unlike an RDD.

If the preceding `Row(...)` object looks similar to a dictionary to you, you are not wrong. Any `Row(...)` object can be converted into a dictionary using the `.asDict(...)` method. For more information, check out http://spark.apache.org/docs/latest/api/python/pyspark.sql. html#pyspark.sql.Row.

If, however, we were to have a look at the data within the `sample_data_df` DataFrame, using the `.show(...)` method, we would see the following:

```
+---+-----------+----+----------+----+----------+-----+----+----+------+------------+
| Id|      Model|Year|ScreenSize| RAM|       HDD|    W|   D|   H|Weight|    HDDSplit|
+---+-----------+----+----------+----+----------+-----+----+----+------+------------+
|  1|MacBook Pro|2015|     "15""|16GB|512GB SSD|13.75|9.48|0.61|  4.02|[512GB, SSD]|
|  2|    MacBook|2016|     "12""| 8GB|256GB SSD|11.04|7.74|0.52|  2.03|[256GB, SSD]|
|  3|MacBook Air|2016|   "13.3""| 8GB|128GB SSD| 12.8|8.94|0.68|  2.96|[128GB, SSD]|
|  4|       iMac|2017|     "27""|64GB|   1TB SSD| 25.6| 8.0|20.3|  20.8|  [1TB, SSD]|
+---+-----------+----+----------+----+----------+-----+----+----+------+------------+
```

Since DataFrames have schema, let's see the schema of our `sample_data_df` using the `.printSchema()` method:

```
root
 |-- D: double (nullable = true)
 |-- H: double (nullable = true)
 |-- HDD: string (nullable = true)
 |-- Model: string (nullable = true)
 |-- RAM: string (nullable = true)
 |-- ScreenSize: string (nullable = true)
 |-- W: double (nullable = true)
 |-- Weight: double (nullable = true)
 |-- Year: long (nullable = true)
 |-- Id: long (nullable = true)
```

As you can see, the columns in our DataFrame have the datatypes matching the datatypes of the original `sample_data` RDD.

 Even though Python is not a strongly-typed language, DataFrames in PySpark are. Unlike RDDs, every element of a DataFrame column has a specified type (these are all listed in the `pyspark.sql.types` submodule) and all the data must conform to the specified schema.

There's more...

When you use the `.read` attribute of `SparkSession`, it returns a `DataFrameReader` object. `DataFrameReader` is an interface to read data into a DataFrame.

From JSON

To read data from a JSON-formatted file, you can simply do the following:

```
sample_data_json_df = (
    spark
    .read
    .json('../Data/DataFrames_sample.json')
)
```

The only drawback (although a minor one) of reading the data from a JSON-formatted file is the fact that all the columns will be ordered alphabetically. See for yourself by running `sample_data_json_df.show()`:

```
+----+----+---------+-----------+----+-----------+-----+-------+-----+---+
|   D|   H|      HDD|      Model| RAM| ScreenSize|    W| Weight| Year| Id|
+----+----+---------+-----------+----+-----------+-----+-------+-----+---+
|9.48|0.61|512GB SSD|MacBook Pro|16GB|        15"|13.75|   4.02| 2015|  1|
|7.74|0.52|256GB SSD|    MacBook| 8GB|        12"|11.04|   2.03| 2016|  2|
|8.94|0.68|128GB SSD|MacBook Air| 8GB|      13.3"| 12.8|   2.96| 2016|  3|
| 8.0|20.3|  1TB SSD|       iMac|64GB|        27"| 25.6|   20.8| 2017|  4|
+----+----+---------+-----------+----+-----------+-----+-------+-----+---+
```

The datatypes, however, remain unchanged: `sample_data_json_df.printSchema()`

```
root
 |-- D: double (nullable = true)
 |-- H: double (nullable = true)
 |-- HDD: string (nullable = true)
 |-- Model: string (nullable = true)
 |-- RAM: string (nullable = true)
 |-- ScreenSize: string (nullable = true)
 |-- W: double (nullable = true)
 |-- Weight: double (nullable = true)
 |-- Year: long (nullable = true)
 |-- Id: long (nullable = true)
```

From CSV

Reading from a CSV file is equally simple:

```
sample_data_csv = (
    spark
    .read
    .csv(
        '../Data/DataFrames_sample.csv'
        , header=True
        , inferSchema=True)
)
```

The only additional parameters passed make sure that the method treats the first row as column names (the `header` parameter) and that it will attempt to assign the right datatype to each column based on the content (the `inferSchema` parameter assigns strings by default).

In contrast to reading the data from a JSON-formatted file, reading from a CSV file preserves the order of columns.

See also

- Check Spark's documentation for a full list of supported data formats: `http://
  spark.apache.org/docs/latest/api/python/pyspark.sql.html#pyspark.sql.
  DataFrameReader`

Accessing underlying RDDs

Switching to using DataFrames does not mean we need to completely abandon RDDs.
Under the hood, DataFrames still use RDDs, but of `Row(...)` objects, as explained earlier.
In this recipe, we will learn how to interact with the underlying RDD of a DataFrame.

Getting ready

To execute this recipe, you need to have a working Spark 2.3 environment. Also, you
should have already gone through the previous recipe as we will reuse the data we created
there.

There are no other requirements.

How to do it...

In this example, we will extract the size of the HDD and its type into separate columns, and
will then calculate the minimum volume needed to put each computer in boxes:

```
import pyspark.sql as sql
import pyspark.sql.functions as f

sample_data_transformed = (
    sample_data_df
    .rdd
    .map(lambda row: sql.Row(
        **row.asDict()
        , HDD_size=row.HDD.split(' ')[0]
        )
    )
    .map(lambda row: sql.Row(
        **row.asDict()
        , HDD_type=row.HDD.split(' ')[1]
        )
```

```
            )
            .map(lambda row: sql.Row(
                **row.asDict()
                , Volume=row.H * row.D * row.W
                )
            )
            .toDF()
            .select(
                sample_data_df.columns +
                [
                    'HDD_size'
                    , 'HDD_type'
                    , f.round(
                        f.col('Volume')
                    ).alias('Volume_cuIn')
                ]
            )
        )
```

How it works...

As pointed out earlier, each element of the RDD inside the DataFrame is a Row(...) object. You can check it by running these two statements:

```
sample_data_df.rdd.take(1)
```

And:

```
sample_data.take(1)
```

The first one produces a single-item list where the element is Row(...):

```
[Row(Id=1, Model='MacBook Pro', Year=2015, ScreenSize='15"', RAM='16GB', HDD='512GB SSD', W=13.75, D=9.48, H=0.61, Weight=4.02)]
```

The other also produces a single-item list, but the item is a tuple:

```
[(1, 'MacBook Pro', 2015, '15"', '16GB', '512GB SSD', 13.75, 9.48, 0.61, 4.02)]
```

 The sample_data RDD is the first RDD we created in the previous recipe.

With that in mind, let's now turn our attention to the code.

First, we load the necessary modules: to work with the `Row(...)` objects, we need `pyspark.sql`, and we will use the `.round(...)` method later, so we need the `pyspark.sql.functions` submodule.

Next, we extract `.rdd` from `sample_data_df`. Using the `.map(...)` transformation, we first add the `HDD_size` column to the schema.

Since we are working with RDDs, we want to retain all the other columns. Thus, we first convert the row (which is a `Row(...)` object) into a dictionary using the `.asDict()` method, so then we can later unpack it using `**`.

In Python, the single `*` preceding a list of tuples, if passed as a parameter to a function, passes each element of a list as a separate argument to the function. The double `**` takes the first element and turns it into a keyword parameter, and uses the second element as the value to be passed.

The second argument follows a simple convention: we pass the name of the column we want to create (the `HDD_size`), and set it to the desired value. In our first example, we split the `.HDD` column and extract the first element since it is `HDD_size`.

We repeat this step twice more: first, to create the `HDD_type` column, and second, to create the `Volume` column.

Next, we use the `.toDF(...)` method to convert our RDD back to a DataFrame. Note that you can still use the `.toDF(...)` method to convert a regular RDD (that is, where each element is not a `Row(...)` object) to a DataFrame, but you will you need to pass a list of column names to the `.toDF(...)` method or you end up with unnamed columns.

Finally, we `.select(...)` the columns so we can `.round(...)` the newly created `Volume` column. The `.alias(...)` method produces a different name for the resulting column.

The resulting DataFrame looks as follows:

```
+---+-----------+----+----------+----+----------+-----+----+----+------+--------+--------+-----------+
| Id|      Model|Year|ScreenSize| RAM|       HDD|    W|   D|   H|Weight|HDD_size|HDD_type|Volume_cuIn|
+---+-----------+----+----------+----+----------+-----+----+----+------+--------+--------+-----------+
|  1|MacBook Pro|2015|       15"|16GB|512GB SSD|13.75|9.48|0.61|  4.02|   512GB|     SSD|       80.0|
|  2|    MacBook|2016|       12"| 8GB|256GB SSD|11.04|7.74|0.52|  2.03|   256GB|     SSD|       44.0|
|  3|MacBook Air|2016|     13.3"| 8GB|128GB SSD| 12.8|8.94|0.68|  2.96|   128GB|     SSD|       78.0|
|  4|       iMac|2017|       27"|64GB|  1TB SSD| 25.6| 8.0|20.3|  20.8|     1TB|     SSD|     4157.0|
+---+-----------+----+----------+----+----------+-----+----+----+------+--------+--------+-----------+
```

Unsurprisingly, the desktop iMac would require the biggest box.

Performance optimizations

Starting with Spark 2.0, the performance of PySpark using DataFrames was on apar with that of Scala or Java. However, there was one exception: using **User Defined Functions** (**UDFs**); if a user defined a pure Python method and registered it as a UDF, under the hood, PySpark would have to constantly switch runtimes (Python to JVM and back). This was the main reason for an enormous performance hit compared with Scala, which does not need to convert the JVM object to a Python object.

Things have changed significantly in Spark 2.3. First, Spark started using the new Apache project. Arrow creates a single memory space used by all environments, thus removing the need for constant copying and converting between objects.

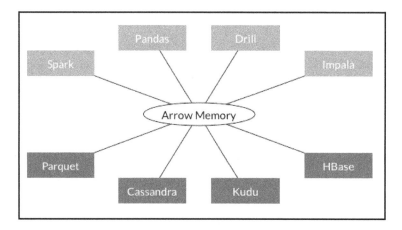

Source: https://arrow.apache.org/img/shared.png

 For an overview of Apache Arrow, go to `https://arrow.apache.org`.

Second, Arrow stores columnar objects in memory giving a big performance boost. Thus, in order to further leverage that, portions of the PySpark code have been refactored and that brought us vectorized UDFs.

In this recipe, we will learn how to use them and test the performance of both: the old, row-by-row UDFs, and the new vectorized ones.

Getting ready

To execute this recipe, you need to have a working Spark 2.3 environment.

There are no other requirements.

How to do it...

In this example, we will use SciPy to return a value of a normal probability distribution function (PDF) for a set of 1,000,000 random numbers between 0 and 1:

```
import pyspark.sql.functions as f
import pandas as pd
from scipy import stats

big_df = (
    spark
    .range(0, 1000000)
    .withColumn('val', f.rand())
)

big_df.cache()
big_df.show(3)

@f.pandas_udf('double', f.PandasUDFType.SCALAR)
def pandas_pdf(v):
    return pd.Series(stats.norm.pdf(v))

(
    big_df
    .withColumn('probability', pandas_pdf(big_df.val))
    .show(5)
)
```

How it works...

First, as always, we import all the modules we will need to run this example:

- `pyspark.sql.functions` gives us access to PySpark SQL functions. We will use it to create our DataFrame with random numbers.
- The `pandas` framework will give us access to the `.Series(...)` datatype so we can return a column from our UDF.

- `scipy.stats` give us access to statistical methods. We will use it to calculate the normal PDF for our random numbers.

Next, our `big_df`. `SparkSession` has a convenience method, `.range(...)`, which allows us to create a range of numbers within specified bounds; in this example, we simply create a DataFrame with one million records.

In the next line, we add another column to our DataFrame using the `.withColumn(...)` method; the column's name is `val` and it will contain one million `.rand()` numbers.

 The `.rand()` method returns pseudo-random numbers drawn from a uniform distribution that ranges between 0 and 1.

Finally, we `.cache()` the DataFrame so it all remains fully in memory (for speeding up the process).

Next, we define the `pandas_cdf(...)` method. Note the `@f.pandas_udf` decorator preceding the method's declaration as this is key to registering a vectorized UDF in PySpark and has only became available in Spark 2.3.

 Note that we did not have to decorate our method; we could have instead registered our vectorized method as `f.pandas_udf(f=pandas_pdf, returnType='double', functionType=f.PandasUDFType.SCALAR)`.

The first parameter to the decorator method is the return type of the UDF, in our case a `double`. This can be either a DDL-formatted type string or `pyspark.sql.types.DataType`. The second parameter is the function type; if we return a single column from our method (such as pandas' `.Series(...)` in our example), it will be `.PandasUDFType.SCALAR` (by default). If, on the other hand, we operate on multiple columns (such as pandas' `DataFrame(...)`), we would define `.PandasUDFType.GROUPED_MAP`.

Our `pandas_pdf(...)` method simply accepts a single column and returns a pandas' `.Series(...)` object with values of normal CDF-corresponding numbers.

Finally, we simply use the new method to transform our data. Here's what the top five records look like (yours most likely will look different since we are creating one million random numbers):

```
+---+-------------------+------------------+
| id|                val|       probability|
+---+-------------------+------------------+
|  0|  0.9453946488613437| 0.2551703151423011|
|  1| 0.39388041568859766| 0.3691657960230967|
|  2|  0.1356767412456391| 0.3952872266471388|
|  3|0.050985087503938376|0.39842409615712904|
|  4|  0.5167556509690651|  0.349079100100191|
+---+-------------------+------------------+
only showing top 5 rows
```

There's more...

Let's now compare the performance of the two approaches:

```python
def test_pandas_pdf():
    return (big_df
            .withColumn('probability', pandas_pdf(big_df.val))
            .agg(f.count(f.col('probability')))
            .show()
           )

%timeit -n 1 test_pandas_pdf()

# row-by-row version with Python-JVM conversion
@f.udf('double')
def pdf(v):
    return float(stats.norm.pdf(v))

def test_pdf():
    return (big_df
            .withColumn('probability', pdf(big_df.val))
            .agg(f.count(f.col('probability')))
            .show()
           )

%timeit -n 1 test_pdf()
```

The `test_pandas_pdf()` method simply uses the `pandas_pdf(...)` method to retrieve the PDF from the normal distribution, performs the `.count(...)` operation, and prints out the results using the `.show(...)` method. The `test_pdf()` method does the same but uses the `pdf(...)` method instead, which is the row-by-row way of using the UDFs.

The `%timeit` decorator simply runs the `test_pandas_pdf()` or the `test_pdf()` methods seven times, multiplied by each execution. Here's a sample output (abbreviated as it is, as you might have expected, highly repetitive) for running the `test_pandas_pdf()` method:

```
+------------------+
|count(probability)|
+------------------+
|           1000000|
+------------------+

23.1 s ± 937 ms per loop (mean ± std. dev. of 7 runs, 1 loop each)
```

The timings for the `test_pdf()` method are quoted as follows:

```
+------------------+
|count(probability)|
+------------------+
|           1000000|
+------------------+

23.1 s ± 937 ms per loop (mean ± std. dev. of 7 runs, 1 loop each)
```

As you can see, the vectorized UDFs provide ~100x performance improvements! Don't get too excited, as such speedups are only expected for more complex queries, such as the one we used previously.

See also

- To learn more, check out this blog post from Databricks announcing the vectorized UDFs: https://databricks.com/blog/2017/10/30/introducing-vectorized-udfs-for-pyspark.html

Inferring the schema using reflection

DataFrames have schema, RDDs don't. That is, unless RDDs are composed of `Row(...)` objects.

In this recipe, we will learn how to create DataFrames by inferring the schema using reflection.

Getting ready

To execute this recipe, you need to have a working Spark 2.3 environment.

There are no other requirements.

How to do it...

In this example, we will first read our CSV sample data into an RDD and then create a DataFrame from it. Here's the code:

```
import pyspark.sql as sql

sample_data_rdd = sc.textFile('../Data/DataFrames_sample.csv')

header = sample_data_rdd.first()

sample_data_rdd_row = (
    sample_data_rdd
    .filter(lambda row: row != header)
    .map(lambda row: row.split(','))
    .map(lambda row:
        sql.Row(
            Id=int(row[0])
            , Model=row[1]
            , Year=int(row[2])
            , ScreenSize=row[3]
            , RAM=row[4]
            , HDD=row[5]
            , W=float(row[6])
            , D=float(row[7])
            , H=float(row[8])
            , Weight=float(row[9])
        )
    )
)
```

How it works...

First, we load the SQL module of PySpark.

Next, we read the `DataFrames_sample.csv` file using the `.textFile(...)` method of SparkContext.

Review the previous chapter if you do not yet know how to read data into RDDs.

The resulting RDD looks as follows:

```
['Id, Model, Year, ScreenSize, RAM, HDD, W, D, H, Weight',
 '1,MacBook Pro,2015,"15\\"",16GB,512GB SSD,13.75,9.48,0.61,4.02']
```

As you can see, the RDD still contains the row with column names. In order to get rid of it, we first extract it using the `.first()` method and then later using the `.filter(...)` transformation to remove any row that is equal to the header.

Next, we split each row with a comma and create a `Row(...)` object for each observation. Note here that we convert all of the fields to the proper datatypes. For example, the `Id` column should be an integer, the `Model` name is a string, and `W` (width) is a float.

Finally, we simply call the `.createDataFrame(...)` method of SparkSession to convert our RDD of `Row(...)` objects into a DataFrame. Here's the final result:

```
+----+----+----------+---+-----------+----+----------+-----+------+----+
|   D|   H|       HDD| Id|      Model| RAM|ScreenSize|    W|Weight|Year|
+----+----+----------+---+-----------+----+----------+-----+------+----+
|9.48|0.61|512GB SSD|  1|MacBook Pro|16GB|    "15\""|13.75|  4.02|2015|
|7.74|0.52|256GB SSD|  2|    MacBook| 8GB|    "12\""|11.04|  2.03|2016|
|8.94|0.68|128GB SSD|  3|MacBook Air| 8GB|  "13.3\""| 12.8|  2.96|2016|
+----+----+----------+---+-----------+----+----------+-----+------+----+
only showing top 3 rows
```

See also

- Check out Spark's documentation to learn more: https://spark.apache.org/docs/latest/sql-programming-guide.html#inferring-the-schema-using-reflection

Specifying the schema programmatically

In the previous recipe, we learned how to infer the schema of a DataFrame using reflection.

In this recipe, we will learn how to specify the schema programmatically.

Getting ready

To execute this recipe, you need to have a working Spark 2.3 environment.

There are no other requirements.

How to do it...

In this example, we will learn how to specify the schema programmatically:

```python
import pyspark.sql.types as typ

sch = typ.StructType([
      typ.StructField('Id', typ.LongType(), False)
    , typ.StructField('Model', typ.StringType(), True)
    , typ.StructField('Year', typ.IntegerType(), True)
    , typ.StructField('ScreenSize', typ.StringType(), True)
    , typ.StructField('RAM', typ.StringType(), True)
    , typ.StructField('HDD', typ.StringType(), True)
    , typ.StructField('W', typ.DoubleType(), True)
    , typ.StructField('D', typ.DoubleType(), True)
    , typ.StructField('H', typ.DoubleType(), True)
    , typ.StructField('Weight', typ.DoubleType(), True)
])

sample_data_rdd = sc.textFile('../Data/DataFrames_sample.csv')

header = sample_data_rdd.first()

sample_data_rdd = (
    sample_data_rdd
    .filter(lambda row: row != header)
    .map(lambda row: row.split(','))
    .map(lambda row: (
                int(row[0])
                , row[1]
                , int(row[2])
                , row[3]
```

```
                        , row[4]
                        , row[5]
                        , float(row[6])
                        , float(row[7])
                        , float(row[8])
                        , float(row[9])
                )
        )
)

sample_data_schema = spark.createDataFrame(sample_data_rdd, schema=sch)
sample_data_schema.show()
```

How it works...

First, we create a list of `.StructField(...)` objects. `.StructField(...)` is a programmatic way of adding a field to a schema in PySpark. The first parameter is the name of the column we want to add.

The second parameter is the datatype of the data we want to store in the column; some of the types available include `.LongType()`, `.StringType()`, `.DoubleType()`, `.BooleanType()`, `.DateType()`, and `.BinaryType()`.

 For a full list of available datatypes in PySpark, go to `http://spark.apache.org/docs/latest/api/python/pyspark.sql.html#module-pyspark.sql.types`.

The last parameter of `.StructField(...)` indicates whether the column can contain null values or not; if set to `True`, it means it can.

Next, we read in the `DataFrames_sample.csv` file using the `.textFile(...)` method of SparkContext. We filter out the header, as we will specify the schema explicitly and we do not need the name columns that are stored in the first row. Next, we split each row with a comma and impose the right datatypes on each element so it conforms to the schema we just specified.

Finally, we call the `.createDataFrame(...)` method but this time, along with the RDD, we also pass `schema`. The resulting DataFrame looks as follows:

```
+---+-----------+----+----------+----+----------+-----+----+----+------+
| Id|      Model|Year|ScreenSize| RAM|       HDD|    W|   D|   H|Weight|
+---+-----------+----+----------+----+----------+-----+----+----+------+
|  1|MacBook Pro|2015|       15"|16GB|512GB SSD |13.75|9.48|0.61|  4.02|
|  2|    MacBook|2016|       12"| 8GB|256GB SSD |11.04|7.74|0.52|  2.03|
|  3|MacBook Air|2016|     13.3"| 8GB|128GB SSD | 12.8|8.94|0.68|  2.96|
|  4|       iMac|2017|       27"|64GB|  1TB SSD | 25.6| 8.0|20.3|  20.8|
+---+-----------+----+----------+----+----------+-----+----+----+------+
```

See also

- Check out Spark's documentation for more: `https://spark.apache.org/docs/latest/sql-programming-guide.html#programmatically-specifying-the-schema`

Creating a temporary table

DataFrames can easily be manipulated with SQL queries in Spark.

In this recipe, we will learn how to create a temporary view so you can access the data within DataFrame using SQL.

Getting ready

To execute this recipe, you need to have a working Spark 2.3 environment. You should have gone through the previous recipe, as we will be using the `sample_data_schema` DataFrame we created there.

There are no other requirements.

How to do it...

We simply use the `.createTempView(...)` method of a DataFrame:

```
sample_data_schema.createTempView('sample_data_view')
```

How it works...

The `.createTempView(...)` method is the simplest way to create a temporary view that later can be used to query the data. The only required parameter is the name of the view.

Let's see how such a temporary view can now be used to extract data:

```
spark.sql('''
    SELECT Model
         , Year
         , RAM
         , HDD
    FROM sample_data_view
''').show()
```

We simply use the `.sql(...)` method of SparkSession, which allows us to write ANSI-SQL code to manipulate data within a DataFrame. In this example, we simply extract four columns. Here's what we get back:

```
+-----------+----+----+---------+
|      Model|Year| RAM|      HDD|
+-----------+----+----+---------+
|MacBook Pro|2015|16GB|512GB SSD|
|    MacBook|2016| 8GB|256GB SSD|
|MacBook Air|2016| 8GB|128GB SSD|
|       iMac|2017|64GB|  1TB SSD|
+-----------+----+----+---------+
```

There's more...

Once you have created a temporary view, you cannot create another view with the same name. However, Spark provides another method that allows us to either create or update a view: `.createOrReplaceTempView(...)`. As the name suggests, by calling this method, we either create a new view if one does not exist, or we replace an already existing one with the new one:

```
sample_data_schema.createOrReplaceTempView('sample_data_view')
```

As before, we can now use it to interact with the data using SQL queries:

```
spark.sql('''
    SELECT Model
         , Year
         , RAM
         , HDD
         , ScreenSize
```

```
    FROM sample_data_view
''').show()
```

Here's what we get back:

```
+-----------+----+----+---------+----------+
|      Model|Year| RAM|      HDD|ScreenSize|
+-----------+----+----+---------+----------+
|MacBook Pro|2015|16GB|512GB SSD|    "15\""|
|    MacBook|2016| 8GB|256GB SSD|    "12\""|
|MacBook Air|2016| 8GB|128GB SSD|  "13.3\""|
|       iMac|2017|64GB|  1TB SSD|    "27\""|
+-----------+----+----+---------+----------+
```

Using SQL to interact with DataFrames

In the previous recipe, we learned how to create or replace temporary views.

In this recipe, we will learn how to play with the data within a DataFrame using SQL queries.

Getting ready

To execute this recipe, you need to have a working Spark 2.3 environment. You should have gone through the *Specifying the schema programmatically* recipe, as we will be using the sample_data_schema DataFrame we created there.

There are no other requirements.

How to do it...

In this example, we will extend our original data with the form factor for each model of Apple's computer:

```
models_df = sc.parallelize([
      ('MacBook Pro', 'Laptop')
    , ('MacBook', 'Laptop')
    , ('MacBook Air', 'Laptop')
    , ('iMac', 'Desktop')
]).toDF(['Model', 'FormFactor'])

models_df.createOrReplaceTempView('models')
```

```
sample_data_schema.createOrReplaceTempView('sample_data_view')

spark.sql('''
    SELECT a.*
        , b.FormFactor
    FROM sample_data_view AS a
    LEFT JOIN models AS b
        ON a.Model == b.Model
    ORDER BY Weight DESC
''').show()
```

How it works...

First, we create a simple DataFrame with two columns: `Model` and `FormFactor`. In this example, we use the `.toDF(...)` method of an RDD to quickly convert it into a DataFrame. The list that we pass is simply a list of column names and the schema will be inferred automatically.

Next, we create the model's view and replace `sample_data_view`.

Finally, to append `FormFactor` to our original data, we simply join the two views on the `Model` column. As the `.sql(...)` method accepts regular SQL expressions, we also use the `ORDER BY` clause so we can order by weight.

Here's what we get back:

```
+---+-----------+----+----------+----+---------+-----+----+----+------+-----------+----------+
| Id|      Model|Year|ScreenSize| RAM|      HDD|    W|   D|   H|Weight|      Model|FormFactor|
+---+-----------+----+----------+----+---------+-----+----+----+------+-----------+----------+
|  2|    MacBook|2016|     "12\""| 8GB|256GB SSD|11.04|7.74|0.52|  2.03|    MacBook|    Laptop|
|  1|MacBook Pro|2015|     "15\""|16GB|512GB SSD|13.75|9.48|0.61|  4.02|MacBook Pro|    Laptop|
|  3|MacBook Air|2016|   "13.3\""| 8GB|128GB SSD| 12.8|8.94|0.68|  2.96|MacBook Air|    Laptop|
|  4|       iMac|2017|     "27\""|64GB|   1TB SSD| 25.6| 8.0|20.3|  20.8|       iMac|   Desktop|
+---+-----------+----+----------+----+---------+-----+----+----+------+-----------+----------+
```

There's more...

The SQL queries are not limited to extracting data only. We can also run some aggregations:

```
spark.sql('''
    SELECT b.FormFactor
        , COUNT(*) AS ComputerCnt
```

```
    FROM sample_data_view AS a
    LEFT JOIN models AS b
        ON a.Model == b.Model
    GROUP BY FormFactor
''').show()
```

In this simple example, we will count how many different computers of different FormFactors we have. The COUNT(*) operator counts how many computers we have and works in conjunction with the GROUP BY clause that specifies the aggregation columns.

Here's what we get from this query:

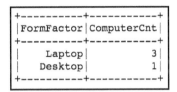

Overview of DataFrame transformations

Just like RDDs, DataFrames have both transformations and actions. As a reminder, transformations convert one DataFrame into another, while actions perform some computation on a DataFrame and normally return the result to the driver. Also, just like the RDDs, transformations in DataFrames are lazy.

In this recipe, we will review the most common transformations.

Getting ready

To execute this recipe, you need to have a working Spark 2.3 environment. You should have gone through the *Specifying schema programmatically* recipe, as we will be using the sample_data_schema DataFrame we created there.

There are no other requirements.

How to do it...

In this section, we will list some of the most common transformations available for DataFrames. The purpose of this list is not to provide a comprehensive enumeration of all available transformations, but to give you some intuition behind the most common ones.

The .select(...) transformation

The .select(...) transformation allows us to extract column or columns from a DataFrame. It works the same way as SELECT found in SQL.

Look at the following code snippet:

```
# select Model and ScreenSize from the DataFrame

sample_data_schema.select('Model', 'ScreenSize').show()
```

It produces the following output:

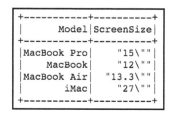

In SQL syntax, this would look like the following:

```
SELECT Model
     , ScreenSize
FROM sample_data_schema;
```

The .filter(...) transformation

The .filter(...) transformation, in contrast to .select(...), selects only rows that pass the condition specified. It can be compared with the WHERE statement from SQL.

Look at the following code snippet:

```
# extract only machines from 2015 onwards

(
    sample_data_schema
    .filter(sample_data_schema.Year > 2015)
    .show()
)
```

It produces the following output:

```
+---+-----------+----+----------+----+----------+-----+----+----+------+
| Id|      Model|Year|ScreenSize| RAM|       HDD|    W|   D|   H|Weight|
+---+-----------+----+----------+----+----------+-----+----+----+------+
|  2|    MacBook|2016|    "12\""| 8GB|256GB SSD|11.04|7.74|0.52|  2.03|
|  3|MacBook Air|2016|  "13.3\""| 8GB|128GB SSD| 12.8|8.94|0.68|  2.96|
|  4|       iMac|2017|    "27\""|64GB|  1TB SSD| 25.6| 8.0|20.3|  20.8|
+---+-----------+----+----------+----+----------+-----+----+----+------+
```

In SQL syntax, the preceding would be equivalent to:

```
SELECT *
FROM sample_data_schema
WHERE Year > 2015
```

The .groupBy(...) transformation

The `.groupBy(...)` transformation performs data aggregation based on the value (or values) from a column (or multiple columns). In SQL syntax, this equates to GROUP BY.

Look at the following code:

```
(
    sample_data_schema
    .groupBy('RAM')
    .count()
    .show()
)
```

It produces this result:

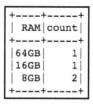

In SQL syntax, this would be:

```
SELECT RAM
    , COUNT(*) AS count
FROM sample_data_schema
GROUP BY RAM
```

The .orderBy(...) transformation

The `.orderBy(...)` transformation sorts the results given the columns specified. An equivalent from the SQL world would also be `ORDER BY`.

Look at the following code snippet:

```
# sort by width (W)

sample_data_schema.orderBy('W').show()
```

It produces the following output:

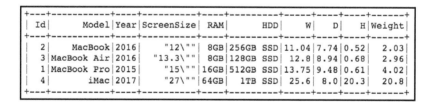

The SQL equivalent would be:

```
SELECT *
FROM sample_data_schema
ORDER BY W
```

You can also change the order of sorting to descending by using the `.desc()` switch of a column (the `.col(...)` method). Look at the following snippet:

```
# sort by height (H) in descending order

sample_data_schema.orderBy(f.col('H').desc()).show()
```

It produces the following output:

```
+---+-----------+----+----------+----+----------+-----+----+----+------+
| Id|      Model|Year|ScreenSize| RAM|       HDD|    W|   D|   H|Weight|
+---+-----------+----+----------+----+----------+-----+----+----+------+
|  4|       iMac|2017|   "27\""| 64GB|   1TB SSD| 25.6| 8.0|20.3|  20.8|
|  3|MacBook Air|2016| "13.3\""|  8GB|128GB SSD| 12.8|8.94|0.68|  2.96|
|  1|MacBook Pro|2015|   "15\""|16GB|512GB SSD|13.75|9.48|0.61|  4.02|
|  2|    MacBook|2016|   "12\""|  8GB|256GB SSD|11.04|7.74|0.52|  2.03|
+---+-----------+----+----------+----+----------+-----+----+----+------+
```

Put in SQL syntax, the preceding expression would be:

```
SELECT *
FROM sample_data_schema
ORDER BY H DESC
```

The .withColumn(...) transformation

The `.withColumn(...)` transformation applies a function to some other columns and/or literals (using the `.lit(...)` method) and stores it as a new function. In SQL, this could be any method that applies any transformation to any of the columns and uses `AS` to assign a new column name. This transformation extends the original DataFrame.

Look at the following code snippet:

```
# split the HDD into size and type

(
    sample_data_schema
    .withColumn('HDDSplit', f.split(f.col('HDD'), ' '))
    .show()
)
```

It produces the following output:

```
+---+-----------+----+----------+----+---------+-----+----+----+------+-----------+
| Id|      Model|Year|ScreenSize| RAM|      HDD|    W|   D|   H|Weight|   HDDSplit|
+---+-----------+----+----------+----+---------+-----+----+----+------+-----------+
|  1|MacBook Pro|2015|     "15\""|16GB|512GB SSD|13.75|9.48|0.61|  4.02|[512GB, SSD]|
|  2|    MacBook|2016|     "12\""| 8GB|256GB SSD|11.04|7.74|0.52|  2.03|[256GB, SSD]|
|  3|MacBook Air|2016|   "13.3\""| 8GB|128GB SSD| 12.8|8.94|0.68|  2.96|[128GB, SSD]|
|  4|       iMac|2017|     "27\""|64GB|   1TB SSD| 25.6| 8.0|20.3|  20.8|  [1TB, SSD]|
+---+-----------+----+----------+----+---------+-----+----+----+------+-----------+
```

You could achieve the same result with the `.select(...)` transformation. The following code will produce the same result:

```
# do the same as withColumn

(
    sample_data_schema
    .select(
        f.col('*')
        , f.split(f.col('HDD'), ' ').alias('HDD_Array')
    ).show()
)
```

The SQL (T-SQL) equivalent would be:

```
SELECT *
    , STRING_SPLIT(HDD, ' ') AS HDD_Array
FROM sample_data_schema
```

The .join(...) transformation

The `.join(...)` transformation allow us to join two DataFrames. The first parameter is the other DataFrame we want to join with, while the second parameter specifies the columns on which to join, and the final parameter specifies the nature of the join. Available types are `inner`, `cross`, `outer`, `full`, `full_outer`, `left`, `left_outer`, `right`, `right_outer`, `left_semi`, and `left_anti`. In SQL, the equivalent is the `JOIN` statement.

 If you're not familiar with the `ANTI` and `SEMI` joins, check out this blog: `https://blog.jooq.org/2015/10/13/semi-join-and-anti-join-should-have-its-own-syntax-in-sql/`.

Look at the following code as follows:

```
models_df = sc.parallelize([
      ('MacBook Pro', 'Laptop')
    , ('MacBook', 'Laptop')
    , ('MacBook Air', 'Laptop')
    , ('iMac', 'Desktop')
]).toDF(['Model', 'FormFactor'])

(
    sample_data_schema
    .join(
        models_df
        , sample_data_schema.Model == models_df.Model
        , 'left'
    ).show()
)
```

It produces the following output:

```
+---+-----------+----+----------+----+----------+-----+----+----+------+-----------+----------+
| Id|      Model|Year|ScreenSize| RAM|       HDD|    W|   D|   H|Weight|      Model|FormFactor|
+---+-----------+----+----------+----+----------+-----+----+----+------+-----------+----------+
|  2|    MacBook|2016|     "12\""| 8GB|256GB SSD|11.04|7.74|0.52|  2.03|    MacBook|    Laptop|
|  1|MacBook Pro|2015|     "15\""|16GB|512GB SSD|13.75|9.48|0.61|  4.02|MacBook Pro|    Laptop|
|  3|MacBook Air|2016|   "13.3\""| 8GB|128GB SSD| 12.8|8.94|0.68|  2.96|MacBook Air|    Laptop|
|  4|       iMac|2017|     "27\""|64GB|  1TB SSD| 25.6| 8.0|20.3|  20.8|       iMac|   Desktop|
+---+-----------+----+----------+----+----------+-----+----+----+------+-----------+----------+
```

In SQL syntax, this would be:

```
SELECT a.*
     , b,FormFactor
FROM sample_data_schema AS a
LEFT JOIN models_df AS b
    ON a.Model == b.Model
```

If we had a DataFrame that would not list every `Model` (note that the `MacBook` is missing), then the following code is:

```
models_df = sc.parallelize([
      ('MacBook Pro', 'Laptop')
    , ('MacBook Air', 'Laptop')
    , ('iMac', 'Desktop')
]).toDF(['Model', 'FormFactor'])

(
    sample_data_schema
```

```
        .join(
            models_df
            , sample_data_schema.Model == models_df.Model
            , 'left'
        ).show()
    )
```

This will generate a table with some missing values:

```
+---+-----------+----+----------+----+----------+-----+----+----+------+-----------+----------+
| Id|      Model|Year|ScreenSize| RAM|       HDD|    W|   D|   H|Weight|      Model|FormFactor|
+---+-----------+----+----------+----+----------+-----+----+----+------+-----------+----------+
|  2|    MacBook|2016|     "12\""| 8GB|256GB SSD|11.04|7.74|0.52|  2.03|       null|      null|
|  1|MacBook Pro|2015|     "15\""|16GB|512GB SSD|13.75|9.48|0.61|  4.02|MacBook Pro|    Laptop|
|  3|MacBook Air|2016|   "13.3\""| 8GB|128GB SSD| 12.8|8.94|0.68|  2.96|MacBook Air|    Laptop|
|  4|       iMac|2017|     "27\""|64GB|  1TB SSD| 25.6| 8.0|20.3|  20.8|       iMac|   Desktop|
+---+-----------+----+----------+----+----------+-----+----+----+------+-----------+----------+
```

The RIGHT join keeps only the records that are matched with the records in the right DataFrame. Thus, look at the following code:

```
    (
        sample_data_schema
        .join(
            models_df
            , sample_data_schema.Model == models_df.Model
            , 'right'
        ).show()
    )
```

This produces a table as follows:

```
+---+-----------+----+----------+----+----------+-----+----+----+------+-----------+----------+
| Id|      Model|Year|ScreenSize| RAM|       HDD|    W|   D|   H|Weight|      Model|FormFactor|
+---+-----------+----+----------+----+----------+-----+----+----+------+-----------+----------+
|  1|MacBook Pro|2015|     "15\""|16GB|512GB SSD|13.75|9.48|0.61|  4.02|MacBook Pro|    Laptop|
|  3|MacBook Air|2016|   "13.3\""| 8GB|128GB SSD| 12.8|8.94|0.68|  2.96|MacBook Air|    Laptop|
|  4|       iMac|2017|     "27\""|64GB|  1TB SSD| 25.6| 8.0|20.3|  20.8|       iMac|   Desktop|
+---+-----------+----+----------+----+----------+-----+----+----+------+-----------+----------+
```

The SEMI and ANTI joins are somewhat recent additions. The SEMI join keeps all the records from the left DataFrame that are matched with the records in the right DataFrame (as with the RIGHT join) but *only keeps the columns from the left DataFrame*; the ANTI join is the opposite of the SEMI join—it keeps only the records that are not found in the right DataFrame. So, the following example of a SEMI join is:

```
(
    sample_data_schema
    .join(
        models_df
        , sample_data_schema.Model == models_df.Model
        , 'left_semi'
    ).show()
)
```

This will produce the following result:

```
+---+-----------+----+----------+----+---------+-----+----+----+------+
| Id|      Model|Year|ScreenSize| RAM|      HDD|    W|   D|   H|Weight|
+---+-----------+----+----------+----+---------+-----+----+----+------+
|  1|MacBook Pro|2015|    "15\""|16GB|512GB SSD|13.75|9.48|0.61|  4.02|
|  3|MacBook Air|2016|  "13.3\""| 8GB|128GB SSD| 12.8|8.94|0.68|  2.96|
|  4|       iMac|2017|    "27\""|64GB|  1TB SSD| 25.6| 8.0|20.3|  20.8|
+---+-----------+----+----------+----+---------+-----+----+----+------+
```

Whereas the example of an ANTI join is:

```
(
    sample_data_schema
    .join(
        models_df
        , sample_data_schema.Model == models_df.Model
        , 'left_anti'
    ).show()
)
```

This will generate the following:

```
+---+-------+----+----------+---+---------+-----+----+----+------+
| Id|  Model|Year|ScreenSize|RAM|      HDD|    W|   D|   H|Weight|
+---+-------+----+----------+---+---------+-----+----+----+------+
|  2|MacBook|2016|    "12\""|8GB|256GB SSD|11.04|7.74|0.52|  2.03|
+---+-------+----+----------+---+---------+-----+----+----+------+
```

The .unionAll(...) transformation

The `.unionAll(...)` transformation appends values from another DataFrame. An equivalent in SQL syntax is `UNION ALL`.

Look at the following code:

```
another_macBookPro = sc.parallelize([
    (5, 'MacBook Pro', 2018, '15"', '16GB', '256GB SSD', 13.75, 9.48,
0.61, 4.02)
]).toDF(sample_data_schema.columns)

sample_data_schema.unionAll(another_macBookPro).show()
```

It produces the following result:

```
+---+-----------+----+----------+----+----------+-----+----+----+------+
| Id|      Model|Year|ScreenSize| RAM|       HDD|    W|   D|   H|Weight|
+---+-----------+----+----------+----+----------+-----+----+----+------+
|  1|MacBook Pro|2015|     "15\""|16GB|512GB SSD|13.75|9.48|0.61|  4.02|
|  2|    MacBook|2016|     "12\""| 8GB|256GB SSD|11.04|7.74|0.52|  2.03|
|  3|MacBook Air|2016|   "13.3\""| 8GB|128GB SSD| 12.8|8.94|0.68|  2.96|
|  4|       iMac|2017|     "27\""|64GB|   1TB SSD| 25.6| 8.0|20.3|  20.8|
|  5|MacBook Pro|2018|       15"|16GB|256GB SSD|13.75|9.48|0.61|  4.02|
+---+-----------+----+----------+----+----------+-----+----+----+------+
```

In SQL syntax, the preceding would read as:

```
SELECT *
FROM sample_data_schema

UNION ALL
SELECT *
FROM another_macBookPro
```

The .distinct(...) transformation

The `.distinct(...)` transformation returns a list of distinct values from a column. An equivalent in SQL would be `DISTINCT`.

Look at the following code:

```
# select the distinct values from the RAM column

sample_data_schema.select('RAM').distinct().show()
```

It produces the following result:

In SQL syntax, this would be:

```
SELECT DISTINCT RAM
FROM sample_data_schema
```

The .repartition(...) transformation

The `.repartition(...)` transformation shuffles the data around the cluster and combines it into a specified number of partitions. You can also specify the column or columns you want to use to perform the partitioning on. There is no direct equivalent in the SQL world.

Look at the following code:

```
sample_data_schema_rep = (
    sample_data_schema
    .repartition(2, 'Year')
)

sample_data_schema_rep.rdd.getNumPartitions()
```

It produces (as expected) this result:

2

The .fillna(...) transformation

The `.fillna(...)` transformation fills in the missing values in a DataFrame. You can either specify a single value and all the missing values will be filled in with it, or you can pass a dictionary where each key is the name of the column, and the values are to fill the missing values in the corresponding column. No direct equivalent exists in the SQL world.

Look at the following code:

```
missing_df = sc.parallelize([
    (None, 36.3, 24.2)
    , (1.6, 32.1, 27.9)
    , (3.2, 38.7, 24.7)
    , (2.8, None, 23.9)
    , (3.9, 34.1, 27.9)
    , (9.2, None, None)
]).toDF(['A', 'B', 'C'])

missing_df.fillna(21.4).show()
```

It produces the following output:

```
+----+----+----+
|   A|   B|   C|
+----+----+----+
|21.4|36.3|24.2|
| 1.6|32.1|27.9|
| 3.2|38.7|24.7|
| 2.8|21.4|23.9|
| 3.9|34.1|27.9|
| 9.2|21.4|21.4|
+----+----+----+
```

We could also specify the dictionary, as the `21.4` value does not really fit the `A` column. In the following code, we first calculate averages for each of the columns:

```
miss_dict = (
    missing_df
    .agg(
        f.mean('A').alias('A')
        , f.mean('B').alias('B')
```

```
        , f.mean('C').alias('C')
    )
).toPandas().to_dict('records')[0]

missing_df.fillna(miss_dict).show()
```

The `.toPandas()` method is an action (that we will cover in the next recipe) and it returns a pandas DataFrame. The `.to_dict(...)` method of the pandas DataFrame converts it into a dictionary, where the `records` parameter produces a regular dictionary where each column is the key and each value is the record.

The preceding code produces the following result:

```
+----+------------------+-----+
|   A|                 B|    C|
+----+------------------+-----+
|4.14|              36.3| 24.2|
| 1.6|              32.1| 27.9|
| 3.2|              38.7| 24.7|
| 2.8|35.300000000000004| 23.9|
| 3.9|              34.1| 27.9|
| 9.2|35.300000000000004|25.72|
+----+------------------+-----+
```

The .dropna(...) transformation

The `.dropna(...)` transformation removes records that have missing values. You can specify the threshold that translates to a minimum number of missing observations in the record that qualifies it to be removed. As with `.fillna(...)`, there is no direct equivalent in the SQL world.

Look at the following code:

```
missing_df.dropna().show()
```

It produces the following result:

```
+---+----+----+
|  A|   B|   C|
+---+----+----+
|1.6|32.1|27.9|
|3.9|34.1|27.9|
|3.2|38.7|24.7|
+---+----+----+
```

Specifying `thresh=2`:

```
missing_df.dropna(thresh=2).show()
```

It retains the first and the fourth records:

```
+----+----+----+
|   A|   B|   C|
+----+----+----+
|null|36.3|24.2|
| 1.6|32.1|27.9|
| 3.2|38.7|24.7|
| 2.8|null|23.9|
| 3.9|34.1|27.9|
+----+----+----+
```

The .dropDuplicates(...) transformation

The `.dropDuplicates(...)` transformation, as the name suggests, removes duplicated records. You can also specify a subset parameter as a list of column names; the method will remove duplicated records based on the values found in those columns.

Look at the following code:

```
dupes_df = sc.parallelize([
        (1.6, 32.1, 27.9)
      , (3.2, 38.7, 24.7)
      , (3.9, 34.1, 27.9)
      , (3.2, 38.7, 24.7)
]).toDF(['A', 'B', 'C'])

dupes_df.dropDuplicates().show()
```

It produces the following result

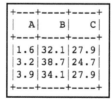

```
+---+----+----+
|  A|   B|   C|
+---+----+----+
|1.6|32.1|27.9|
|3.2|38.7|24.7|
|3.9|34.1|27.9|
+---+----+----+
```

The .summary() and .describe() transformations

The .summary() and .describe() transformations produce similar descriptive statistics, with the .summary() transformation additionally producing quartiles.

Look at the following code:

```
sample_data_schema.select('W').summary().show()
sample_data_schema.select('W').describe().show()
```

It produces the following result:

```
+-------+------------------+
|summary|                 W|
+-------+------------------+
|  count|                 4|
|   mean|15.797500000000001|
| stddev| 6.630738395281983|
|    min|             11.04|
|    25%|             11.04|
|    50%|              12.8|
|    75%|             13.75|
|    max|              25.6|
+-------+------------------+

+-------+------------------+
|summary|                 W|
+-------+------------------+
|  count|                 4|
|   mean|15.797500000000001|
| stddev| 6.630738395281983|
|    min|             11.04|
|    max|              25.6|
+-------+------------------+
```

The .freqItems(...) transformation

The .freqItems(...) transformation returns a list of frequent items from a column. You can also specify a minSupport parameter that will throw away items that are below a certain threshold.

Look at the following code:

```
sample_data_schema.freqItems(['RAM']).show()
```

It produces this result:

```
+-------+------------------+
|summary|                 W|
+-------+------------------+
|  count|                 4|
|   mean|15.797500000000001|
| stddev| 6.630738395281983|
|    min|             11.04|
|    25%|             11.04|
|    50%|              12.8|
|    75%|             13.75|
|    max|              25.6|
+-------+------------------+


+-------+------------------+
|summary|                 W|
+-------+------------------+
|  count|                 4|
|   mean|15.797500000000001|
| stddev| 6.630738395281983|
|    min|             11.04|
|    max|              25.6|
+-------+------------------+
```

See also

- Refer to Spark's documentation for more transformations: http://spark.apache.org/docs/latest/api/python/pyspark.sql.html#pyspark.sql.DataFrame

Overview of DataFrame actions

Transformations listed in the previous recipe transform one DataFrame into another. However, they only get executed once an action is called on a **DataFrame**.

In this recipe, we will provide an overview of the most popular actions.

Getting ready

To execute this recipe, you need to have a working Spark 2.3 environment. You should have gone through the previous recipe, *Specifying schema programmatically*, as we will be using the `sample_data_schema` DataFrame we created there.

There are no other requirements.

How to do it...

In this section, we will list some of the most common actions available for DataFrames. The purpose of this list is not to provide a comprehensive enumeration of all available transformations, but to give you some intuition behind the most common ones.

The .show(...) action

The `.show(...)` action, by default, shows the top five rows in tabular form. You can specify how many records to retrieve by passing an integer as a parameter.

Look at the following code:

```
sample_data_schema.select('W').describe().show()
```

It produces this result:

```
+-------+------------------+
|summary|                 W|
+-------+------------------+
|  count|                 4|
|   mean|15.797500000000001|
| stddev| 6.630738395281983|
|    min|             11.04|
|    max|              25.6|
+-------+------------------+
```

The .collect() action

The `.collect()` action, as the name suggests, collects all the results from all the worker nodes, and returns them to the driver. Beware of using this method on a big dataset as your driver will most likely break if you try to return the whole DataFrame of billions of records; use this method only to return small, aggregated data.

Look at the following code:

```
sample_data_schema.groupBy('Year').count().collect()
```

It produces the following result:

```
[Row(Year=2015, count=1), Row(Year=2016, count=2), Row(Year=2017, count=1)]
```

The .take(...) action

The `.take(...)` action works in the same as in RDDs–it returns the specified number of records to the driver node:

```
Look at the following code:sample_data_schema.take(2)
```

It produces this result:

```
[Row(Id=1, Model='MacBook Pro', Year=2015, ScreenSize='"15\\""', RAM='16GB', HDD='512GB SSD', W=13.75, D=9.48, H=0.61, Weight=4.02),
 Row(Id=2, Model='MacBook', Year=2016, ScreenSize='"12\\""', RAM='8GB', HDD='256GB SSD', W=11.04, D=7.74, H=0.52, Weight=2.03)]
```

The .toPandas() action

The `.toPandas()` action, as the name suggests, converts the Spark DataFrame into a pandas DataFrame. The same warning needs to be issued here as with the `.collect()` action – the `.toPandas()` action collects all the records from all the workers, returns them to the driver, and then converts the results into a pandas DataFrame.

Since our sample data is tiny, we can do this without any problems:

```
sample_data_schema.toPandas()
```

This is what the results look like:

	Id	Model	Year	ScreenSize	RAM	HDD	W	D	H	Weight
0	1	MacBook Pro	2015	"15\""	16GB	512GB SSD	13.75	9.48	0.61	4.02
1	2	MacBook	2016	"12\""	8GB	256GB SSD	11.04	7.74	0.52	2.03
2	3	MacBook Air	2016	"13.3\""	8GB	128GB SSD	12.80	8.94	0.68	2.96
3	4	iMac	2017	"27\""	64GB	1TB SSD	25.60	8.00	20.30	20.80

See also

- Refer to Spark's documentation for more actions: `http://spark.apache.org/docs/latest/api/python/pyspark.sql.html#pyspark.sql.DataFrame`

Preparing Data for Modeling

4

In this chapter, we will cover how to clean up your data and prepare it for modeling. You will learn the following recipes:

- Handling duplicates
- Handling missing observations
- Handling outliers
- Exploring descriptive statistics
- Computing correlations
- Drawing histograms
- Visualizing interactions between features

Introduction

Now that we have a thorough understanding of how RDDs and DataFrames work and what they can do, we can start preparing ourselves and our data for modeling.

Someone famous (Albert Einstein) once said (paraphrasing):

> *"The universe and the problems with any dataset are infinite, and I am not sure about the former."*

The preceding is of course a joke. However, any dataset you work with, be it acquired at work, found online, collected yourself, or obtained through any other means, is dirty until proven otherwise; you should not trust it, you should not play with it, you should not even look at it until such time that you have proven to yourself that it is sufficiently clean (there is no such thing as totally clean).

What problems can your dataset have? Well, to name a few:

- **Duplicated observations**: These arise through systemic and operator's faults
- **Missing observations**: These can emerge due to sensor problems, respondents' unwillingness to provide an answer to a question, or simply some data corruption
- **Aanomalous observations**: Observations that, when you look at them, stand out when compared with the rest of the dataset or a population
- **Encoding**: Text fields that are not normalized (for example, words are not stemmed or use synonyms), in different languages, or you can encounter gibberish text input, and date and date time fields may not encoded the same way
- **Untrustworthy answers (true especially for surveys)**: When respondents lie for any reason; this type of dirty data is much harder to work with and clean up

As you can see, your data might be plagued by thousands upon thousands of traps that are just waiting for you to fall for them. Cleaning up the data and getting familiar with it is what we (as data scientists) do 80% of the time (the remaining 20% we spend building models and complaining about cleaning data). So fasten your seatbelt and prepare for *a bumpy ride* that is necessary for us to trust the data that we have and get familiar with it.

In this chapter, we will work with a small dataset of 22 records:

```
dirty_data = spark.createDataFrame([
        (1,'Porsche','Boxster S','Turbo',2.5,4,22,None)
    , (2,'Aston Martin','Vanquish','Aspirated',6.0,12,16,None)
    , (3,'Porsche','911 Carrera 4S Cabriolet','Turbo',3.0,6,24,None)
    , (3,'General Motors','SPARK ACTIV','Aspirated',1.4,None,32,None)
    , (5,'BMW','COOPER S HARDTOP 2 DOOR','Turbo',2.0,4,26,None)
    , (6,'BMW','330i','Turbo',2.0,None,27,None)
    , (7,'BMW','440i Coupe','Turbo',3.0,6,23,None)
    , (8,'BMW','440i Coupe','Turbo',3.0,6,23,None)
    , (9,'Mercedes-Benz',None,None,None,None,27,None)
    , (10,'Mercedes-Benz','CLS 550','Turbo',4.7,8,21,79231)
    , (11,'Volkswagen','GTI','Turbo',2.0,4,None,None)
    , (12,'Ford Motor Company','FUSION AWD','Turbo',2.7,6,20,None)
    , (13,'Nissan','Q50 AWD RED SPORT','Turbo',3.0,6,22,None)
    , (14,'Nissan','Q70 AWD','Aspirated',5.6,8,18,None)
    , (15,'Kia','Stinger RWD','Turbo',2.0,4,25,None)
    , (16,'Toyota','CAMRY HYBRID LE','Aspirated',2.5,4,46,None)
    , (16,'Toyota','CAMRY HYBRID LE','Aspirated',2.5,4,46,None)
    , (18,'FCA US LLC','300','Aspirated',3.6,6,23,None)
    , (19,'Hyundai','G80 AWD','Turbo',3.3,6,20,None)
    , (20,'Hyundai','G80 AWD','Turbo',3.3,6,20,None)
```

```
    , (21,'BMW','X5 M','Turbo',4.4,8,18,121231)
    , (22,'GE','K1500 SUBURBAN 4WD','Aspirated',5.3,8,18,None)
], ['Id','Manufacturer','Model','EngineType','Displacement',
    'Cylinders','FuelEconomy','MSRP'])
```

Throughout the subsequent recipes, we will clean up the preceding dataset and learn a little bit more about it.

Handling duplicates

Duplicates show up in data for many reasons, but sometimes it's really hard to spot them. In this recipe, we will show you how to spot the most common ones and handle them using Spark.

Getting ready

To execute this recipe, you need to have a working Spark environment. If you do not have one, you might want to go back to `Chapter 1`, *Installing and Configuring Spark,* and follow the recipes you will find there.

We will work on the dataset from the introduction. All the code that you will need in this chapter can be found in the GitHub repository we set up for the book: `http://bit.ly/2ArlBck`. Go to `Chapter04` and open the `4.Preparing data for modeling.ipynb` notebook.

No other prerequisites are required.

How to do it...

A duplicate is a record in your dataset that appears more than once. It is an exact copy. Spark DataFrames have a convenience method to remove the duplicated rows, the `.dropDuplicates()` transformation:

1. Check whether any rows are duplicated, as follows:

    ```
    dirty_data.count(), dirty_data.distinct().count()
    ```

2. If any are duplicates, remove them:

    ```
    full_removed = dirty_data.dropDuplicates()
    ```

How it works...

You should know this one by now, but the `.count()` method counts how many rows there are in our DataFrame. The second command checks how many distinct rows we have. Execute these two commands on our `dirty_data`. DataFrame produces (22, 21) as the result. So, we now know that we have two records in our dataset that are exact copies of each other. Let's see which ones:

```
(
    dirty_data
    .groupby(dirty_data.columns)
    .count()
    .filter('count > 1')
    .show()
)
```

Let's unpack what's happening here. First, we use the `.groupby(...)` method to define what columns to use for the aggregation; in this example, we essentially use all of them as we want to find all the distinct combinations of all the columns in our dataset. Next, we count how many times such a combination of values occurs using the `.count()` method; the method adds the `count` column to our dataset. Using the `.filter(...)` method, we select all the rows that occur in our dataset more than once and print them to the screen using the `.show()` action.

This produces the following result:

```
+---+------------+----------------+----------+------------+---------+-----------+----+-----+
| Id|Manufacturer|           Model|EngineType|Displacement|Cylinders|FuelEconomy|MSRP|count|
+---+------------+----------------+----------+------------+---------+-----------+----+-----+
| 16|      Toyota|CAMRY HYBRID LE| Aspirated|         2.5|        4|         46|null|    2|
+---+------------+----------------+----------+------------+---------+-----------+----+-----+
```

So, the row with `Id` equal to `16` is the duplicated one. So, let's drop it using the `.dropDuplicates(...)` method. Finally, running the `full_removed.count()` command confirms that we now have 21 records.

There's more...

Well, there's more to it, as you might imagine. There are still some records that are duplicated in our `full_removed` DataFrame. Let's have a closer look.

Only IDs differ

If you collect data over time, you might record the same data but with different IDs. Let's check whether our DataFrame has any such records. The following snippet will help you do this:

```
(
    full_removed
    .groupby([col for col in full_removed.columns if col != 'Id'])
    .count()
    .filter('count > 1')
    .show()
)
```

Just like before, we first group by all the columns but we exclude the `'Id'` column, then count how many records we get given from this grouping, and finally we extract those with `'count > 1'` and show them on the screen. After running the preceding code, here's what we get:

Manufacturer	Model	EngineType	Displacement	Cylinders	FuelEconomy	MSRP	count
BMW	440i Coupe	Turbo	3.0	6	23	null	2
Hyundai	G80 AWD	Turbo	3.3	6	20	null	2

As you can see, we have four records with different IDs but that are the same cars: the BMW 440i Coupe and the Hyundai G80 AWD.

We could also check the counts, like before:

```
no_ids = (
    full_removed
    .select([col for col in full_removed.columns if col != 'Id'])
)

no_ids.count(), no_ids.distinct().count()
```

First, we only select all the columns except the `'Id'` one, and then count the total number of rows and the total number of distinct rows. After running the previous snippet, you should see `(21, 19)`, indicating that we have four records that are duplicated, just like we saw earlier.

The .dropDuplicates(...) method can handle such situations easily. All we need to do is to pass to the subset parameter a list of all the columns we want it to consider while searching for the duplicates. Here's how:

```
id_removed = full_removed.dropDuplicates(
    subset = [col for col in full_removed.columns if col != 'Id']
)
```

Once again, we select all the columns but the 'Id' columns to define which columns to use to determine the duplicates. If we now count the total number of rows in the id_removed DataFrame, we should get 19:

```
In [9]: # count
        id_removed.count()

        19
```

And that's precisely what we got!

ID collisions

You might also assume that if there are two records with the same ID, they are duplicated. Well, while this might be true, we would have already removed them by now when dropping the records based on all the columns. Thus, at this point, any duplicated IDs are more likely collisions.

Duplicated IDs might arise for a multitude of reasons: an instrumentation error or insufficient data structure to store the IDs, or if the IDs represent some hash function of the record elements, there might be collisions arising from the choice of the hash function. These are just a few of the reasons why you might have duplicated IDs but the records are not really duplicated.

Let's check whether this is true for our dataset:

```
import pyspark.sql.functions as fn

id_removed.agg(
      fn.count('Id').alias('CountOfIDs')
    , fn.countDistinct('Id').alias('CountOfDistinctIDs')
).show()
```

In this example, instead of subsetting records and then counting the records, then counting the distinct records, we will use the `.agg(...)` method. To this end, we first import all the functions from the `pyspark.sql.functions` module.

 For a list of all the functions available in `pyspark.sql.functions`, please refer to `https://spark.apache.org/docs/latest/api/python/pyspark.sql.html#module-pyspark.sql.functions`.

The two functions we'll use will allow us to do the counting in one go: the `.count(...)` method counts all the records with non-null values in the specified column, while the `.countDistinct(...)` returns a count of distinct values in such a column. The `.alias(...)` method allows us to specify a friendly name for the columns resulting from the counting. Here's what we get after counting:

```
+----------+------------------+
|CountOfIDs|CountOfDistinctIDs|
+----------+------------------+
|        19|                18|
+----------+------------------+
```

OK, so we have two records with the same IDs. Again, let's check which IDs are duplicated:

```
(
    id_removed
    .groupby('Id')
    .count()
    .filter('count > 1')
    .show()
)
```

As before, we first group by the values in the `'Id'` column, and then show all the records with a `count` greater than 1. Here's what we get:

```
+---+-----+
| Id|count|
+---+-----+
|  3|    2|
+---+-----+
```

Well, it looks like we have two records with `'Id == 3'`. Let's check whether they're the same:

```
+---+--------------+--------------------+----------+------------+----------+-----------+----+
| Id|  Manufacturer|               Model|EngineType|Displacement|Cylinders|FuelEconomy|MSRP|
+---+--------------+--------------------+----------+------------+----------+-----------+----+
|  3|General Motors|          SPARK ACTIV| Aspirated|         1.4|     null|         32|null|
|  3|        Porsche|911 Carrera 4S Ca...|     Turbo|         3.0|        6|         24|null|
+---+--------------+--------------------+----------+------------+----------+-----------+----+
```

These are definitely not the same records but they share the same ID. In this situation, we can create a new ID that will be unique (we have already made sure we do not have other duplicates in our dataset). PySpark's SQL functions module offers a `.monotonically_increasing_id()` method that creates a unique stream of IDs.

 The `.monotonically_increasing_id()`—generated ID is guaranteed to be unique as long as your data lives in less than one billion partitions and with less than eight billion records in each. That's a pretty big number.

Here's a snippet that will create and replace our ID column with a unique one:

```
new_id = (
    id_removed
    .select(
        [fn.monotonically_increasing_id().alias('Id')] +
        [col for col in id_removed.columns if col != 'Id'])
)

new_id.show()
```

We are creating the ID column first and then selecting all the other columns except the original `'Id'` column. Here's what the new IDs look like:

```
+-------------+------------------+--------------------+----------+------------+---------+-----------+------+
|          Id|      Manufacturer|               Model|EngineType|Displacement|Cylinders|FuelEconomy|  MSRP|
+-------------+------------------+--------------------+----------+------------+---------+-----------+------+
|   8589934592|    General Motors|         SPARK ACTIV| Aspirated|         1.4|     null|         32|  null|
|  188978561024|    Mercedes-Benz|             CLS 550|     Turbo|         4.7|        8|         21| 79231|
|  197568495616|    Mercedes-Benz|                null|      null|        null|     null|         27|  null|
|  206158430208|Ford Motor Company|          FUSION AWD|     Turbo|         2.7|        6|         20|  null|
|  438086664192|               BMW|COOPER S HARDTOP ...|     Turbo|         2.0|        4|         26|  null|
|  523986010112|     Aston Martin|            Vanquish| Aspirated|         6.0|       12|         16|  null|
|  721554505728|       Volkswagen|                 GTI|     Turbo|         2.0|        4|       null|  null|
|  764504178688|               Kia|         Stinger RWD|     Turbo|         2.0|        4|         25|  null|
|  919123001344|               BMW|                330i|     Turbo|         2.0|     null|         27|  null|
|  944892805120|           Porsche|           Boxster S|     Turbo|         2.5|        4|         22|  null|
|  970662608896|        FCA US LLC|                 300| Aspirated|         3.6|        6|         23|  null|
| 1030792151040|           Hyundai|             G80 AWD|     Turbo|         3.3|        6|         20|  null|
| 1039382085632|               BMW|          440i Coupe|     Turbo|         3.0|        6|         23|  null|
| 1116691496960|            Nissan|   Q50 AWD RED SPORT|     Turbo|         3.0|        6|         22|  null|
| 1211180777472|               BMW|                X5 M|     Turbo|         4.4|        8|         18|121231|
| 1331439861760|            Nissan|             Q70 AWD| Aspirated|         5.6|        8|         18|  null|
| 1606317768704|           Porsche| 911 Carrera 4S Ca...|     Turbo|         3.0|        6|         24|  null|
| 1614907703296|            Toyota|     CAMRY HYBRID LE| Aspirated|         2.5|        4|         46|  null|
| 1700807049216|                GE|  K1500 SUBURBAN 4WD| Aspirated|         5.3|        8|         18|  null|
+-------------+------------------+--------------------+----------+------------+---------+-----------+------+
```

The numbers are definitely unique. We are now ready to handle the other problems in our dataset.

Handling missing observations

Missing observations are pretty much the second-most-common issue in datasets. These arise for many reasons, as we have already alluded to in the introduction. In this recipe, we will learn how to deal with them.

Getting ready

To execute this recipe, you need to have a working Spark environment. Also, we will be working off of the `new_id` DataFrame we created in the previous recipe, so we assume you have followed the steps to remove the duplicated records.

No other prerequisites are required.

How to do it...

Since our data has two dimensions (rows and columns), we need to check the percentage of data missing in each row and each column to make a determination of what to keep, what to drop, and what to (potentially) impute:

1. To calculate how many missing observations there are in a row, use the following snippet:

```
(
    spark.createDataFrame(
        new_id
        .rdd
        .map(
            lambda row: (
                    row['Id']
                , sum([c == None for c in row])
            )
        )
        .collect()
        .filter(lambda el: el[1] > 1)
        ,['Id', 'CountMissing']
    )
    .orderBy('CountMissing', ascending=False)
    .show()
)
```

2. To calculate how much data is missing in each column, use the following code:

```
for k, v in sorted(
    merc_out
        .agg(*[
                (1 - (fn.count(c) / fn.count('*')))
                    .alias(c + '_miss')
                for c in merc_out.columns
            ])
        .collect()[0]
        .asDict()
        .items()
    , key=lambda el: el[1]
    , reverse=True
):
    print(k, v)
```

Let's walk through these step by step.

How it works...

Let's now take a look at how to handle missing observations in rows and columns in detail in the following sections.

Missing observations per row

To calculate how much data is missing from a row, it is easier to work with RDDs as we can loop through each element of an RDD's record and count how many values are missing. Thus, the first thing we do is we access `.rdd` within our `new_id` DataFrame. Using the `.map(...)` transformation, we loop through each row, extract `'Id'`, and count how many times an element is missing using the `sum([c == None for c in row])` expression. The outcome of these operations is an RDD of elements that each has two values: the ID of the row and the count of missing values.

Next, we only select those that have more than one missing value and `.collect()` those records on the driver. We then create a simple DataFrame, `.orderBy(...)`, by the count of missing values in a descending order and show the records.

The result looks as follows:

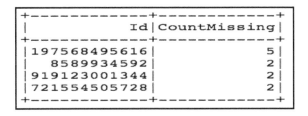

As you can see, one of the records has five out of eight values missing. Let's see that record:

```
(
    new_id
    .where('Id == 197568495616')
    .show()
)
```

The preceding code shows that one of the `Mercedes-Benz` records has most of its values missing:

```
+------------+-------------+-----+----------+------------+---------+-----------+----+
|          Id|  Manufacturer|Model|EngineType|Displacement|Cylinders|FuelEconomy|MSRP|
+------------+-------------+-----+----------+------------+---------+-----------+----+
|197568495616|Mercedes-Benz| null|      null|        null|     null|         27|null|
+------------+-------------+-----+----------+------------+---------+-----------+----+
```

So, we can drop the whole observation as there isn't really much value contained in this record. To achieve this goal, we can use the `.dropna(...)` method of DataFrames: `merc_out = new_id.dropna(thresh=4)`.

> If you use `.dropna()` without passing any parameters, any record that has a missing value will be removed.

We specify `thresh=4`, so we only remove the records that have a minimum of four non-missing values; our record has only three useful pieces of information.

Let's confirm: running `new_id.count()`, `merc_out.count()` produces `(19, 18)`, so yes, indeed, we removed one of the records. Did we really remove the `Mercedes-Benz` one? Let's check:

```
(
    merc_out
    .where('Id == 197568495616')
    .show()
)
```

The preceding code snippet produces an empty table, so it did remove the records with `Id` equal to `197568495616`, as shown in the following screenshot:

```
+---+------------+-----+----------+------------+---------+-----------+----+
| Id|Manufacturer|Model|EngineType|Displacement|Cylinders|FuelEconomy|MSRP|
+---+------------+-----+----------+------------+---------+-----------+----+
+---+------------+-----+----------+------------+---------+-----------+----+
```

Missing observations per column

We also need to check whether there are columns with a particularly low incidence of useful information. There's a lot of things happening in the code we presented, so let's unpack it step by step.

Let's start with the inner list:

```
[
    (1 - (fn.count(c) / fn.count('*')))
        .alias(c + '_miss')
    for c in merc_out.columns
]
```

We loop through all the columns in the `merc_out` DataFrame and count how many non-missing values we find in each column. We then divide it by the total count of all the rows and subtract this from 1 so we get the percentage of missing values.

> We imported `pyspark.sql.functions` as `fn` earlier in the chapter.

However, what we're actually doing here is not really calculating anything. The way Python stores this information, at this time, is just as a list of objects, or pointers, to certain operations. Only after we pass the list to the `.agg(...)` method does it get translated into PySpark's internal execution graph (which only gets executed when we call the `.collect()` action).

> The `.agg(...)` method accepts a set of parameters, not as a list object, but as a comma-separated list of parameters. Therefore, instead of passing the list itself to the `.agg(...)` method, we included `'*'` in front of the list, which unfolds each element of our list and passes it like a parameter to our method.

The `.collect()` method will return a list of one element—a `Row` object with aggregated information. We can transform `Row` into a dictionary using the `.asDict()` method and then extract all the `items` from it. This will result in a list of tuples, where the first element is the column name (we used the `.alias(...)` method to append `'_miss'` to each column) and the second element is the percentage of missing observations.

While looping through the elements of the sorted list, we just print them to the screen:

```
MSRP_miss 0.8888888888888888
Cylinders_miss 0.11111111111111116
FuelEconomy_miss 0.05555555555555558
EngineType_miss 0.0
Manufacturer_miss 0.0
Id_miss 0.0
Model_miss 0.0
Displacement_miss 0.0
```

Well, it looks like most of the information in the MSRP column is missing. Thus, we can drop it, as it will not bring us any useful information:

```
no_MSRP = merc_out.select([col for col in new_id.columns if col != 'MSRP'])
```

We still have two columns with some missing information. Let's do something about them.

There's more...

PySpark allows you to impute the missing observations. You can either pass a value that every null or None in your data will be replaced with, or you can pass a dictionary with different values for each column with missing observations. In this example, we will use the latter approach and will specify a ratio between the fuel economy and displacement, and between the number of cylinders and displacement.

First, let's create our dictionary:

```
multipliers = (
    no_MSRP
    .agg(
        fn.mean(
            fn.col('FuelEconomy') /
            (
                fn.col('Displacement') * fn.col('Cylinders')
            )
        ).alias('FuelEconomy')
        , fn.mean(
            fn.col('Cylinders') /
            fn.col('Displacement')
        ).alias('Cylinders')
    )
).toPandas().to_dict('records')[0]
```

Here, we are effectively calculating our multipliers. In order to replace the missing values in the fuel economy, we will use the following formula:

$$fuel\_economy\_mult = \frac{fuel\_economy}{displacement * cylinders}$$

For the number of cylinders, we will use the following equation:

$$cylinders\_mult = \frac{cylinders}{displacement}$$

Our preceding code uses these two formulas to calculate the multiplier for each row and then takes the average of these.

> This is not going to be totally accurate but given the data we have, it should be accurate enough.

Here, we also present yet another way of creating a dictionary out of your (small!) Spark DataFrame: use the .toPandas() method to convert the Spark DataFrame to a pandas DataFrame. The DataFrame of pandas has a .to_dict(...) method that will allow you to convert our data to a dictionary. The 'records' parameter instructs the method to convert each row to a dictionary where the key is the column name with the corresponding record value.

> Check out this link to read more about the .to_dict(...) method: https://pandas.pydata.org/pandas-docs/stable/generated/pandas.DataFrame.to_dict.html.

Our resulting dictionary looks like this:

```
{'FuelEconomy': 1.4957485048359973, 'Cylinders': 1.8353365984789105}
```

Let's use it now to impute our missing data:

```
imputed = (
    no_MSRP
    .withColumn('FuelEconomy', fn.col('FuelEconomy') /
fn.col('Displacement') / fn.col('Cylinders'))
    .withColumn('Cylinders', fn.col('Cylinders') / fn.col('Displacement'))
    .fillna(multipliers)
    .withColumn('Cylinders', (fn.col('Cylinders') *
fn.col('Displacement')).cast('integer'))
    .withColumn('FuelEconomy', fn.col('FuelEconomy') *
fn.col('Displacement') * fn.col('Cylinders'))
)
```

First, we convert our original data so it also reflects the ratios we specified earlier. Next, we use the multipliers dictionary to fill in the missing values, and finally we revert the columns to their original state.

Note that each time we use the `.withColumn(...)` method, we overwrite the original column names.

The resulting DataFrame looks as follows:

Id	Manufacturer	Model	EngineType	Displacement	Cylinders	FuelEconomy
8589934592	General Motors	SPARK ACTIV	Aspirated	1.4	2	4.188095813552
188978561024	Mercedes-Benz	CLS 550	Turbo	4.7	8	21.0
206158430208	Ford Motor Company	FUSION AWD	Turbo	2.7	5	16.666666666666668
438086664192	BMW	COOPER S HARDTOP ...	Turbo	2.0	4	26.0
523986010112	Aston Martin	Vanquish	Aspirated	6.0	12	16.0
721554505728	Volkswagen	GTI	Turbo	2.0	4	11.96598803872
764504178688	Kia	Stinger RWD	Turbo	2.0	4	25.0
919123001344	BMW	330i	Turbo	2.0	3	8.974491029040001
944892805120	Porsche	Boxster S	Turbo	2.5	4	22.0
970662608896	FCA US LLC	300	Aspirated	3.6	6	23.0
1030792151040	Hyundai	G80 AWD	Turbo	3.3	6	20.0
1039382085632	BMW	440i Coupe	Turbo	3.0	6	23.000000000000004
1116691496960	Nissan	Q50 AWD RED SPORT	Turbo	3.0	6	21.999999999999996
1211180777472	BMW	X5 M	Turbo	4.4	8	18.0
1331439861760	Nissan	Q70 AWD	Aspirated	5.6	8	18.0
1606317768704	Porsche	911 Carrera 4S Ca...	Turbo	3.0	6	24.0
1614907703296	Toyota	CAMRY HYBRID LE	Aspirated	2.5	4	46.0
1700807049216	GE	K1500 SUBURBAN 4WD	Aspirated	5.3	8	18.0

As you can see, the resulting values for the cylinders and the fuel economy are not totally accurate but still are arguably better than replacing them with some predefined value.

See also

- Check out PySpark's documentation on the missing observation methods: `https://spark.apache.org/docs/latest/api/python/pyspark.sql.html#pyspark.sql.DataFrameNaFunctions`

Handling outliers

Observations that differ greatly from the rest of the observations, that is, they are located in the long tail(s) of the data distribution, are outliers. In this recipe, we will learn how to locate and handle the outliers.

Getting ready

To execute this recipe, you need to have a working Spark environment. Also, we will be working off of the `imputed` DataFrame we created in the previous recipe, so we assume you have followed the steps to handle missing observations.

No other prerequisites are required.

How to do it...

Let's start with a popular definition of an outlier.

A point, p, that meets the following criteria:

$$Q^1 - 1.5IQR \leqslant p \leqslant Q^3 + 1.5IQR$$

Is not considered an outlier; any point outside this range is. In the preceding equation, Q^1 is the first quartile (25th percentile), Q^3 is the third quartile, and IQR is the **interquartile range** and is defined as the difference between Q^3 and Q^1 : IQR= Q^3-Q^1.

To flag the outliers, follow these steps:

1. Let's calculate our ranges first:

```
features = ['Displacement', 'Cylinders', 'FuelEconomy']
quantiles = [0.25, 0.75]

cut_off_points = []

for feature in features:
    quants = imputed.approxQuantile(feature, quantiles, 0.05)
    IQR = quants[1] - quants[0]
    cut_off_points.append((feature, [
        quants[0] - 1.5 * IQR,
        quants[1] + 1.5 * IQR,
    ]))
cut_off_points = dict(cut_off_points)
```

2. Next, we flag the outliers:

```
outliers = imputed.select(*['id'] + [
        (
            (imputed[f] < cut_off_points[f][0]) |
            (imputed[f] > cut_off_points[f][1])
        ).alias(f + '_o') for f in features
    ])
```

How it works...

We will only be looking at the numerical variables: the displacement, cylinders, and the fuel economy.

We loop through all these features and calculate the first and third quartiles using the `.approxQuantile(...)` method. The method takes the feature (column) name as its first parameter, the float (or list of floats) of quantiles to calculate as the second parameter, and the third parameter specifies the relative target precision (setting this value to 0 will find exact quantiles but it can be very expensive).

The method returns a list of two (in our case) values: Q^1 and Q^3. We then calculate the interquartile range and append the (`feature_name`, `[lower_bound, upper_bound]`) tuple to the `cut_off_point` list. After converting to a dictionary, our cut-off points are as follows:

```
{    'Cylinders': [-2.0, 14.0],
     'Displacement': [-1.6000000000000005, 8.0],
     'FuelEconomy': [7.166666666666664, 32.50000000000001]}
```

So, now we can use these to flag our outlying observations. We will only select the ID columns and then loop through our features to check whether they fall outside of our calculated bounds. Here's what we get:

```
+--------------+----------------+------------+---------------+
|            id|Displacement_o|Cylinders_o|FuelEconomy_o|
+--------------+----------------+------------+---------------+
|    8589934592|           false|       false|           true|
|  188978561024|           false|       false|          false|
|  206158430208|           false|       false|          false|
|  438086664192|           false|       false|          false|
|  523986010112|           false|       false|          false|
|  721554505728|           false|       false|          false|
|  764504178688|           false|       false|          false|
|  919123001344|           false|       false|          false|
|  944892805120|           false|       false|          false|
|  970662608896|           false|       false|          false|
| 1030792151040|           false|       false|          false|
| 1039382085632|           false|       false|          false|
| 1116691496960|           false|       false|          false|
| 1211180777472|           false|       false|          false|
| 1331439861760|           false|       false|          false|
| 1606317768704|           false|       false|          false|
| 1614907703296|           false|       false|           true|
| 1700807049216|           false|       false|          false|
+--------------+----------------+------------+---------------+
```

So, we have two outliers in the fuel economy column. Let's check the records:

```
with_outliers_flag = imputed.join(outliers, on='Id')

(
    with_outliers_flag
    .filter('FuelEconomy_o')
    .select('Id', 'Manufacturer', 'Model', 'FuelEconomy')
    .show()
)
```

First, we join our `imputed` DataFrame with the `outliers` one and then we filter on the `FuelEconomy_o` flag to select our outlying records only. Finally, we just extract the most relevant columns to show:

```
+------------+-------------+--------------+-------------+
|          Id| Manufacturer|         Model|  FuelEconomy|
+------------+-------------+--------------+-------------+
|  8589934592|General Motors|   SPARK ACTIV|4.188095813552|
|1614907703296|       Toyota|CAMRY HYBRID LE|         46.0|
+------------+-------------+--------------+-------------+
```

So we have SPARK ACTIV and CAMRY HYBRID LE as the outliers. SPARK ACTIV became an outlier due to our imputation logic, as we had to impute its fuel economy values; given that its engine's displacement is 1.4 liters, our logic didn't work out well. Well, there are other ways you can impute the values. The Camry, being a hybrid, is definitely an outlier in a dataset dominated by large and turbo-charged engines; it should not surprise us to see it here.

Trying to build a machine learning model based on data with outliers can lead to some untrustworthy results or a model that does not generalize well, so we normally remove these from our dataset:

```
no_outliers = (
    with_outliers_flag
    .filter('!FuelEconomy_o')
    .select(imputed.columns)
)
```

The preceding snippet simply filters out all the records that are not outliers in our `FuelEconomy_o` column. That's it!

See also

- Check out this website for more information about outliers: http://www.itl.nist.gov/div898/handbook/prc/section1/prc16.htm

Exploring descriptive statistics

Descriptive statistics are the most fundamental measures you can calculate on your data. In this recipe, we will learn how easy it is to get familiar with our dataset in PySpark.

Getting ready

To execute this recipe, you need to have a working Spark environment. Also, we will be working off of the `no_outliers` DataFrame we created in the *Handling outliers* recipe so we assume you have followed the steps to handle duplicates, missing observations, and outliers.

No other prerequisites are required.

How to do it...

Calculating the descriptive statistics for your data is extremely easy in PySpark. Here's how:

```
descriptive_stats = no_outliers.describe(features)
```

That's it!

How it works...

The preceding code barely needs an explanation. The `.describe(...)` method takes a list of columns you want to calculate the descriptive statistics on and returns a DataFrame with basic descriptive statistics: count, mean, standard deviation, minimum value, and maximum value.

> You can specify both numeric and string columns as input parameters to `.describe(...)`.

Here's what we get from running the `.describe(...)` method on our `features` list of columns:

```
+-------+------------------+------------------+------------------+
|summary|      Displacement|         Cylinders|        FuelEconomy|
+-------+------------------+------------------+------------------+
|  count|                16|                16|                16|
|   mean|           3.44375|             6.125|19.60044660840167|
| stddev|1.354975399530683|2.276693508870558|4.666647767366612|
|    min|               2.0|                 3|8.974491029040001|
|    max|               6.0|                12|              26.0|
+-------+------------------+------------------+------------------+
```

As expected, we have `16` records in total. Our dataset seems to be skewed (used here as a loose term, not in statistical terms) toward larger engines as the mean displacement is `3.44` liters with six cylinders. Fuel economy, for such sizable engines, seems to be decent, though, at 19 MPG.

There's more...

If you do not pass a list of columns to calculate the descriptive statistics over, PySpark will return the statistics for each and every column in your DataFrame. Check out the following snippet:

```
descriptive_stats_all = no_outliers.describe()
descriptive_stats_all.show()
```

It will result in the following table:

summary	Id	Manufacturer	Model	EngineType	Displacement	Cylinders	FuelEconomy
count	16	16	16	16	16	16	16
mean	9.19659872256E11	null	300.0	null	3.44375	6.125	19.60044660840167
stddev	4.396778949583304E11	null	NaN	null	1.354975399530683	2.276693508870558	4.666647767366612
min	188978561024	Aston Martin	300	Aspirated	2.0	3	8.974491029040001
max	1700807049216	Volkswagen	X5 M	Turbo	6.0	12	26.0

As you can see, even the string columns got their descriptive statistics which are, however, fairly questionable to interpret.

Descriptive statistics for aggregated columns

Sometimes you want to calculate some descriptive statistics within a group of values. In this example, we will calculate some basic stats for cars with different numbers of cylinders:

```
(
    no_outliers
    .select(features)
    .groupBy('Cylinders')
    .agg(*[
        fn.count('*').alias('Count')
        , fn.mean('FuelEconomy').alias('MPG_avg')
        , fn.mean('Displacement').alias('Disp_avg')
        , fn.stddev('FuelEconomy').alias('MPG_stdev')
```

```
        , fn.stddev('Displacement').alias('Disp_stdev')
    ])
    .orderBy('Cylinders')
).show()
```

First, we select our `features` list of columns so we reduce the number of data we need to analyze. Next, we aggregate our data over the cylinders column and use the (already familiar) `.agg(...)` method to calculate the count, mean, and standard deviation over fuel economy and displacement.

> There are more aggregation functions available in the `pyspark.sql.functions` module: `avg(...)`, `count(...)`, `countDistinct(...)`, `first(...)`, `kurtosis(...)`, `max(...)`, `mean(...)`, `min(...)`, `skewness(...)`, `stddev_pop(...)`, `stddev_samp(...)`, `sum(...)`, `sumDistinct(...)`, `var_pop(...)`, `var_samp(...)`, and `variance(...)`.

Here's the resulting table:

```
+---------+-----+------------------+------------------+------------------+-------------------+
|Cylinders|Count|           MPG_avg|          Disp_avg|        MPG_stdev|         Disp_stdev|
+---------+-----+------------------+------------------+------------------+-------------------+
|        3|    1| 8.974491029040001|               2.0|              NaN|                NaN|
|        4|    4|   21.24149700968|             2.125| 6.413009924983552|0.24999999999999994|
|        5|    1|16.666666666666668|               2.7|              NaN|                NaN|
|        6|    5|              22.4|3.1799999999999997|1.5165750888103104|0.26832815729997467|
|        8|    4|             18.75|               5.0|               1.5| 0.5477225575051655|
|       12|    1|              16.0|               6.0|              NaN|                NaN|
+---------+-----+------------------+------------------+------------------+-------------------+
```

We can read two things from this table:

- Our imputation method is truly inaccurate, so next time we should come up with a better method.
- `MPG_avg` for six cylinder cars is higher than for four cylinder cars and it would be suspicious. This is why you should be getting intimate with your data, as you can then spot such hidden traps in your data.

What to do with such finding goes beyond the scope of this book. But, the point is that this is why a data scientist would spend 80% of their time cleaning the data and getting familiar with it, so the model that is built with such data can be relied on.

See also

- There are many other statistics you can calculate on your data that we did not cover here (but that PySpark will allow you to calculate). For a more comprehensive overview, we suggest you check out this website: `https://www.socialresearchmethods.net/kb/statdesc.php`.

Computing correlations

Features correlated with the outcome are desirable, but those that are also correlated among themselves can make the model unstable. In this recipe, we will show you how to calculate correlations between features.

Getting ready

To execute this recipe, you need to have a working Spark environment. Also, we will be working off of the `no_outliers` DataFrame we created in the *Handling outliers* recipe, so we assume you have followed the steps to handle duplicates, missing observations, and outliers.

No other prerequisites are required.

How to do it...

To calculate the correlations between two features, all you have to do is to provide their names:

```
(
    no_outliers
    .corr('Cylinders', 'Displacement')
)
```

That's it!

How it works...

The `.corr(...)` method takes two parameters, the names of the two features you want to calculate the correlation coefficient between.

Currently, only the Pearson correlation coefficient is available.

The preceding command will produce a correlation coefficient equal to `0.938` for our dataset.

There's more...

If you want to calculate a correlation matrix, you need to do this somewhat manually. Here's our solution:

```
n_features = len(features)

corr = []

for i in range(0, n_features):
    temp = [None] * i

    for j in range(i, n_features):
        temp.append(no_outliers.corr(features[i], features[j]))
    corr.append([features[i]] + temp)

correlations = spark.createDataFrame(corr, ['Column'] + features)
```

The preceding code is effectively looping through the list of our `features` and computing the pair-wise correlations between them to fill the upper-triangular portion of the matrix.

 We introduced the `features` list in the *Handling outliers* recipe earlier.

The calculated coefficient is then appended to the `temp` list which, in return, gets added to the `corr` list. Finally, we create the correlations DataFrame. Here's what it looks like:

```
+------------+------------+------------------+--------------------+
|      Column|Displacement|         Cylinders|         FuelEconomy|
+------------+------------+------------------+--------------------+
|Displacement|         1.0|0.9381829964408113|-0.10757908872489412|
|   Cylinders|        null|               1.0|-0.04218546545131555|
| FuelEconomy|        null|              null|                 1.0|
+------------+------------+------------------+--------------------+
```

As you can see, the only strong correlation is between `Displacement` and `Cylinders` and this, of course, comes as no surprise. `FuelEconomy` is not really correlated with the displacement as there are other factors that affect `FuelEconomy`, such as drag and weight of the car. However, if you were trying to predict, for example, maximum speed and assuming (and it is a fair assumption to make) that both `Displacement` and `Cylinders` would be highly positively correlated with the maximum speed, then you should only use one of them.

Drawing histograms

Histograms are the easiest way to visually *inspect* the distribution of your data. In this recipe, we will show you how to do this in PySpark.

Getting ready

To execute this recipe, you need to have a working Spark environment. Also, we will be working off of the `no_outliers` DataFrame we created in the *Handling outliers* recipe, so we assume you have followed the steps to handle duplicates, missing observations, and outliers.

No other prerequisites are required.

How to do it...

There are two ways to produce histograms in PySpark:

- Select feature you want to visualize, `.collect()` it on the driver, and then use the matplotlib's native `.hist(...)` method to draw the histogram
- Calculate the counts in each histogram bin in PySpark and only return the counts to the driver for visualization

The former solution will work for small datasets (such as ours in this chapter) but it will break your driver if the data is too big. Moreover, there's a good reason why we distribute the data so we can do the computations in parallel instead of in a single thread. Thus, in this recipe, we will only show you the second solution. Here's the snippet that does all the calculations for us:

```
histogram_MPG = (
    no_outliers
    .select('FuelEconomy')
    .rdd
    .flatMap(lambda record: record)
    .histogram(5)
)
```

How it works...

The preceding code is pretty self-explanatory. First, we select the feature of interest (in our case, the fuel economy).

The Spark DataFrames do not have a native histogram method, so that's why we switch to the underlying RDD.

Next, we flatten our results into a long list (instead of a `Row` object) and use the `.histogram(...)` method to calculate our histogram.

The `.histogram(...)` method accepts either an integer that would specify the number of buckets to allocate our data to or a list with a specified bucket limit.

Check out PySpark's documentation on the `.histogram(...)` at https:/
/spark.apache.org/docs/latest/api/python/pyspark.html#pyspark.
RDD.histogram.

The method returns a tuple of two elements: the first element is a list of bin bounds, and the other element is the counts of elements in the corresponding bins. Here's what this looks like for our fuel economy feature:

```
([8.974491029040001, 12.379592823232, 15.784694617424, 19.189796411616, 22.594898205808, 26.0], [2, 0, 5, 4, 5])
```

Note that we specified that we want the `.histogram(...)` method to bucketize our data into five bins, but there are six elements in the first list. However, we still have five buckets in our dataset: *[8.97, 12.38), [12.38, 15.78), [15.78, 19.19), [19.19, 22.59),* and *[22.59, 26.0).*

We cannot create any plots in PySpark natively without going through a lot of setting up (see, for example, this: https://plot.ly/python/apache-spark/). The easier way is to prepare a DataFrame with our data and use some *magic* (well, sparkmagics, but it still counts!) locally on the driver.

First, we need to extract our data and create a temporary `histogram_MPG` table:

```
(
    spark
    .createDataFrame(
        [(bins, counts)
         for bins, counts
         in zip(
             histogram_MPG[0],
             histogram_MPG[1]
         )]
        , ['bins', 'counts']
    )
    .registerTempTable('histogram_MPG')
)
```

We create a two-column DataFrame where the first column contains the bin lower bound and the second column contains the corresponding count. The `.registerTempTable(...)` method (as the name suggests) registers a temporary table so we can actually use it with the `%%sql` magic:

```
%%sql -o hist_MPG -q
SELECT * FROM histogram_MPG
```

The preceding command selects all the records from our temporary `histogram_MPG` table and outputs it to the locally-accessible `hist_MPG` variable; the `-q` switch is there so nothing gets printed out to the notebook.

With `hist_MPG` locally accessible, we can now use it to produce our plot:

```
%%local
import matplotlib.pyplot as plt
%matplotlib inline
plt.style.use('ggplot')

fig = plt.figure(figsize=(12,9))
ax = fig.add_subplot(1, 1, 1)
ax.bar(hist_MPG['bins'], hist_MPG['counts'], width=3)
ax.set_title('Histogram of fuel economy')
```

`%%local` executes whatever is located in that notebook cell in local mode. First, we import the `matplotlib` library and specify that it produces the plots inline within the notebook instead of popping up a new window each time a plot is produced. `plt.style.use(...)` changes the styles of our charts.

For a full list of available styles, check out `https://matplotlib.org/`
`devdocs/gallery/style_sheets/style_sheets_reference.html`.

Next, we create a figure and add a subplot to it that we will be drawing in. Finally, we use
the `.bar(...)` method to plot our histogram and set the title. Here's what the chart looks
like:

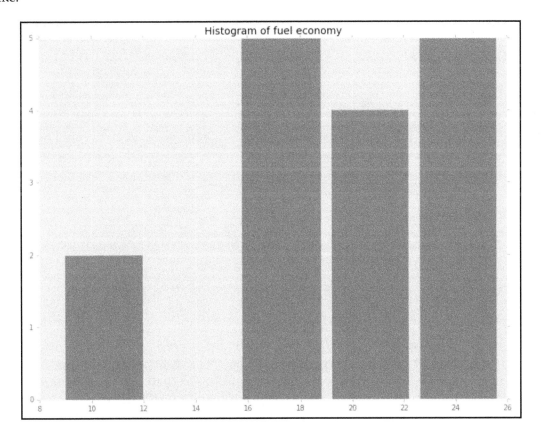

That's it!

There's more...

Matplotlib is not the only library we can use to plot histograms. Bokeh (available at `https:/ /bokeh.pydata.org/en/latest/`) is another powerful plotting library, built on top of `D3.js`, which allows you to interactively *play* with your charts.

 Check out the gallery of examples at `https://bokeh.pydata.org/en/ latest/docs/gallery.html`.

Here's how you plot with Bokeh:

```
%%local
from bokeh.io import show
from bokeh.plotting import figure
from bokeh.io import output_notebook
output_notebook()

labels = [str(round(e, 2)) for e in hist_MPG['bins']]

p = figure(
    x_range=labels,
    plot_height=350,
    title='Histogram of fuel economy'
)

p.vbar(x=labels, top=hist_MPG['counts'], width=0.9)

show(p)
```

First, we load all the necessary components of Bokeh; the `output_notebook()` method makes sure that we produce the chart inline in the notebook instead of opening a new window each time. Next, we produce the labels to put on our chart. Then, we define our figure: the `x_range` parameter specifies the number of points on the *x* axis and the `plot_height` sets the height of our plot. Finally, we use the `.vbar(...)` method to draw the bars of our histogram; the `x` parameter is the labels to put on our plot, and the `top` parameter specifies the counts.

The result looks as follows:

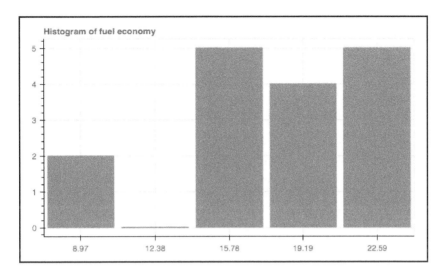

It's the same information, but you can interact with this chart in your browser.

See also

- If you want to further customize your histograms, here is a page that might be useful: https://plot.ly/matplotlib/histograms/

Visualizing interactions between features

Plotting the interactions between features can further your understanding of not only the distribution of your data, but also how the features relate to each other. In this recipe, we will show you how to create scatter plots from your data.

Getting ready

To execute this recipe, you need to have a working Spark environment. Also, we will be working off of the no_outliers DataFrame we created in the *Handling outliers* recipe, so we assume you have followed the steps to handle duplicates, missing observations, and outliers.

No other prerequisites are required.

How to do it...

Once again, we will select our data from the DataFrame and expose it locally:

```
scatter = (
    no_outliers
    .select('Displacement', 'Cylinders')
)

scatter.registerTempTable('scatter')

%%sql -o scatter_source -q
SELECT * FROM scatter
```

How it works...

First, we select the two features we want to learn more about to see how they interact with each other; in our case they are the displacement and cylinders features.

Our example here is small so we can work with all our data. However, in the real world, you should sample your data first before attempting to plot billions of data points.

After registering the temp table, we use the %%sql magic to select all the data from the scatter table and expose it locally as a scatter_source. Now, we can start plotting:

```
%%local
import matplotlib.pyplot as plt
%matplotlib inline
plt.style.use('ggplot')

fig = plt.figure(figsize=(12,9))
ax = fig.add_subplot(1, 1, 1)
ax.scatter(
      list(scatter_source['Cylinders'])
    , list(scatter_source['Displacement'])
    , s = 200
    , alpha = 0.5
)

ax.set_xlabel('Cylinders')
ax.set_ylabel('Displacement')

ax.set_title('Relationship between cylinders and displacement')
```

First, we load the Matplotlib library and set it up.

See the *Drawing histograms* recipe for a more detailed explanation of what these Matplotlib commands do.

Next, we create a figure and add a subplot to it. Then, we draw a scatter plot using our data; the x axis will represent the number of cylinders and the y axis will represent the displacement. Finally, we set the axes labels and the chart title.

Here's what the final result looks like:

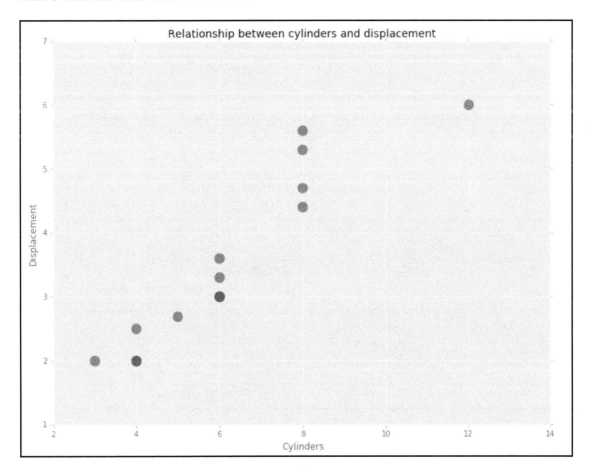

There's more...

You can create an interactive version of the preceding chart using bokeh:

```
%%local
from bokeh.io import show
from bokeh.plotting import figure
from bokeh.io import output_notebook
output_notebook()

p = figure(title = 'Relationship between cylinders and displacement')
p.xaxis.axis_label = 'Cylinders'
p.yaxis.axis_label = 'Displacement'

p.circle( list(scatter_source['Cylinders'])
        , list(scatter_source['Displacement'])
        , fill_alpha=0.2, size=10)

show(p)
```

First, we create the canvas, the figure we will be plotting on. Next, we set our labels. Finally, we use the .circle(...) method to plot the dots on the canvas.

The final result looks as follows:

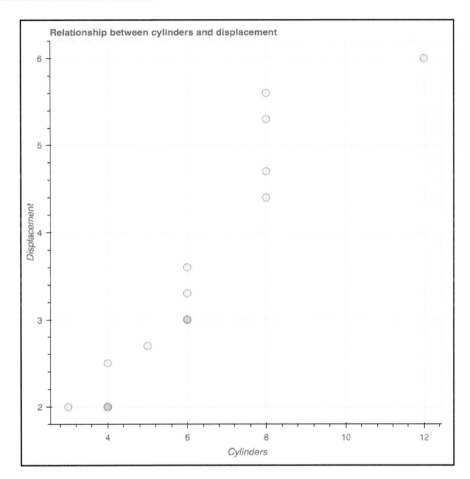

Machine Learning with MLlib

5

In this chapter, we will cover how to build machine learning models with PySpark's MLlib module. Even though it is now being deprecated and most of the models are now being moved to the ML module, if you store your data in RDDs, you can use MLlib to do machine learning. You will learn the following recipes:

- Loading the data
- Exploring the data
- Testing the data
- Transforming the data
- Standardizing the data
- Creating an RDD for training
- Predicting hours of work for census respondents
- Forecasting the income level of census respondents
- Building a clustering model
- Computing performance statistics

Loading the data

In order to build a machine learning model, we need data. Thus, before we start, we need to read some data. In this recipe, and throughout this chapter, we will be using the 1994 census income data.

Getting ready

To execute this recipe, you need to have a working Spark environment. If you do not have one, you might want to go back to `Chapter 1`, *Installing and Configuring Spark* and follow the recipes you will find there.

The dataset was sourced from `http://archive.ics.uci.edu/ml/datasets/Census+Income`.

 The dataset is located in the `data` folder in the GitHub repository for the book.

All the code that you will need in this chapter can be found in the GitHub repository we set up for the book: `http://bit.ly/2ArlBck`; go to `Chapter05` and open the `5. Machine Learning with MLlib.ipynb` notebook.

No other prerequisites are required.

How to do it...

We will read the data into a DataFrame so it is easier for us to work with. Later on, we will convert it into an RDD of labeled points. To read the data, execute the following:

```
census_path = '../data/census_income.csv'

census = spark.read.csv(
    census_path
    , header=True
    , inferSchema=True
)
```

How it works...

First, we specify the path to our dataset. In our case, as with all the other datasets we use in this book, `census_income.csv` is located in the `data` folder, accessible from the parent folder.

Next, we use the `.read` property of `SparkSession`, which returns the `DataFrameReader` object. The first parameter to the `.csv(...)` method specifies the path to the data. Our dataset has the column names in the first row, so we use the `header` option to instruct the reader to use the first row for column names. The `inferSchema` parameter instructs the `DataFrameReader` to automatically detect the datatype of each column.

Let's check whether the datatype inference is correct:

```
census.printSchema()
```

The preceding code produces the following output:

```
root
 |-- age: integer (nullable = true)
 |-- workclass: string (nullable = true)
 |-- fnlwgt: integer (nullable = true)
 |-- education: string (nullable = true)
 |-- education-num: integer (nullable = true)
 |-- marital-status: string (nullable = true)
 |-- occupation: string (nullable = true)
 |-- relationship: string (nullable = true)
 |-- race: string (nullable = true)
 |-- sex: string (nullable = true)
 |-- capital-gain: integer (nullable = true)
 |-- capital-loss: integer (nullable = true)
 |-- hours-per-week: integer (nullable = true)
 |-- native-country: string (nullable = true)
 |-- label: string (nullable = true)
```

As you can see, the datatype of certain columns was detected properly; without the `inferSchema` parameter, all the columns would default to strings.

There's more...

However, there's a small problem with our dataset: most of the string columns have either leading or trailing white spaces. Here's how you can correct this:

```
import pyspark.sql.functions as func

for col, typ in census.dtypes:
    if typ == 'string':
        census = census.withColumn(
            col
            , func.ltrim(func.rtrim(census[col]))
        )
```

We loop through all the columns in the `census` DataFrame.

 The `.dtypes` property of a DataFrame is a list of tuples where the first element is the column name and the second element is the datatype.

If the type of the column is equal to string, we apply two functions: `.ltrim(...)`, which removes any leading whitespaces in a string, and `.rtrim(...)`, which removes any trailing whitespaces. The `.withColumn(...)` method does not append any new columns as we reuse the same name for the column: `col`.

Exploring the data

Jumping straight into modeling the data is a misstep almost every new data scientist makes; we get too eager to get to the reward stage, so we forget about the fact that most of the time is actually spent doing the boring stuff of cleaning up our data and getting familiar with it. In this recipe, we will explore the census dataset.

Getting ready

To execute this recipe, you need to have a working Spark environment. You should have already gone through the previous recipe where we loaded the census data into a DataFrame.

No other prerequisites are required.

How to do it...

First, we list all the columns we want to keep:

```
cols_to_keep = census.dtypes

cols_to_keep = (
    ['label','age'
     ,'capital-gain'
     ,'capital-loss'
     ,'hours-per-week'
    ] + [
        e[0] for e in cols_to_keep[:-1]
        if e[1] == 'string'
    ]
)
```

Next, we select the numerical and categorical features as we will be exploring these separately:

```
census_subset = census.select(cols_to_keep)

cols_num = [
    e[0] for e in census_subset.dtypes
    if e[1] == 'int'
]
cols_cat = [
    e[0] for e in census_subset.dtypes[1:]
    if e[1] == 'string'
]
```

How it works...

First, we extract all the columns with their corresponding datatypes.

 We have already discussed the .dtypes property of DataFrame stores in the previous recipe.

We will only keep label, which is the column that holds an identifier regarding whether a person makes more than $50,000 or not, and a handful of other numeric columns. In addition, we carry over all the string features.

Next, we create a DataFrame with only the selected columns and extract all the numeric and categorical columns; we store these in the cols_num and cols_cat lists, respectively.

Numerical features

Let's explore the numerical features. Just like in Chapter 4, *Preparing Data for Modeling*, for the numerical variables, we will calculate some basic descriptive statistics:

```
import pyspark.mllib.stat as st
import numpy as np

rdd_num = (
    census_subset
    .select(cols_num)
    .rdd
    .map(lambda row: [e for e in row])
```

```
)

stats_num = st.Statistics.colStats(rdd_num)

for col, min_, mean_, max_, var_ in zip(
        cols_num
    , stats_num.min()
    , stats_num.mean()
    , stats_num.max()
    , stats_num.variance()
):
    print('{0}: min->{1:.1f}, mean->{2:.1f}, max->{3:.1f}, stdev->{4:.1f}'
        .format(col, min_, mean_, max_, np.sqrt(var_)))
```

First, we further subset our `census_subset` to include only the numerical columns. Next, we extract the underlying RDD. Since every element of this RDD is a row, we first need to create a list so we can work with it; we achieve that using the `.map(...)` method.

 For documentation on the `Row` class, check out `http://spark.apache.org/docs/latest/api/python/pyspark.sql.html#pyspark.sql.Row`.

Now that we have our RDD ready, we simply call the `.colStats(...)` method from the statistics module of MLlib. `.colStats(...)` accepts an RDD of numeric values; these can be either lists or vectors (either dense or sparse, see the documentation on `pyspark.mllib.linalg.Vectors` at `http://spark.apache.org/docs/latest/api/python/pyspark.mllib.html#pyspark.mllib.linalg.Vectors`). A `MultivariateStatisticalSummary` trait is returned, which contains data such as count, max, mean, min, norms L1 and L2, number of nonzero observations, and the variance.

 If you are familiar with C++ or Java, traits can be viewed as virtual classes (C++) or interfaces (Java). You can read more about traits at `https://docs.scala-lang.org/tour/traits.html`.

In our example, we only select the min, mean, max, and variance. Here's what we get back:

```
age: min->17.0, mean->38.6, max->90.0, stdev->13.6
capital-gain: min->0.0, mean->1077.6, max->99999.0, stdev->7385.3
capital-loss: min->0.0, mean->87.3, max->4356.0, stdev->403.0
hours-per-week: min->1.0, mean->40.4, max->99.0, stdev->12.3
```

So, the average age is about 39 years old. However, we definitely have an outlier in our dataset of 90 years old. In terms of capital gain or loss, the census respondents seem to be making more money than losing. On average, the respondents worked 40 hours per week but we had someone working close to 100-hour weeks.

Categorical features

For the categorical data, we cannot calculate simple descriptive statistics. Thus, we are going to calculate frequencies for each distinct value in each categorical column. Here's a code snippet that will achieve this:

```
rdd_cat = (
    census_subset
    .select(cols_cat + ['label'])
    .rdd
    .map(lambda row: [e for e in row])
)

results_cat = {}

for i, col in enumerate(cols_cat + ['label']):
    results_cat[col] = (
        rdd_cat
        .groupBy(lambda row: row[i])
        .map(lambda el: (el[0], len(el[1])))
        .collect()
    )
```

First, we repeat what we have just done for the numerical columns but for the categorical ones: we subset `census_subset` to only the categorical columns and the label, access the underlying RDD, and transform each row into a list. We're going to store the results in the `results_cat` dictionary. We loop through all the categorical columns and aggregate the data using the `.groupBy(...)` transformation. Finally, we create a list of tuples where the first element is the value (`el[0]`) and the second element is the frequency (`len(el[1])`).

The `.groupBy(...)` transformation outputs a list where the first element is the value and the second is a `pyspark.resultIterable.ResultIterable` object that is effectively a list of all elements from the RDD that contains the value.

Now that we have our data aggregated, let's see what we deal with:

```
sex [('Male', 21790), ('Female', 10771)]

race [('White', 27816), ('Black', 3124), ('Asian-Pac-Islander', 1039), ('Amer-Indian-Eskimo', 311)
, ('Other', 271)]

label [('<=50K', 24720), ('>50K', 7841)]

native-country [('United-States', 29170), ('Mexico', 643), ('?', 583), ('Philippines', 198), ('Ger
many', 137), ('Canada', 121), ('Puerto-Rico', 114), ('El-Salvador', 106), ('India', 100), ('Cuba',
95), ('England', 90), ('Jamaica', 81), ('South', 80), ('China', 75), ('Italy', 73), ('Dominican-Re
public', 70), ('Vietnam', 67), ('Guatemala', 64), ('Japan', 62), ('Poland', 60), ('Columbia', 59),
('Taiwan', 51), ('Haiti', 44), ('Iran', 43), ('Portugal', 37), ('Nicaragua', 34), ('Peru', 31), ('
France', 29), ('Greece', 29), ('Ecuador', 28), ('Ireland', 24), ('Hong', 20), ('Trinadad&Tobago',
19), ('Cambodia', 19), ('Laos', 18), ('Thailand', 18), ('Yugoslavia', 16), ('Outlying-US(Guam-USVI
-etc)', 14), ('Hungary', 13), ('Honduras', 13), ('Scotland', 12), ('Holand-Netherlands', 1)]
```

The preceding list is abbreviated for brevity. Check (or run the code in) the 5. `Machine Learning with MLlib.ipynb` notebook present in our GitHub repository.

As you can see, we are dealing with an imbalanced sample: it is heavily skewed toward males and mostly white people. Also, in 1994 there were not many people earning more than $50,000, only about a quarter.

There's more...

Another important metric you might want to check is the correlations between numerical variables. Calculating correlations with MLlib is very easy:

```
correlations = st.Statistics.corr(rdd_num)
```

The `.corr(...)` action returns a NumPy array or arrays, or, in other words, a matrix where each element is a Pearson (by default) or Spearman correlation coefficient.

To print it out, we just loop through all the elements:

```
for i, el_i in enumerate(abs(correlations) > 0.05):
    print(cols_num[i])
    for j, el_j in enumerate(el_i):
        if el_j and j != i:
            print(
                '
```

```
                        , cols_num[j]
                        , correlations[i][j]
                )
        print()
```

We only print the upper triangular portion of the matrix without the diagonal. Using the enumerate allows us to print out the column names since the correlations NumPy matrix does not list them. Here's what we get:

```
age
        capital-gain 0.077674498166
        capital-loss 0.057774539479
        hours-per-week 0.0687557075095

capital-gain
        age 0.077674498166
        hours-per-week 0.0784086153901

capital-loss
        age 0.057774539479
        hours-per-week 0.0542563622727

hours-per-week
        age 0.0687557075095
        capital-gain 0.0784086153901
        capital-loss 0.0542563622727
```

As you can see, there is not much correlation between our numerical variables. This is actually a good thing, as we can use all of them in our model since we will not suffer from much multicollinearity.

If you do not know what multicollinearity, is check out this lecture: https://onlinecourses.science.psu.edu/stat501/node/343.

See also

- You might also want to check out this tutorial from Berkeley University: http://ampcamp.berkeley.edu/big-data-mini-course/data-exploration-using-spark.html

Testing the data

In order to build a successful statistical or machine learning model, we need to follow a simple (but hard!) rule: make it as simple as possible (so it generalizes the phenomenon being modeled well) but not too simple (so it loses its main ability to predict). A visual example of how this manifests is as follows (from `http://bit.ly/2GpRybB`):

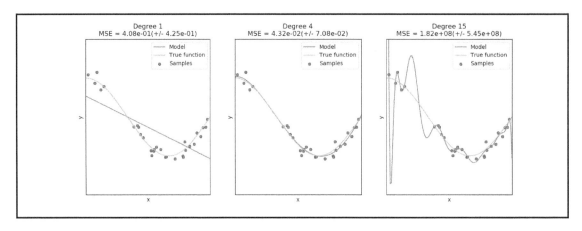

The middle chart shows a good fit: the model line follows the true function well. The model line on the left chart oversimplifies the phenomenon and has literally no predictive power (apart from a handful of points)—a perfect example of underfitting. The model line on the right follows the training data almost perfectly but if new data was presented, it would most likely misrepresent it—a concept known as overfitting, that is, it does not generalize well. As you can see from these three charts, the complexity of the model needs to be just right so it models the phenomenon well.

Some machine learning models have a tendency to overtrain. For example, any models that try to find a mapping (a function) between the input data and the independent variable (or a label) have a tendency to overfit; these include parametric regression models, such as linear or generalized regression models, as well as recently (again!) popular neural networks (or deep learning models). On the other hand, some decision tree-based models (such as random forests) are less prone to overfitting even with more complex models.

So, how do we get the model just right? There are four rules of thumb:

- Select your features wisely
- Do not overtrain, or select a model that is less prone to overfitting

- Run multiple model estimations with randomly selected data from your dataset
- Tune hyperparameters

In this recipe, we will focus on the first point, the remaining points will be covered in some of the recipes found in this and the two next chapters.

Getting ready

To execute this recipe, you need to have a working Spark environment. You would have already gone through the *Loading the data* recipe where we loaded the census data into a DataFrame.

No other prerequisites are required.

How to do it...

In order to find the best features for the problem at hand, we first need to understand what problem we are dealing with, as different methods will be used for selecting features in regression problems or for classifiers:

- **Regression**: In regression, your target (or ground truth) is a *continuous* variable (such as number of work hours per week). You have two methods to select your best features:
    - **Pearson's correlation**: We covered this one in the previous recipe. As noted there, the correlation can only be calculated between two numerical (continuous) features.
    - **Analysis of variance (ANOVA)**: It is a tool to explain (or test) the distribution of observations conditional on some categories. Thus, it can be used to select the most discriminatory (categorical) features of the continuous dependent variable.
- **Classification**: In classification, your target (or label) is a discrete variable of two (binomial) or many (multinomial) levels. There are also two methods that help to select the best features:
    - **Linear discriminant analysis (LDA)**: This helps to find a linear combination of continuous features that best explains the variance of the categorical label
    - χ^2 **test**: A test that tests the independence between two categorical variables

Spark, for now, allows us to test (or select) the best features between comparable variables; it only implements the correlations (the `pyspark.mllib.stat.Statistics.corr(...)` we covered earlier) and the χ^2 test (the `pyspark.mllib.stat.Statistics.chiSqTest(...)` or the `pyspark.mllib.feature.ChiSqSelector(...)` methods).

In this recipe, we will use `.chiSqTest(...)` to test the independence between our label (that is, an indicator that someone is earning more than \$50,000) and the occupation of the census responder. Here's a snippet that does this for us:

```
import pyspark.mllib.linalg as ln

census_occupation = (
    census
    .groupby('label')
    .pivot('occupation')
    .count()
)

census_occupation_coll = (
    census_occupation
    .rdd
    .map(lambda row: (row[1:]))
    .flatMap(lambda row: row)
    .collect()
)

len_row = census_occupation.count()
dense_mat = ln.DenseMatrix(
    len_row
    , 2
    , census_occupation_coll
    , True)
chi_sq = st.Statistics.chiSqTest(dense_mat)

print(chi_sq.pValue)
```

How it works...

First, we import the linear algebra portion of MLlib; we will be using some matrix representations later.

Next, we build a pivot table where we group by the `occupation` feature and pivot by the `label` column (either <=50K or >50K). Each occurrence is counted and this results in the following table:

```
+-----------------+-----+----+
|       occupation|<=50K|>50K|
+-----------------+-----+----+
|            Sales| 2667| 983|
|   Exec-managerial| 2098|1968|
|    Prof-specialty| 2281|1859|
| Handlers-cleaners| 1284|  86|
|   Farming-fishing|  879| 115|
|      Craft-repair| 3170| 929|
|   Transport-moving| 1277| 320|
|    Priv-house-serv|  148|   1|
|    Protective-serv|  438| 211|
|     Other-service| 3158| 137|
|      Tech-support|  645| 283|
| Machine-op-inspct| 1752| 250|
|      Armed-Forces|    8|   1|
|                ?| 1652| 191|
|      Adm-clerical| 3263| 507|
+-----------------+-----+----+
```

Next, we flatten the output by accessing the underlying RDD and selecting only the counts with the map transformation: `.map(lambda row: (row[1:]))`. The `.flatMap(...)` transformation creates a long list of all the values we need. We collect all the data on the driver so we can later create `DenseMatrix`.

> You should be cautious about using the `.collect(...)` action since it brings all the data to the driver. As you can see, we are only bringing the heavily aggregated representation of our dataset.

Once we have all our numbers on the driver, we can create their matrix representation; we will have a matrix of 15 rows and 2 columns. First, we check how many distinct occupation values there are by checking the count of the `census_occupation` elements. Next, we call the `DenseMatrix(...)` constructor to create our matrix. The first parameter specifies the number of rows, the second one the number of columns. The third parameter specifies the data, and the final one indicates whether the data is transposed or not. The dense representation looks as follows:

```
DenseMatrix(15, 2, [2667.0, 983.0, 2098.0, 1968.0, 2281.0, 1859.0, 1284.0, 86.0, ..., 1752.0, 250.0, 8.0, 1.0, 1652.0
, 191.0, 3263.0, 507.0], True)
```

And in a more readable format (as a NumPy matrix), it looks like this:

```
array([[  2.66700000e+03,   9.83000000e+02],
       [  2.09800000e+03,   1.96800000e+03],
       [  2.28100000e+03,   1.85900000e+03],
       [  1.28400000e+03,   8.60000000e+01],
       [  8.79000000e+02,   1.15000000e+02],
       [  3.17000000e+03,   9.29000000e+02],
       [  1.27700000e+03,   3.20000000e+02],
       [  1.48000000e+02,   1.00000000e+00],
       [  4.38000000e+02,   2.11000000e+02],
       [  3.15800000e+03,   1.37000000e+02],
       [  6.45000000e+02,   2.83000000e+02],
       [  1.75200000e+03,   2.50000000e+02],
       [  8.00000000e+00,   1.00000000e+00],
       [  1.65200000e+03,   1.91000000e+02],
       [  3.26300000e+03,   5.07000000e+02]])
```

Now, we simply call the `.chiSqTest(...)` and pass our matrix as its only parameter. What is left is to check `pValue` and whether `nullHypothesis` was rejected or not:

```
0.0
the occurrence of the outcomes is statistically independent.
```

So, as you can see, `pValue` is `0.0`, so we can reject the null hypothesis that states the distribution of occupation between those that earn more than $50,000 versus those that earn less than $50,000 is the same. Thus, we can conclude, as Spark tells us, that the occurrence of the outcomes is statistically independent, that is, occupation should be a strong indicator for someone who earns more than $50,000.

See also...

- There are many statistical tests that help to establish whether two populations (or samples) are similar or not, or whether they follow certain distributions. For a good overview, we suggest the following document: http://www.statstutor. ac.uk/resources/uploaded/tutorsquickguidetostatistics.pdf.

Transforming the data

Machine learning (**ML**) is a field of study that aims at using machines (computers) to understand world phenomena and predict their behavior. In order to build an ML model, all our data needs to be numeric. Since almost all of our features are categorical, we need to transform our features. In this recipe, we will learn how to use a hashing trick and dummy encoding.

Getting ready

To execute this recipe, you need to have a working Spark environment. You would have already gone through the *Loading the data* recipe where we loaded the census data into a DataFrame.

No other prerequisites are required.

How to do it...

We will be reducing the dimensionality of our dataset roughly by half, so first we need to extract the total number of distinct values in each column:

```
len_ftrs = []

for col in cols_cat:
    (
        len_ftrs
        .append(
            (col
            , census
                .select(col)
                .distinct()
                .count()
            )
        )
    )
len_ftrs = dict(len_ftrs)
```

Next, for each feature, we will use the .HashingTF(...) method to encode our data:

```
import pyspark.mllib.feature as feat
```

```
final_data = (     census
    .select(cols_to_keep)
    .rdd
    .map(lambda row: [
        list(
            feat.HashingTF(int(len_ftrs[col] / 2.0))
            .transform(row[i])
            .toArray()
        ) if i >= 5
        else [row[i]]
        for i, col in enumerate(cols_to_keep)]
    )
)

final_data.take(3)
```

How it works...

First, we loop through all the categoricals and append a tuple of the column name (the `col`) and the count of distinct values found in that column. The latter is achieved by selecting the column of interest, running the `.distinct()` transformation, and counting the resulting number of values. `len_ftrs` is now a list of tuples. By calling the `dict(...)` method, Python will create a dictionary that will take the first element of the tuple as a key and the second element as the corresponding value. The resulting dictionary looks as follows:

```
{'sex': 2, 'race': 5, 'native-country': 42, 'marital-status': 7, 'workclass': 9, 'education': 16, 'occupation': 15, '
relationship': 6}
```

Now that we know the total number of distinct values in each feature, we can use the hashing trick. First, we import the feature component of the MLlib as that is where the `.HashingTF(...)` is located. Next, we subset the census DataFrame to only the columns we want to keep. We then use the `.map(...)` transformation on the underlying RDD: for each element, we enumerate all the columns and if the index of the column is greater than or equal to five, we create a new instance of `.HashingTF(...)`, which we then use to transform the value and convert it into an NumPy array. The only thing you need to specify for the `.HashingTF(...)` method is the output number of elements; in our case, we roughly halve the number of the number of distinct values so we will have some hashing collisions, but that is fine.

For your reference, our `cols_to_keep` looks as follows:

```
['label', 'age', 'capital-gain', 'capital-loss', 'hours-per-week', 'workclass', 'education', 'marital-status', 'occup
ation', 'relationship', 'race', 'sex', 'native-country']
```

After doing the preceding to our current dataset, `final_data`, it looks as follows; note the format might look a bit odd but we will soon be getting it ready for creating the training RDD:

```
[[['<=50K'], [39], [2174], [0], [40], [1.0, 2.0, 1.0, 5.0], [3.0, 3.0, 0.0, 0.0, 1.0, 0.0, 1.0, 1.0], [2.0, 3.0, 8.0]
, [0.0, 3.0, 3.0, 1.0, 4.0, 1.0, 0.0], [5.0, 5.0, 3.0], [3.0, 2.0], [4.0], [1.0, 0.0, 0.0, 3.0, 0.0, 1.0, 0.0, 0.0, 0
.0, 0.0, 0.0, 2.0, 0.0, 0.0, 0.0, 1.0, 1.0, 2.0, 1.0, 1.0, 0.0]], [[['<=50K'], [50], [0], [0], [13], [4.0, 3.0, 1.0, 8
.0], [3.0, 3.0, 0.0, 0.0, 1.0, 0.0, 1.0, 1.0], [5.0, 5.0, 8.0], [0.0, 1.0, 2.0, 2.0, 8.0, 1.0, 1.0], [4.0, 2.0, 1.0],
[3.0, 2.0], [4.0], [1.0, 0.0, 0.0, 3.0, 0.0, 1.0, 0.0, 0.0, 0.0, 0.0, 0.0, 2.0, 0.0, 0.0, 0.0, 1.0, 1.0, 2.0, 1.0, 1.
0, 0.0]], [['<=50K'], [38], [0], [0], [40], [2.0, 2.0, 0.0, 3.0], [2.0, 2.0, 0.0, 0.0, 0.0, 0.0, 2.0, 1.0], [3.0, 2.0
, 3.0], [2.0, 3.0, 1.0, 3.0, 7.0, 0.0, 1.0], [5.0, 5.0, 3.0], [3.0, 2.0], [4.0], [1.0, 0.0, 0.0, 3.0, 0.0, 1.0, 0.0,
0.0, 0.0, 0.0, 0.0, 2.0, 0.0, 0.0, 0.0, 1.0, 1.0, 2.0, 1.0, 1.0, 0.0]]]
```

There's more...

The only thing that's left is to handle our label; as you can see, it is still a categorical variable. However, since it only takes two values, we can encode it as follows:

```
def labelEncode(label):
    return [int(label[0] == '>50K')]

final_data = (
    final_data
    .map(lambda row: labelEncode(row[0])
        + [item
            for sublist in row[1:]
            for item in sublist]
        )
)
```

The `labelEncode(...)` method takes the label and checks whether it is `'>50k'` or not; if yes, we get a Boolean true, otherwise we get false. We can represent the Boolean data as integers by simply wrapping it inside Python's `int(...)` method.

Finally, we again use `.map(...)`, where we pass the first element of our `row`—the label—to the `labelEncode(...)` method. We then loop through all the remaining lists and combine them together. That portion of the code might look a bit peculiar at first, but it is actually fairly easy to understand. We loop through all the remaining elements (the `row[1:]`) and since each element is a list (hence we name it `sublist`), we create another loop (the `for item in sublist` portion) to extract the individual items. The resulting RDD looks as follows:

```
[[0, 39, 2174, 0, 40, 1.0, 2.0, 1.0, 5.0, 3.0, 3.0, 0.0, 0.0, 1.0, 0.0, 1.0, 1.0, 2.0, 3.0, 8.0, 0.0, 3.0, 3.0, 1.0,
4.0, 1.0, 0.0, 5.0, 5.0, 3.0, 3.0, 2.0, 4.0, 1.0, 0.0, 0.0, 3.0, 0.0, 1.0, 0.0, 0.0, 0.0, 0.0, 0.0, 2.0, 0.0, 0.0, 0.
0, 1.0, 1.0, 2.0, 1.0, 1.0, 0.0], [0, 50, 0, 0, 13, 4.0, 3.0, 1.0, 8.0, 3.0, 3.0, 0.0, 0.0, 1.0, 0.0, 1.0, 1.0, 5.0,
5.0, 8.0, 0.0, 1.0, 2.0, 2.0, 8.0, 1.0, 1.0, 4.0, 2.0, 1.0, 3.0, 2.0, 4.0, 1.0, 0.0, 0.0, 3.0, 0.0, 1.0, 0.0, 0.0, 0.
0, 0.0, 0.0, 2.0, 0.0, 0.0, 0.0, 1.0, 1.0, 2.0, 1.0, 1.0, 0.0], [0, 38, 0, 0, 40, 2.0, 2.0, 0.0, 3.0, 2.0, 2.0, 0.0,
0.0, 0.0, 0.0, 2.0, 1.0, 3.0, 2.0, 3.0, 2.0, 3.0, 1.0, 3.0, 7.0, 0.0, 1.0, 5.0, 5.0, 3.0, 3.0, 2.0, 4.0, 1.0, 0.0, 0.
0, 3.0, 0.0, 1.0, 0.0, 0.0, 0.0, 0.0, 0.0, 2.0, 0.0, 0.0, 0.0, 1.0, 1.0, 2.0, 1.0, 1.0, 0.0]]
```

See also...

- Check out this link for a nice overview of how to deal with categorical features in Python: `http://pbpython.com/categorical-encoding.html`

Standardizing the data

Data standardization (or normalization) is important for a number of reasons:

- Some algorithms converge faster on standardized (or normalized) data
- If your input variables are on vastly different scales, the interpretability of coefficients might be hard or conclusions drawn might be wrong
- For some models, the optimal solution might be wrong if you do not standardize

In this recipe, we will show you how to standardize the data so if your modeling project requires standardized data, you will know how to do it.

Getting ready

To execute this recipe, you need to have a working Spark environment. You would have already gone through the previous recipe where we encoded the census data.

No other prerequisites are required.

How to do it...

MLlib offers a method to do most of this work for us. Even though the following code might be confusing at first, we will walk through it step by step:

```python
standardizer = feat.StandardScaler(True, True)
sModel = standardizer.fit(final_data.map(lambda row: row[1:]))
final_data_scaled = sModel.transform(final_data.map(lambda row: row[1:]))

final_data = (
    final_data
    .map(lambda row: row[0])
    .zipWithIndex()
    .map(lambda row: (row[1], row[0]))
    .join(
        final_data_scaled
        .zipWithIndex()
        .map(lambda row: (row[1], row[0]))
    )
    .map(lambda row: row[1])
)

final_data.take(1)
```

How it works...

First, we create the `StandardScaler(...)` object. The two parameters set to `True`—the former stands for mean, the latter stands for standard deviation—indicate that we want the model to standardize our features using Z-score: $z_i^f = \dfrac{x_i^f - \mu^f}{\sigma^f}$, where x_i^f is the ith observation of the f feature, μ^f is the mean of all the observations in the f feature, and σ^f is the standard deviation of all the observations in the f feature.

Next, we `.fit(...)` the data using `StandardScaler(...)`. Note that we do not standardize the first feature as it is actually our label. Finally, we `.transform(...)` our dataset so we get the scaled features.

However, since we do not scale our label, we need to somehow bring it back to our scaled dataset. So first, from `final_data`, we extract the label (using the `.map(lamba row: row[0])` transformation). However, we would not be able to join it with the `final_data_scaled` as it is since there is no key to join on. Note, we essentially want to join in a row-by-row fashion. So, we use the `.zipWithIndex()` method, which gives us a tuple in return, with the first element being the data and the second element being the row number. Since we want to join on the row number, we need to bring it to the first position in the tuple since that is how the `.join(...)` works for RDDs; we achieve this with the second `.map(...)` operation.

> In RDDs, the `.join(...)` operation cannot specify the key explicitly; both RDDs need to be two-element tuples, where the first element is the key and the second element is the data.

Once the join is complete, we simply extract the joined data by using the `.map(lambda row: row[1])` transformation.

Here's how our data looks now:

```
[(0, DenseVector([0.0307, 0.1485, -0.2167, -0.0354, -1.2635, 0.008, 1.7796, 1.0001, 0.83, 0.5743, -0.3473, -0.443, 0.
6826, -0.4007, -0.3862, -0.4685, -1.1369, -0.4555, 0.4551, -1.1329, 2.0776, 1.8713, -1.0381, -0.3381, -0.2381, -0.775
, 0.9805, 1.5207, 0.3083, -0.0634, -0.2574, -0.7031, 0.3208, -0.0901, -0.1263, 0.3355, -0.1223, 0.3378, -0.0853, -0.0
937, -0.0887, -0.2104, 0.0, 0.1286, -0.1976, -0.1433, -0.1419, 0.1895, 0.298, 0.2896, 0.1638, 0.1221, 0.0]))]
```

We can also peek into `sModel` to see what means and standard deviations were used to transform our data:

```
(DenseVector([38.5816, 1077.6488, 87.3038, 40.4375, 2.2307, 1.9942, 0.2391, 3.4004, 2.2001, 2.2522, 0.1836, 0.2528, 0
.5707, 0.1384, 1.2445, 1.5914, 3.6564, 3.6415, 7.1161, 1.0957, 0.838, 1.4236, 2.461, 4.7319, 1.223, 0.4287, 3.8206, 2
.8271, 2.472, 3.0508, 2.4882, 4.6616, 0.9066, 0.008, 0.0157, 2.7153, 0.0157, 0.8967, 0.0072, 0.0108, 0.0078, 0.0432,
0.0, 1.9416, 0.0445, 0.0238, 0.0197, 0.9444, 0.9136, 1.8534, 0.9618, 0.964, 0.0]), DenseVector([13.6404, 7385.2921, 4
02.9602, 12.3474, 0.974, 0.722, 0.4276, 1.5994, 0.9637, 1.3021, 0.5285, 0.5706, 0.6288, 0.3453, 0.6331, 1.2623, 1.457
, 1.4084, 1.9423, 0.9671, 1.0407, 0.8424, 1.4074, 2.1649, 0.9365, 0.5532, 1.2029, 1.4289, 1.7124, 0.8013, 1.8969, 0.9
41, 0.2911, 0.0893, 0.1243, 0.8486, 0.1281, 0.3057, 0.0846, 0.1151, 0.088, 0.2055, 0.0, 0.4543, 0.2251, 0.1658, 0.139
1, 0.2935, 0.29, 0.5062, 0.2331, 0.2945, 0.0]))
```

Creating an RDD for training

Before we can train an ML model, we need to create an RDD where each element is a labeled point. In this recipe, we will use the `final_data` RDD we created in the previous recipe to prepare our RDD for training.

Getting ready

To execute this recipe, you need to have a working Spark environment. You would have already gone through the previous recipe when we standardized the encoded census data.

No other prerequisites are required.

How to do it...

Many of the MLlib models require an RDD of labeled points to train. The next code snippets will create such an RDD for us to build classification and regression model.

Classification

Here's the snippet to create the classification RDD of labeled points that we will be using to predict whether someone is making more than $50,000:

```
final_data_income = (
    final_data
    .map(lambda row: reg.LabeledPoint(
        row[0]
        , row[1:]
        )
    )
)
```

Regression

Here's the snippet to create the regression RDD of labeled points that we will be using to predict the number of hours people work:

```
mu, std = sModel.mean[3], sModel.std[3]

final_data_hours = (
    final_data
    .map(lambda row: reg.LabeledPoint(
        row[1][3] * std + mu
        , ln.Vectors.dense([row[0]] + list(row[1][0:3]) + list(row[1][4:]))
        )
    )
)
```

How it works...

Before we create the RDDs, we have to import the `pyspark.mllib.regression` submodule, as that is where we can access the `LabeledPoint` class:

```
import pyspark.mllib.regression as reg
```

Next, we simply loop through all the elements of the `final_data` RDD and create a labeled point for each element using the `.map(...)` transformation.

The first parameter of `LabeledPoint(...)` is the label. If you look at the the two code snippets, the only difference between them is what we consider labels and features.

 As a reminder, a classification problem aims to find the probability of an observation belonging to a specific class; thus, the label is normally a categorical or, in other words, discrete. On the other hand, the regression problem aims to predict a value given an observation; thus, the label is normally numerical, or continuous if you will.

So, in the `final_data_income` case, we are using the binary indicator for whether the census respondent earns more (a value of 1) or less (the label equal to 0) than $50,000, whereas in the `final_data_hours`, we use the `hours-per-week` feature (see the *Loading the data* recipe), which, in our case, is the fifth piece of each of the elements of the `final_data` RDD. Note for this label we need to scale it back, so we need to multiply by the standard deviation and add the mean.

 We assume here that you are working through the `5. Machine Learning with MLlib.ipynb` notebook and have the `sModel` object already created. If you do not, please go back to the previous recipe and follow the steps outlined there.

The second parameter of the `LabeledPoint(...)` is a vector of all the features. You can pass either a NumPy array, list, `scipy.sparse` column matrix, or `pyspark.mllib.linalg.SparseVector` or `pyspark.mllib.linalg.DenseVector`; in our case, we encoded our features into `DenseVector` as we have already encoded all our features using the hashing trick.

There's more...

We could use the full dataset to train our models, but we would then run into another problem: how do we evaluate how good our model is? Therefore, any data scientist normally performs a split of the data into two subsets: training and testing.

 See the *See also* section of this recipe for why this often isn't good enough, and you should actually be splitting the data into training, testing, and validation datasets.

Here are two code snippets that show how easily this can be done in PySpark:

```
(
    final_data_income_train
    , final_data_income_test
) = (
    final_data_income.randomSplit([0.7, 0.3])
)
```

Here is the second:

```
(
    final_data_hours_train
    , final_data_hours_test
) = (
    final_data_hours.randomSplit([0.7, 0.3])
)
```

By simply calling the `.randomSplit(...)` method of an RDD, we can quickly divide our RDDs into training and testing subsets. The only required parameter for the `.randomSplit(...)` method is a list where each element specifies the proportion of the dataset to randomly select. Note, these proportions need to sum up to 1.

 We could have passed a list of three elements if we wanted to get the training, testing, and validation subsets.

See also

- Why you should be splitting into three datasets, and not two, is nicely explained here: http://bit.ly/2GFyvtY

Predicting hours of work for census respondents

In this recipe, we will build a simple linear regression model that will aim to predict the number of hours each of the census respondents works per week.

Getting ready

To execute this recipe, you need to have a working Spark environment. You would have already gone through the previous recipe where we created training and testing datasets for estimating regression models.

No other prerequisites are required.

How to do it...

Training models with MLlib is pretty straightforward. See the following code snippet:

```
workhours_model_lm =
reg.LinearRegressionWithSGD.train(final_data_hours_train)
```

How it works...

As you can see, we first create the `LinearRegressionWithSGD` object and call its `.train(...)` method.

For a very good overview of different derivatives of stochastic gradient descent, check this out: `http://ruder.io/optimizing-gradient-descent/`.

The first, and the only, required parameter we pass to the method is an RDD of labeled points that we created earlier. There is a host of parameters, though, that you can specify:

- Number of iterations; the default is `100`
- Step is the parameter used in SGD; the default is `1.0`
- `miniBatchFraction` specifies the proportion of data to be used in each SGD iteration; the default is `1.0`

- The `initialWeights` parameter allows us to initialize the coefficients to some specific values; it has no defaults and the algorithm will start with the weights equal to `0.0`
- The regularizer type parameter, `regType`, allows us to specify the type of the regularizer used: `'l1'` for L1 regularization and `'l2'` for L2 regularization; the default is `None`, no regularization
- The `regParam` parameter specifies the regularizer parameter; the default is `0.0`
- The model can also fit the intercept but it is not set by default; the default is false
- Before training, the model by default can validate data
- You can also specify `convergenceTol`; the default is `0.001`

Let's now see how well our model predicts working hours:

```
small_sample_hours = sc.parallelize(final_data_hours_test.take(10))

for t,p in zip(
    small_sample_hours
        .map(lambda row: row.label)
        .collect()
    , workhours_model_lm.predict(
        small_sample_hours
            .map(lambda row: row.features)
    ).collect()):
    print(t,p)
```

First, from our full testing dataset, we select 10 observations (so we can print them on the screen). Next, we extract the true value from the testing dataset, whereas for the prediction we simply call the `.predict(...)` method of the `workhours_model_lm` model and pass the `.features` vector. Here is what we get:

```
16.0 3.28395400384
40.0 45.7930482573
35.0 19.46708583
60.0 41.8838718837
52.0 11.0061417631
43.0 1.28423467636
35.0 9.96743282811
40.0 -9.36306561637
60.0 10.8259138175
40.0 1.09195397136
```

As you can see, our model does not do very well, so further refining would be necessary. This, however, goes beyond the scope of this chapter and the book itself.

Forecasting the income levels of census respondents

In this recipe, we will show you how to solve a classification problem with MLlib by building two models: the ubiquitous logistic regression and a slightly more sophisticated model, the **SVM (Support Vector Machine)**.

Getting ready

To execute this recipe, you need to have a working Spark environment. You would have already gone through the *Creating an RDD for training* recipe where we created training and testing datasets for estimating classification models.

No other prerequisites are required.

How to do it...

Just like with the linear regression, building a logistic regression starts with creating a `LogisticRegressionWithSGD` object:

```
import pyspark.mllib.classification as cl

income_model_lr =
cl.LogisticRegressionWithSGD.train(final_data_income_train)
```

How it works...

As with the `LinearRegressionWithSGD` model, the only required parameter is the RDD with labeled points. Also, you can specify the same set of parameters:

- The number of iterations; the default is `100`
- The step is the parameter used in SGD; the default is `1.0`

- `miniBatchFraction` specifies the proportion of data to be used in each SGD iteration; the default is `1.0`
- The `initialWeights` parameter allows us to initialize the coefficients to some specific values; it has no defaults and the algorithm will start with the weights equal to `0.0`
- The regularizer type parameter, `regType`, allows us to specify the type of the regularizer used: `l1` for L1 regularization and `l2` for L2 regularization; the default is `None`, no regularization
- The `regParam` parameter specifies the regularizer parameter; the default is `0.0`
- The model can also fit the intercept but it is not set by default; the default is false
- Before training, the model by default can validate data
- You can also specify `convergenceTol`; the default is `0.001`

The `LogisticRegressionModel(...)` object that is returned upon finalizing the training allows us to utilize the model. By passing a vector of features to the `.predict(...)` method, we can predict the class the observations will most likely be associated with.

Any classification model produces a set of probabilities and logistic regression is not an exception. In the binary case, we can specify a threshold that, once breached, would indicate that the observation would be assigned with the class equal to 1 rather than 0; this threshold is normally set to `0.5`. `LogisticRegressionModel(...)` assumes `0.5` by default, but you can change it by calling the `.setThreshold(...)` method and passing a desired threshold value that is between 0 and 1 (not inclusive).

Let's see how our model performs:

```
small_sample_income = sc.parallelize(final_data_income_test.take(10))

for t,p in zip(
    small_sample_income
        .map(lambda row: row.label)
        .collect()
    , income_model_lr.predict(
        small_sample_income
            .map(lambda row: row.features)
    ).collect()):
    print(t,p)
```

As with the linear regression example, we first extract 10 records from our test dataset so we can fit them on the screen. Next, we extract the desired label and call the `income_model_lr` model of `.predict(...)` the class. Here's what we get back:

```
1.0 1
1.0 1
1.0 1
0.0 0
0.0 0
0.0 1
0.0 0
0.0 0
0.0 0
0.0 0
```

So, out of 10 records, we got 9 right. Not bad.

 In the *Computing performance statistics* recipe, we will learn how to use the full testing dataset to more formally evaluate our models.

There's more...

Logistic regression is normally the benchmark used to asses the relative performance of other classification models, that is, whether they are performing better or worse. The drawback of logistic regression, however, is that it cannot handle cases where two classes cannot be separated by a line. SVMs do not have these kinds of problem, as their kernel can be expressed in quite flexible ways:

```
income_model_svm = cl.SVMWithSGD.train(
    final_data_income
    , miniBatchFraction=1/2.0
)
```

In this example, just like with the `LogisticRegressionWithSGD` model, we can specify a host of parameters (we will not be repeating them here). However, the `miniBatchFraction` parameter instructs the SVM model to only use half of the data in each iteration; this helps preventing overfitting.

The results for the 10 observations from the `small_sample_income` RDD are calculated the same way as with the logistic regression model:

```
for t,p in zip(
    small_sample_income
        .map(lambda row: row.label)
        .collect()
    , income_model_svm.predict(
        small_sample_income
            .map(lambda row: row.features)
    ).collect()):
    print(t,p)
```

The model produces the same results as the logistic regression model, so we will not be repeating them here. However, in the *Computing performance statistics* recipe, we will see how these differ.

Building a clustering models

Often, it is hard to get our hands on data that is labeled. Also, sometimes you might want to find underlying patterns in your dataset. In this recipe, we will learn how to build the popular k-means clustering model in Spark.

Getting ready

To execute this recipe, you need to have a working Spark environment. You should have already gone through the *Standardizing the data* recipe where we standardized the encoded census data.

No other prerequisites are required.

How to do it...

Just like with classification or regression models, building clustering models is pretty straightforward in Spark. Here's the code that aims to find patterns in the census data:

```
import pyspark.mllib.clustering as clu

model = clu.KMeans.train(
```

```
      final_data.map(lambda row: row[1])
    , 2
    , initializationMode='random'
    , seed=666
)
```

How it works...

First, we need to import the clustering submodule of MLlib. Just like before, we first create the clustering estimator object, `KMeans`. The `.train(...)` method requires two parameters: the RDD we want to use to find the clusters in, and the number of clusters we expect. We also chose to randomly initialize the centroids of the clusters by specifying `initializationMode`; the default for this one is `k-means||`. Other parameters include:

- `maxIterations` specifies after how many iterations the estimation should stop; the default is `100`
- `initializationSteps` is only useful if the default initialization mode is used; the default for this parameter is `2`
- `epsilon` is a stopping criteria—if all the centers of the centroids move (in terms of the Euclidean distance) less than this, the iterations stop; the default is `0.0001`
- `initialModel` allows you to specify the centers previously estimated in the form of `KMeansModel`; the default is `None`

There's more...

Once the model is estimated, we can use it to predict the clusters and see how good our model actually is. However, at the moment, Spark does not provide the means to evaluate clustering models. Thus, we will use the metrics provided by scikit-learn:

```
import sklearn.metrics as m

predicted = (
    model
        .predict(
            final_data.map(lambda row: row[1])
        )
)
predicted = predicted.collect()
```

```
true = final_data.map(lambda row: row[0]).collect()

print(m.homogeneity_score(true, predicted))
print(m.completeness_score(true, predicted))
```

The clustering metrics are located in the `.metrics` submodule of scikit-learn. We are using two of the metrics available: homogeneity and completeness. Homogeneity measures whether all the points in a cluster come from the same class whereas the completeness score estimates whether, for a given class, all the points end up in the same cluster; a value of 1 for either of the scores means a perfect model.

Let's see what we get:

```
0.153472872815
0.122339061021
```

Well, our clustering model did not do so well: the homogeneity score of 15% means that the remaining 85% of observations were misclustered, and we only clustered ~12% properly of all those that belong to the same class.

See also

- For more on the evaluation of clustering models, you might want to check out https://nlp.stanford.edu/IR-book/html/htmledition/evaluation-of-clustering-1.html

Computing performance statistics

In the previous recipes, we have already seen some values predicted by our classification and regression models and how far or how close they were from/to the original values. In this recipe, we will learn how to fully calculate the performance statistics for these models.

Getting ready

In order to execute this recipe, you need to have a working Spark environment and you should have gone through the *Predicting hours of work for census respondents* and *Forecasting income levels of census respondents* recipes presented earlier in this chapter.

No other prerequisites are required.

How to do it...

Getting the performance metrics for regression and classification in Spark is extremely simple:

```
import pyspark.mllib.evaluation as ev

(...)

metrics_lm = ev.RegressionMetrics(true_pred_reg)

(...)

metrics_lr = ev.BinaryClassificationMetrics(true_pred_class_lr)
```

How it works...

First, we load the evaluation module; doing this exposes the `.RegressionMetrics(...)` and the `.BinaryClassificationMetrics(...)` methods, which we can use.

Regression metrics

`true_pred_reg` is an RDD of tuples where the first element is the prediction from our linear regression model and the second element is the expected value (the number of hours worked per week). Here's how we create it:

```
true_pred_reg = (
    final_data_hours_test
    .map(lambda row: (
        float(workhours_model_lm.predict(row.features))
        , row.label))
)
```

The `metrics_lm` object contains a variety of metrics: `explainedVariance`, `meanAbsouteError`, `meanSquaredError`, `r2`, and `rootMeanSquaredError`. Here, we will only print out a couple of them:

```
print('R^2: ', metrics_lm.r2)
print('Explained Variance: ', metrics_lm.explainedVariance)
print('meanAbsoluteError: ', metrics_lm.meanAbsoluteError)
```

Let's see what we got for the linear regression model:

```
R^2:  -6.754451242767173
Explained Variance:  1145.7421086452416
meanAbsoluteError:  29.866629018908615
```

Not unexpectedly, the model performs really poorly, given what we have already seen. Do not be too surprised by the negative R-squared; it can turn negative, that is, a nonsensical value for R-squared, if the predictions of the model are nonsensical.

Classification metrics

We will evaluate the two models we built earlier; here is the logistic regression:

```
true_pred_class_lr = (
    final_data_income_test
    .map(lambda row: (
        float(income_model_lr.predict(row.features))
        , row.label))
)

metrics_lr = ev.BinaryClassificationMetrics(true_pred_class_lr)

print('areaUnderPR: ', metrics_lr.areaUnderPR)
print('areaUnderROC: ', metrics_lr.areaUnderROC)
```

And here is the SVM:

```
true_pred_class_svm = (
    final_data_income_test
    .map(lambda row: (
        float(income_model_svm.predict(row.features))
        , row.label))
)

metrics_svm = ev.BinaryClassificationMetrics(true_pred_class_svm)

print('areaUnderPR: ', metrics_svm.areaUnderPR)
print('areaUnderROC: ', metrics_svm.areaUnderROC)
```

The two metrics—the area under the **Precision-Recall (PR)** and the area under the **Receiver Operating Characteristics (ROC)** curve—allow us to compare the two models.

Check out this interesting discussion about the two metrics on stack exchange: `https://stats.stackexchange.com/questions/7207/roc-vs-precision-and-recall-curves`.

Let's see what we got. For the logistic regression, we have:

```
areaUnderPR:   0.7050195379236808
areaUnderROC:  0.7951114398791014
```

And for the SVM, we have:

```
areaUnderPR:   0.6911561138639338
areaUnderROC:  0.7794154787088152
```

It comes a bit as a surprise that the SVM performed a bit worse than the logistic regression. Let's see the confusion matrix to see where these two models differ. For the logistic regression, we achieve this with the following code:

```
(
    true_pred_class_lr
    .map(lambda el: ((el), 1))
    .reduceByKey(lambda x,y: x+y)
    .take(4)
)
```

And we get:

```
[((0.0, 0.0), 4967), ((1.0, 1.0), 2163), ((0.0, 1.0), 196), ((1.0, 0.0), 2410)]
```

For the SVM, the code looks pretty much the same, with the exception of the input RDD:

```
(
    true_pred_class_svm
    .map(lambda el: ((el), 1))
    .reduceByKey(lambda x,y: x+y)
    .take(4)
)
```

With the preceding, we get:

```
[((0.0, 0.0), 4848), ((1.0, 1.0), 2127), ((0.0, 1.0), 232), ((1.0, 0.0), 2529)]
```

As you can see, the logistic regression is more accurate in predicting both the positive and negative cases, thus achieving fewer of the misclassified (false positives and false negatives) observations. However, the differences are not that dramatic.

To calculate the overall error rate, we can use the following code:

```
trainErr = (
    true_pred_class_lr
    .filter(lambda lp: lp[0] != lp[1]).count()
    / float(true_pred_class_lr.count())
)
print("Training Error = " + str(trainErr))
```

For the SVM, the preceding code looks the same, with an exception of using `true_pred_class_svm` instead of `true_pred_class_lr`. The preceding produces the following. For the logistic regression, we get:

```
Training Error = 0.26766639276910437
```

For the SVM, the results look as follows:

```
Training Error = 0.28358668857847164
```

The error is slightly higher for the SVM, but still a fairly reasonable model.

See also

- If you want to learn more about various performance metrics, we suggest you visit the following URL: https://machinelearningmastery.com/metrics-evaluate-machine-learning-algorithms-python/

Machine Learning with the ML Module

6

In this chapter, we will move on to the currently supported machine learning module of PySpark—the ML module. The ML module, like MLLib, exposes a vast array of machine learning models, almost completely covering the spectrum of the most-used (and usable) models. The ML module, however, operates on Spark DataFrames, making it much more performant as it can leverage the tungsten execution optimizations.

In this chapter, you will learn about the following recipes:

- Introducing Transformers
- Introducing Estimators
- Introducing Pipelines
- Selecting the most predictable features
- Predicting forest coverage types
- Estimating forest elevation
- Clustering forest cover types
- Tuning hyperparameters
- Extracting features from text
- Discretizing continuous variables
- Standardizing continuous variables
- Topic mining

In this chapter, we will use data we downloaded from `https://archive.ics.uci.edu/ml/datasets/covertype`. The dataset is located in the GitHub repository for this book: `/data/forest_coverage_type.csv`.

We load the data in the same manner as before:

```
forest_path = '../data/forest_coverage_type.csv'

forest = spark.read.csv(
    forest_path
    , header=True
    , inferSchema=True
)
```

Introducing Transformers

The `Transformer` class, introduced in Spark 1.3, transforms one dataset into another by normally appending one or more columns to the existing DataFrame. Transformers are an abstraction around methods that actually transform features; the abstraction also includes trained machine learning models (as we will see in the following recipes).

In this recipe, we will introduce two Transformers: `Bucketizer` and `VectorAssembler`.

 TIP We will not be introducing all the Transformers; throughout the rest of this chapter, the most useful ones will show up. For the rest, the Spark documentation is a good place to learn what they do and how to use them.

Here is a list of all of the Transformers that convert one feature into another:

- `Binarizer` is a method that, given a threshold, transforms a continuous numerical feature into a binary one.
- `Bucketizer`, similarly to `Binarizer`, uses a list of thresholds to transform a continuous numerical variable into a discrete one (with as many levels as the length of the list of thresholds plus one).
- `ChiSqSelector` helps to select a predefined number of features that explain the most of the variance of a categorical target (a classification model).
- `CountVectorizer` converts many lists of strings into a `SparseVector` of counts, where each column is a flag for each distinct string found in the lists, and the value indicates how many times the string was found in the current list.
- `DCT` stands for the **Discrete Cosine Transform**. It takes a vector of real values and returns a vector of cosine functions oscillating at different frequencies.
- `ElementwiseProduct` can be used to scale your numerical features as it takes a vector of values and multiplies it (element by element, as the name suggests) by another vector with weights for each value.

- `HashingTF` is a hashing trick transformer that returns a vector (of specified length) representation for a tokenized text.
- `IDF` computes an **Inverse Document Frequency** for a list of records, where each record is a numerical representation of a body of text (see either `CountVectorizer` or `HashingTF`).
- `IndexToString` uses the encoding from the `StringIndexerModel` object to reverse the string index to original values.
- `MaxAbsScaler` rescales the data to be within the –1 to 1 range.
- `MinMaxScaler` rescales the data to be within the 0 to 1 range.
- `NGram` returns pairs, triplets, or *n*-mores of subsequent words of a tokenized text.
- `Normalizer` scales the data to be of unit norm (by default, L2).
- `OneHotEncoder` encodes a categorical variable into a vector representation where only one element is hot, that is, equal to 1 (all others are 0).
- `PCA` is a dimensionality reduction method to extract principal components from data.
- `PolynomialExpansion` returns a polynomial expansion of an input vector.
- `QuantileDiscretizer` is a similar method to `Bucketizer`, but instead of defining the thresholds, only the number of returned bins needs to be specified; the method will use quantiles to decide the thresholds.
- `RegexTokenizer` is a string tokenizer the uses regular expressions to process text.
- `RFormula` is a method to pass R-syntax formula to transform data.
- `SQLTransformer` is a method to pass SQL syntax formula to transform data.
- `StandardScaler` converts a numerical feature to have a 0 mean and a standard deviation of 1.
- `StopWordsRemover` is used to remove words such as `a` or `the` from tokenized text.
- `StringIndexer` produces a vector of indices given a list of all words in a column.
- `Tokenizer` is a default tokenizer that takes a sentence (a string), splits it on a space, and normalizes the words.
- `VectorAssembler` combines the specified (separate) features into a single feature.
- `VectorIndexer` takes a categorical variable (already encoded to be numbers) and returns a vector of indices.

- VectorSlicer can be thought of as a converse of VectorAssembler, as it extracts the data from the vector of features given indices.
- Word2Vec converts a sentence (or string) into a map of {string, vector} representation.

Getting ready

To execute this recipe, you will need a working Spark environment and you would have already loaded the data into the forest DataFrame.

No other prerequisites are required.

How to do it...

First, let's learn how to use the .Bucketizer(...) transformer. Here's the snippet that allows us to transform the Horizontal_Distance_To_Hydrology column into 10 equidistant buckets:

```
import pyspark.sql.functions as f
import pyspark.ml.feature as feat
import numpy as np

buckets_no = 10

dist_min_max = (
    forest.agg(
        f.min('Horizontal_Distance_To_Hydrology')
            .alias('min')
        , f.max('Horizontal_Distance_To_Hydrology')
            .alias('max')
    )
    .rdd
    .map(lambda row: (row.min, row.max))
    .collect()[0]
)

rng = dist_min_max[1] - dist_min_max[0]

splits = list(np.arange(
    dist_min_max[0]
    , dist_min_max[1]
    , rng / (buckets_no + 1)))
```

```
bucketizer = feat.Bucketizer(
    splits=splits
    , inputCol= 'Horizontal_Distance_To_Hydrology'
    , outputCol='Horizontal_Distance_To_Hydrology_Bkt'
)

(
    bucketizer
    .transform(forest)
    .select(
        'Horizontal_Distance_To_Hydrology'
        ,'Horizontal_Distance_To_Hydrology_Bkt'
    ).show(5)
)
```

Any ideas why we could not use `.QuantileDiscretizer(...)` to achieve this?

How it works...

As always, we first load the necessary module we will use throughout, `pyspark.sql.functions`, which will allow us to calculate minimum and maximum values of the `Horizontal_Distance_To_Hydrology` feature. `pyspark.ml.feature` exposes the `.Bucketizer(...)` transformer for us to use, while NumPy will help us to create an equispaced list of thresholds.

We want to bucketize our numerical variable into 10 buckets, hence our `buckets_no` is equal to `10`. Next, we calculate the minimum and maximum values for the `Horizontal_Distance_To_Hydrology` feature and return these two values to the driver. On the driver, we create the list of thresholds (the `splits` list); the first parameter to the `np.arange(...)` method is the minimum, the second one is the maximum, and the third one defines the size of each step.

Now that we have the splits list defined, we pass it to the `.Bucketizer(...)` method.

Each transformer (Estimators work similarly) has a very similar API, but two parameters are always required: `inputCol` and `outputCol`, which define the input and output columns to be consumed and their output, respectively. The two classes—`Transformer` and `Estimator`—also universally implement the `.getOutputCol()` method, which returns the name of the output column.

Finally, we use the `bucketizer` object to transform our DataFrame. Here's what we expect to see:

```
+-------------------------------+-----------------------------------+
|Horizontal_Distance_To_Hydrology|Horizontal_Distance_To_Hydrology_Bkt|
+-------------------------------+-----------------------------------+
|                            258|                                2.0|
|                            212|                                1.0|
|                            268|                                2.0|
|                            242|                                1.0|
|                            153|                                1.0|
+-------------------------------+-----------------------------------+
```

There's more...

Almost exclusively, every estimator (or, in other words, an ML model) found in the ML module expects to see a *single* column as an input; the column should contain all the features a data scientist wants such a model to use. The `.VectorAssembler(...)` method, as the name suggests, collates multiple features into a single column.

Consider the following example:

```
vectorAssembler = (
    feat.VectorAssembler(
        inputCols=forest.columns,
        outputCol='feat'
    )
)

pca = (
    feat.PCA(
        k=5
        , inputCol=vectorAssembler.getOutputCol()
        , outputCol='pca_feat'
    )
)
```

```
(
    pca
    .fit(vectorAssembler.transform(forest))
    .transform(vectorAssembler.transform(forest))
    .select('feat','pca_feat')
    .take(1)
)
```

First, we use the `.VectorAssembler(...)` method to collate all columns from our `forest` DataFrame.

Note that the `.VectorAssembler(...)` method, unlike other Transformers, has the `inputCols` parameter, not `inputCol`, as it accepts a list of columns, not just a single column.

We then use the `feat` column (which is now a `SparseVector` of all the features) in the `PCA(...)` method to extract the top five most significant principal components.

Notice how we can now use the `.getOutputCol()` method to get the name of the output column? It should become more apparent why we do this when we introduce pipelines.

The output of the preceding code should look somewhat as follows:

```
[Row(feat=SparseVector(55, {0: 2596.0, 1: 51.0, 2: 3.0, 3: 258.0, 5: 510.0, 6: 221.0, 7: 232.0, 8: 148.0, 9: 6279.0, 1
0: 1.0, 42: 1.0, 54: 5.0}), pca_feat=DenseVector([-3887.7711, 4996.8103, 2323.0932, 1014.5873, -135.1702]))]
```

See also

- For an example of a transformer (and more) check this blog post: `https://blog.insightdatascience.com/spark-pipelines-elegant-yet-powerful-7be93afcdd42`

Introducing Estimators

The `Estimator` class, just like the `Transformer` class, was introduced in Spark 1.3. The Estimators, as the name suggests, estimate the parameters of a model or, in other words, fit the models to data.

In this recipe, we will introduce two models: the linear SVM acting as a classification model, and a linear regression model predicting the forest elevation.

Here is a list of all of the Estimators, or machine learning models, available in the ML module:

- Classification:

  - `LinearSVC` is an SVM model for linearly separable problems. The SVM's kernel has the $\vec{w} \cdot \vec{x} - b = 0$ form (a hyperplane), where $\vec{w}$ is the coefficients (or a normal vector to the hyperplane), $\vec{x}$ is the records, and b is the offset.

  - `LogisticRegression` is a default, *go-to* classification model for linearly separable problems. It uses a logit function to calculate the probability of a record being a member of a particular class.

  - `DecisionTreeClassifier` is a decision tree-based model used for classification purposes. It builds a binary tree with the proportions of classes in the terminal nodes determining the class membership.

  - `GBTClassifier` is a member of the group of ensemble models. The **Gradient-Boosted Trees** (**GBT**) build several weak models that, when combined, form a strong classifier. The model can also be applied to solve regression problems.

  - `RandomForestClassifier` is also a member of an ensemble group of models. Unlike GBT, however, random forests grows fully-grow decision trees and the total error reduction is achieved by reducing variance (while GBTs reduce bias). Just like GBT, these models can also be used to solve regression problems.

- `NaiveBayes` uses the Bayes conditional probability theory, $p(A \mid B) = \dfrac{p(A)p(B \mid A)}{p(B)}$, to classify observations based on evidence and prior assumptions about the probability and likelihood.

- `MultilayerPerceptronClassifier` is derived from the field of artificial intelligence, and, more narrowly, artificial neural networks. The model consists of a directed graph of artificial neurons that mimic (to some extent) the fundamental building blocks of the brain.

- `OneVsRest` is a reduction technique that selects only one class in a multinomial scenario.

- Regression:

  - `AFTSurvivalRegression` is a parametric model that predicts life expectancy and assumes that a marginal effect of one of the features accelerates or decelerates a process failure.

  - `DecisionTreeRegressor`, a counterpart of `DecisionTreeClassifier`, is applicable for regression problems.

  - `GBTRegressor`, a counterpart of `GBTClassifier`, is applicable for regression problems.

  - `GeneralizedLinearRegression` is a family of linear models that allow us to specify different kernel functions (or link functions). Unlike linear regression, which assumes the normality of error terms, the **Generalized Linear Model** (**GLM**) allow models to have other distributions of error terms.

  - `IsotonicRegression` fits a free-form and non-decreasing line to data.

  - `LinearRegression` is the benchmark of regression models. It fits a straight line (or a plane defined in linear terms) through the data.

  - `RandomForestRegressor`, a counterpart of `RandomForestClassifier`, is applicable for regression problems.

- Clustering:
    - BisectingKMeans is a model that begins with all observations in a single cluster and iteratively splits the data into *k* clusters.
    - Kmeans separates data into *k* (defined) clusters by iteratively finding centroids of clusters by shifting the cluster boundaries so the sum of all distances between data points and cluster centroids is minimized.
    - GaussianMixture uses *k* Gaussian distributions to break the dataset down into clusters.
    - LDA: The **Latent Dirichlet Allocation** is a model frequently used in topic mining. It is a statistical model that makes use of some unobserved (or unnamed) groups to cluster observations. For example, a PLANE_linked cluster can have words included, such as engine, flaps, or wings.

Getting ready

To execute this recipe, you will need a working Spark environment and you would have already loaded the data into the forest DataFrame.

No other prerequisites are required.

How to do it...

First, let's learn how to build an SVM model:

```
import pyspark.ml.classification as cl

vectorAssembler = feat.VectorAssembler(
    inputCols=forest.columns[0:-1]
    , outputCol='features')

fir_dataset = (
    vectorAssembler
    .transform(forest)
    .withColumn(
        'label'
        , (f.col('CoverType') == 1).cast('integer'))
    .select('label', 'features')
)
```

```
svc_obj = cl.LinearSVC(maxIter=10, regParam=0.01)
svc_model = svc_obj.fit(fir_dataset)
```

How it works...

The `.LinearSVC(...)` method is available from `pyspark.ml.classification`, so we load it first.

Next, we use `.VectorAssembler(...)` to grab all the columns from the `forest` DataFrame, but the last one (the `CoverType`) will be used as a label. We will predict the forest cover type equal to 1, that is, whether the forest is a spruce-fir type; we achieve this by checking whether `CoverType` is equal to 1 and casting the resulting Boolean to an integer. Finally, we select only `label` and `features`.

Next, we create the `LinearSVC` object. We specify the maximum number of iterations to 10 and set the regularization parameter (type L2, or ridge) to 1%.

 If you are not familiar with regularization in terms of machine learning, check out this website: `http://enhancedatascience.com/2017/07/04/machine-learning-explained-regularization/`.

Other parameters include:

- `featuresCol`: This is set to the name of the features columns, by default it is `features` (like in our dataset)
- `labelCol`: This is set to the name of the label column if something other than `label`
- `predictionCol`: This is set to the name of the prediction column if you want to rename it to something other than `prediction`
- `tol`: This is a stopping parameter that defines the minimum change between iterations in terms of the cost function: if the change (by default) is smaller than 10^{-6}, the algorithm will assume that it has converged
- `rawPredictionCol`: This returns the raw value from the generating function (before the threshold is applied); you can specify a different name than `rawPrediction`
- `fitIntercept`: This instructs the model to fit the intercept (constant) as well, not only the model coefficients; this is set to `True` by default
- `standardization`: This is set to `True` by default, and it standardizes the features before fitting the model

- threshold: This is set by default to 0.0; it is a parameter that decides what is classified as 1 or 0
- weightCol: This is a column name if each observation was to be weighted differently
- aggregationDepth: This is a tree-depth parameter used for aggregation

Finally, we .fit(...) the dataset using the object; the object returns a .LinearSVCModel(...). Once the model is estimated, we can extract the estimated model's coefficients like so: svc_model.coefficients. Here's what we get:

```
DenseVector([-0.0001, -0.0, -0.0023, -0.0, -0.0001, 0.0, -0.001, -0.0017, -0.0003, -0.0, 0.0, 0.0401, -0.0071, -0.0958
, -0.0901, -0.0653, -0.0655, -0.0437, -0.0928, -0.0848, -0.0211, -0.0045, -0.0498, -0.0829, -0.0522, -0.0325, -0.0263,
-0.0923, -0.0889, -0.0275, -0.0606, -0.0595, 0.0341, -0.003, 0.0822, 0.0607, 0.0351, 0.0093, 0.0048, -0.0154, 0.0422,
-0.0673, -0.0039, -0.0142, 0.0036, 0.0078, 0.0, -0.0117, 0.0283, -0.0002, -0.0463, 0.0394, 0.0292, 0.0358])
```

There's more...

Now, let's see whether a linear regression model can be reasonably accurate in estimating forest elevation:

```
import pyspark.ml.regression as rg

vectorAssembler = feat.VectorAssembler(
    inputCols=forest.columns[1:]
    , outputCol='features')

elevation_dataset = (
    vectorAssembler
    .transform(forest)
    .withColumn(
        'label'
        , f.col('Elevation').cast('float'))
    .select('label', 'features')
)
lr_obj = rg.LinearRegression(
    maxIter=10
    , regParam=0.01
    , elasticNetParam=1.00)
lr_model = lr_obj.fit(elevation_dataset)
```

The preceding code is quite similar to the one presented earlier. As a side note, this is true for almost all the ML module models, so testing various models is extremely simple.

The difference is in the `label` column—right now, we are using `Elevation` and casting it as a `float` (since this is a regression problem).

Similarly, the linear regression object, `lr_obj`, instantiates the `.LinearRegression(...)` object.

For the full list of parameters to `.LinearRegression(...)`, please refer to the documentation: `http://bit.ly/2J9OvEJ`.

Once the model is estimated, we can check its coefficients by calling `lr_model.coefficients`. Here's what we get:

```
DenseVector([0.0309, 0.6522, 0.1911, 0.1424, 0.0342, 0.7402, 1.053, -0.0017, -0.0041, 2.7163, 189.0362, 27.8238, -265.
8505, -407.4379, -346.0612, -364.3841, -302.6788, -400.5852, -212.9918, -126.1329, -117.7423, -312.0478, -248.7118, -2
21.4788, -155.1459, -84.5129, -398.0433, -387.8102, -179.4485, -261.3875, -337.7875, 48.0629, -94.7813, 149.8043, 135.
144, 80.0901, 64.3659, 124.0233, -115.0126, 119.1285, -181.7498, 10.8056, -42.7849, 65.5441, 102.2562, 36.9865, -48.11
63, 379.2091, 256.0169, 497.1714, 313.0607, 337.172, 397.0758, -14.4551])
```

In addition, `.LinearRegressionModel(...)` calculates a summary that returns basic performance statistics:

```
summary = lr_model.summary

print(
    summary.r2
    , summary.rootMeanSquaredError
    , summary.meanAbsoluteError
)
```

The preceding code will produce the following result:

```
0.7860412464754236 129.50871925702438 103.34079732698483
```

Surprisingly, the linear regression does well in this application: 78% R-squared is not a bad result.

Introducing Pipelines

The `Pipeline` class helps to sequence, or streamline, the execution of separate blocks that lead to an estimated model; it chains multiple Transformers and Estimators to form a sequential execution workflow.

Pipelines are useful as they avoid explicitly creating multiple transformed datasets as the data gets pushed through different parts of the overall data transformation and model estimation process. Instead, Pipelines abstract distinct intermediate stages by automating the data flow through the workflow. This makes the code more readable and maintainable as it creates a higher abstraction of the system, and it helps with code debugging.

In this recipe, we will streamline the execution of a generalized linear regression model.

Getting ready

To execute this recipe, you will need a working Spark environment and you would have already loaded the data into the `forest` DataFrame.

No other prerequisites are required.

How to do it...

The following code provides a streamlined version of the execution of the linear regression model estimation via GLM:

```
from pyspark.ml import Pipeline

vectorAssembler = feat.VectorAssembler(
    inputCols=forest.columns[1:]
    , outputCol='features')

lr_obj = rg.GeneralizedLinearRegression(
    labelCol='Elevation'
    , maxIter=10
    , regParam=0.01
    , link='identity'
    , linkPredictionCol="p"
)

pip = Pipeline(stages=[vectorAssembler, lr_obj])
```

```
(
    pip
    .fit(forest)
    .transform(forest)
    .select('Elevation', 'prediction')
    .show(5)
)
```

How it works...

The whole code is much shorter than the one we used in the previous example, as we do not need to do the following:

```
elevation_dataset = (
    vectorAssembler
    .transform(forest)
    .withColumn(
        'label'
        , f.col('Elevation').cast('float'))
    .select('label', 'features')
)
```

However, as before, we specify vectorAssembler and lr_obj (the .GeneralizedLinearRegression(...) object). .GeneralizedLinearRegression(...) allows us to specify not only the model's family, but also the link function. In order to decide what link function and family to choose, we can look at the distribution of our Elevation column:

```
import matplotlib.pyplot as plt

transformed_df = forest.select('Elevation')
transformed_df.toPandas().hist()

plt.savefig('Elevation_histogram.png')

plt.close('all')
```

Here's the plot that results from running the preceding code:

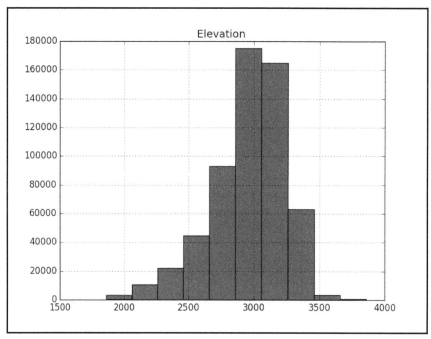

The distribution is a bit skewed, but to a certain degree, we can assume that it follows a normal distribution. Thus, we can use `family = 'gaussian'` (default) and `link = 'identity'`.

Having created the Transformer (`vectorAssembler`) and the Estimator (`lr_obj`), we then put them into a Pipeline. The `stages` parameter is an ordered list of the objects to push our data through; in our case, `vectorAssembler` goes first as we need to collate all the features, and then we estimate our model using `lr_obj`.

Finally, we use the pipeline to estimate the model at the same time. The Pipeline's `.fit(...)` method calls either the `.transform(...)` method if the object is a Transformer, or the `.fit(...)` method if the object is an Estimator. Consequently, calling the `.transform(...)` method on `PipelineModel` calls the `.transform(...)` methods of both the Transformer and Estimator objects.

The final result looks as follows:

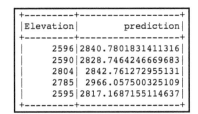

As you can see, the results are not that much different from the actual ones.

See also

- Check out this blog post (even though it's Scala-specific) for an overview of Pipelines: `https://databricks.com/blog/2015/01/07/ml-pipelines-a-new-high-level-api-for-mllib.html`

Selecting the most predictable features

A mantra of (almost) every data scientist is: build a simple model while explaining as much variance in the target as possible. In other words, you can build a model with all your features, but the model may be highly complex and prone to overfitting. What's more, if one of the variables is missing, the whole model might produce an erroneous output and some of the variables might simply be unnecessary, as other variables would already explain the same portion of the variance (a term called *collinearity*).

In this recipe, we will learn how to select the best predicting model when building either classification or regression models. We will be reusing what we learn in this recipe in the recipes that follow.

Getting ready

To execute this recipe, you will need a working Spark environment and you would have already loaded the data into the `forest` DataFrame.

No other prerequisites are required.

How to do it...

Let's begin with a code that will help to select the top 10 features with the most predictive power to find the best class for an observation in our `forest` DataFrame:

```
vectorAssembler = feat.VectorAssembler(
    inputCols=forest.columns[0:-1]
    , outputCol='features'
)

selector = feat.ChiSqSelector(
    labelCol='CoverType'
    , numTopFeatures=10
    , outputCol='selected')

pipeline_sel = Pipeline(stages=[vectorAssembler, selector])
```

How it works...

First, we assemble all the features into a single vector using the `.VectorAssembler(...)` method. Note that we do not use the last column as it is the `CoverType` feature and this is our target.

Next, we use the `.ChiSqSelector(...)` method to select the best features based on the pairwise chi-square test between each variable and the target. Based on the values from the test, `numTopFeatures`, the most predictable features, are selected. The `selected` vector will contain the top 10 (in this case) most predictable features. The `labelCol` specifies the target column.

> You can learn more about the chi-square test here: `http://learntech.uwe.ac.uk/da/Default.aspx?pageid=1440`.

Let's check it out:

```
(
    pipeline_sel
    .fit(forest)
    .transform(forest)
    .select(selector.getOutputCol())
    .show(5)
)
```

Here's what you should see from running the preceding snippet:

```
+--------------------+
|            selected|
+--------------------+
|(10,[0,1,2,3,5,6,...|
|(10,[0,1,2,3,4,5,...|
|(10,[0,1,2,3,4,5,...|
|(10,[0,1,2,3,4,5,...|
|(10,[0,1,2,3,4,5,...|
+--------------------+
```

As you can see, the resulting `SparseVector` has a length of 10 and includes only the most predictable features.

There's more...

We cannot use the `.ChiSqSelector(...)` method to select features against targets that are continuous, that is, the regression problems. One approach to select the best features would be to check correlations between each and every feature and the target and select those that are the most highly correlated with the target but exhibit little to no correlation with other features:

```python
import pyspark.ml.stat as st

features_and_label = feat.VectorAssembler(
    inputCols=forest.columns
    , outputCol='features'
)

corr = st.Correlation.corr(
    features_and_label.transform(forest),
    'features',
    'pearson'
)

print(str(corr.collect()[0][0]))
```

 There is no automatic way to do this in Spark, but starting with Spark 2.2, we can now calculate correlations between features in DataFrames.

The `.Correlation(...)` method is part of the `pyspark.ml.stat` module, so we import it first.

Next, we create `.VectorAssembler(...)`, which collates all the columns of the `forest` DataFrame. We can now use the Transformer and pass the resulting DataFrame to the `Correlation` class. The `.corr(...)` method of the `Correlation` class accepts a DataFrame as its first parameter, the name of the column with all the features as the second, and the type of correlation to calculate as the third; the available values are `pearson` (the default value) and `spearman`.

 Check out this website for more information about the two correlation methods: `http://bit.ly/2xm49s7`.

Here's what we would expect to see from running the method:

```
DenseMatrix([[ 1.          ,  0.01573494, -0.24269664, ...,  0.19359464,
               0.21261232, -0.26955378],
             [ 0.01573494,  1.          ,  0.07872841, ...,  0.00829428,
              -0.00586558,  0.0170798 ],
             [-0.24269664,  0.07872841,  1.          , ...,  0.09360193,
               0.02563691,  0.14828541],
             ...,
             [ 0.19359464,  0.00829428,  0.09360193, ...,  1.          ,
              -0.01929168,  0.15566826],
             [ 0.21261232, -0.00586558,  0.02563691, ..., -0.01929168,
               1.          ,  0.1283513 ],
             [-0.26955378,  0.0170798 ,  0.14828541, ...,  0.15566826,
               0.1283513 ,  1.          ]])
```

Now that we have the correlation matrix, we can extract the top 10 most correlated features with our label:

```
num_of_features = 10
cols = dict([
    (i, e)
    for i, e
    in enumerate(forest.columns)
])

corr_matrix = corr.collect()[0][0]
label_corr_with_idx = [
    (i[0], e)
    for i, e
    in np.ndenumerate(corr_matrix.toArray()[:,0])
```

```
][1:]

label_corr_with_idx_sorted = sorted(
    label_corr_with_idx
    , key=lambda el: -abs(el[1])
)

features_selected = np.array([
    cols[el[0]]
    for el
    in label_corr_with_idx_sorted
])[0:num_of_features]
```

First, we specify the number of features we want to extract and create a dictionary with all the columns from our `forest` DataFrame; note that we ZIP it with the index as the correlation matrix does not propagate the feature names, only the indices.

Next, we extract the first column from the `corr_matrix` (as this is our target, the Elevation feature); the `.toArray()` method converts a DenseMatrix to a NumPy array representation. Note that we also append the index to the elements of this array so we know which element is most correlated with our target.

Next, we sort the list in descending order by looking at the absolute values of the correlation coefficient.

Finally, we loop through the top 10 (in this case) elements of the resulting list and select the column from the `cols` dictionary that corresponds with the selected index.

For our problem that aims at estimating the forest elevation, here's the list of features we get:

```
array(['Wilderness_Area_CacheLaPoudre', 'Soil_type_4703',
       'Horizontal_Distance_To_Roadways',
       'Horizontal_Distance_To_Hydrology', 'CoverType', 'Slope',
       'Wilderness_Area_Neota', 'Soil_type_8771', 'Soil_type_2717',
       'Soil_type_8776'], dtype='<U34')
```

See also

- If you are curious to learn more about feature selection, check out this paper: http://www.stat.wisc.edu/~loh/treeprogs/guide/lchen.pdf

Predicting forest coverage types

In this recipe, we will learn how to process data and build two classification models that aim to forecast the forest coverage type: the benchmark logistic regression model and the random forest classifier. The problem we have at hand is *multinomial*, that is, we have more than two classes that we want to classify our observations into.

Getting ready

To execute this recipe, you will need a working Spark environment and you would have already loaded the data into the `forest` DataFrame.

No other prerequisites are required.

How to do it...

Here's the code that will help us build the logistic regression model:

```
forest_train, forest_test = (
    forest
    .randomSplit([0.7, 0.3], seed=666)
)

vectorAssembler = feat.VectorAssembler(
    inputCols=forest.columns[0:-1]
    , outputCol='features'
)

selector = feat.ChiSqSelector(
    labelCol='CoverType'
    , numTopFeatures=10
    , outputCol='selected'
)

logReg_obj = cl.LogisticRegression(
    labelCol='CoverType'
    , featuresCol=selector.getOutputCol()
    , regParam=0.01
    , elasticNetParam=1.0
    , family='multinomial'
)

pipeline = Pipeline(
```

```
    stages=[
        vectorAssembler
        , selector
        , logReg_obj
    ])

pModel = pipeline.fit(forest_train)
```

How it works...

First, we split the data we have into two subsets: the first one, `forest_train`, we will use for training the model, while `forest_test` will be used for testing the performance of the model.

Next, we build the usual stages we have already seen earlier in this chapter: we collate all the features we want to use to build our model using `.VectorAssembler(...)` and then pass them through the `.ChiSqSelector(...)` method to select the top 10 most predictive features.

As the last step before building the Pipeline, we create `logReg_obj`: the `.LogisticRegression(...)` object we will use to fit our data with. We use the elastic-net type of regularization in this model: the L2 portion is defined in the `regParam` parameter, and the L1 portion in `elasticNetParam`. Note that we specify the family of the model to be `multinomial` as we are dealing with a multinomial classification problem.

 You can also specify the `family` parameter to be `auto` or `binomial`, if you want the model to self-select, or if you have a binary variable.

Finally, we build the Pipeline and pass the three objects as the list of stages. Next, we push our data through the pipeline using the `.fit(...)` method.

Now that we have the model estimated, we can check how well it performs:

```
import pyspark.ml.evaluation as ev

results_logReg = (
    pModel
    .transform(forest_test)
    .select('CoverType', 'probability', 'prediction')
)
```

```
evaluator = ev.MulticlassClassificationEvaluator(
    predictionCol='prediction'
    , labelCol='CoverType')

(
    evaluator.evaluate(results_logReg)
    , evaluator.evaluate(
        results_logReg
        , {evaluator.metricName: 'weightedPrecision'}
    )
    , evaluator.evaluate(
        results_logReg
        , {evaluator.metricName: 'accuracy'}
    )
)
```

First, we load the `pyspark.ml.evaluation` module as it contains all the evaluation methods we will use throughout the rest of this chapter.

Next, we push `forest_test` through our `pModel` so that we can get the predictions for the dataset that the model has never seen before.

Finally, we create the `MulticlassClassificationEvaluator(...)` object, which will calculate the performance metrics of our model. `predictionCol` specifies the name of the column that contains the predicted class for an observation, and `labelCol` specifies the true label.

The `.evaluate(...)` method of the evaluator, if no other parameters are passed but the results of the model, will return the F1-score. If you want to retrieve either precision, recall, or accuracy, you need to call either `weightedPrecision`, `weightedRecall`, or `accuracy`, respectively.

 If you are not familiar with classification metrics, they are nicely explained here: `https://turi.com/learn/userguide/evaluation/classification.html`.

Here's how our logistic regression model performs:

```
(0.6638467009427569, 0.6632784396900246, 0.691296432850954)
```

The accuracy of almost 70% indicates it's not a totally terrible model.

There's more...

Let's see whether the random forest model can do any better:

```
rf_obj = cl.RandomForestClassifier(
    labelCol='CoverType'
    , featuresCol=selector.getOutputCol()
    , minInstancesPerNode=10
    , numTrees=10
)

pipeline = Pipeline(
    stages=[vectorAssembler, selector, rf_obj]
)

pModel = pipeline.fit(forest_train)
```

As you can see from the preceding code, we will be reusing most of the objects we have already created for the logistic regression model; all we introduced here was `.RandomForestClassifier(...)` and we can reuse the `vectorAssembler` and `selector` objects. This is one examples of how simple it is to work with Pipelines.

The `.RandomForestClassifier(...)` object will build the random forest model for us. In this example, we specified only four parameters, most of which you are most likely familiar with, such as `labelCol` and `featuresCol`. `minInstancesPerNode` specifies the minimum number of records still allowed to split the node into two sub-nodes, while `numTrees` specifies how many trees in the forest to estimate. Other notable parameters include:

- `impurity`: This specifies the criterion used for information gain. By default, it is set to `gini` but can also be `entropy`.
- `maxDepth`: This specifies the maximum depth of any of the trees.
- `maxBins`: This specifies the maximum number of bins in any of the trees.
- `minInfoGain`: This specifies the minimum level of information gain between iterations.

 For a full specification of the class, see `http://bit.ly/2sgQAFa`.

Having estimated the model, let's see how it performs so we can compare it to the logistic regression one:

```
results_rf = (
    pModel
    .transform(forest_test)
    .select('CoverType', 'probability', 'prediction')
)

(
    evaluator.evaluate(results_rf)
    , evaluator.evaluate(
        results_rf
        , {evaluator.metricName: 'weightedPrecision'}
    )
    , evaluator.evaluate(
        results_rf
        , {evaluator.metricName: 'accuracy'}
    )
)
```

The preceding code should produce results similar to the following:

```
(0.6638467009427569, 0.6632784396900246, 0.691296432850954)
```

The results are exactly the same, indicating that the two models perform equally well and we might want to increase the number of selected features in the selector stage to potentially achieve better results.

Estimating forest elevation

In this recipe, we will build two regression models that will predict forest elevation: the random forest regression model and the gradient-boosted trees regressor.

Getting ready

To execute this recipe, you will need a working Spark environment and you would have already loaded the data into the `forest` DataFrame.

No other prerequisites are required.

How to do it...

In this recipe, we will only build a two stage Pipeline with the .VectorAssembler(...) and the .RandomForestRegressor(...) stages. We will skip the feature selection stage as it is not currently an automated process.

You can do this manually. Just check the *Selecting the most predictable features* recipe earlier from in this chapter.

Here's the full code:

```
vectorAssembler = feat.VectorAssembler(
    inputCols=forest.columns[1:]
    , outputCol='features')

rf_obj = rg.RandomForestRegressor(
    labelCol='Elevation'
    , maxDepth=10
    , minInstancesPerNode=10
    , minInfoGain=0.1
    , numTrees=10
)

pip = Pipeline(stages=[vectorAssembler, rf_obj])
```

How it works...

First, as always, we collate all the features we want to use in our model using the .VectorAssembler(...) method. Note that we only use the columns starting from the second one as the first one is our target—the elevation feature.

Next, we specify the .RandomForestRegressor(...) object. The object uses an almost-identical list of parameters as .RandomForestClassifier(...).

See the previous recipe for a list of other notable parameters.

The last step is to build the Pipeline object; pip has only two stages: vectorAssembler and rf_obj.

Next, let's see how our model is performing compared to the linear regression model we estimated in the *Introducing Estimators* recipe:

```
results = (
    pip
    .fit(forest)
    .transform(forest)
    .select('Elevation', 'prediction')
)

evaluator = ev.RegressionEvaluator(labelCol='Elevation')
evaluator.evaluate(results, {evaluator.metricName: 'r2'})
```

`.RegressionEvaluator(...)` calculates the performance metrics of regression models. By default, it returns `rmse`, the root mean-squared error, but it can also return:

- `mse`: This is the mean-squared error
- `r2`: This is the R^2 metric
- `mae`: This is the mean-absolute error

From the preceding code, we got:

```
0.8264236722093034
```

This is better than the linear regression model we built earlier, meaning that our model might not be as linearly separable as we initially thought.

 Check out this website for more information about the different types of regression metrics: `http://bit.ly/2sgpONr`.

There's more...

Let's see whether the gradient-boosted trees model can beat the preceding result:

```
gbt_obj = rg.GBTRegressor(
    labelCol='Elevation'
    , minInstancesPerNode=10
    , minInfoGain=0.1
)

pip = Pipeline(stages=[vectorAssembler, gbt_obj])
```

The only change compared to the random forest regressor is the fact that we now use the
.GBTRegressor(...) class to fit the gradient-boosted trees model to our data. The most
notable parameters for this class include:

- maxDepth: This specifies the maximum depth of the built trees, which by default
  is set to 5
- maxBins: This specifies the maximum number of bins
- minInfoGain: This specifies the minimum level of information gain between
  iterations
- minInstancesPerNode: This specifies the minimum number of instances when
  the tree will still perform a split
- lossType: This specifies the loss type, and accepts the squared or absolute
  values
- impurity: This is, by default, set to variance, and for now (in Spark 2.3) is the
  only option allowed
- maxIter: This specifies the maximum number of iterations—a stopping criterion
  for the algorithm

Let's check the performance now:

```
results = (
    pip
    .fit(forest)
    .transform(forest)
    .select('Elevation', 'prediction')
)

evaluator = ev.RegressionEvaluator(labelCol='Elevation')
evaluator.evaluate(results, {evaluator.metricName: 'r2'})
```

Here's what we got:

```
0.833598109692272
```

As you can see, we have still (even though ever-so-slightly) improved over the random
forest regressor.

Clustering forest cover types

Clustering is an unsupervised family of methods that attempts to find patterns in data without any indication of what a class might be. In other words, the clustering methods find commonalities between records and groups them into clusters, depending on how similar they are to each other, and how dissimilar they are from those found in other clusters.

In this recipe, we will build the most fundamental model of them all—the k-means.

Getting ready

To execute this recipe, you will need a working Spark environment and you would have already loaded the data into the `forest` DataFrame.

No other prerequisites are required.

How to do it...

The process of building a clustering model in Spark does not deviate significantly from what we have already seen in either the classification or regression examples:

```
import pyspark.ml.clustering as clust

vectorAssembler = feat.VectorAssembler(
    inputCols=forest.columns[:-1]
    , outputCol='features')

kmeans_obj = clust.KMeans(k=7, seed=666)

pip = Pipeline(stages=[vectorAssembler, kmeans_obj])
```

How it works...

We, as always, start with importing the relevant modules; in this case, it is the `pyspark.ml.clustering` module.

Next, we collate all the features together that we will use in building the model using the well-known `.VectorAssembler(...)` Transformer.

This is followed by instantiating the `.KMeans(...)` object. We only specified two parameters, but the list of the most notable ones is as follows:

- `k`: This specifies the expected number of clusters and is the only required parameter to build the k-means model
- `initMode`: This specifies the initialization type of the cluster centroids; `k-means||` to use a parallel variant of k-means, or `random` to choose random centroid points
- `initSteps`: This specifies the initialization steps
- `maxIter`: This specifies the maximum number of iterations after which the algorithm stops, even if it had not achieved a convergence

Finally, we build the Pipeline with two stages only.

Once the results are calculated, we can look at what we got. Our aim was to see whether there are any underlying patterns found in the type of forest coverage:

```
results = (
    pip
    .fit(forest)
    .transform(forest)
    .select('features', 'CoverType', 'prediction')
)

results.show(5)
```

Here's what we got from running the preceding code:

```
+--------------------+---------+----------+
|            features|CoverType|prediction|
+--------------------+---------+----------+
|(54,[0,1,2,3,5,6,...|        5|         1|
|(54,[0,1,2,3,4,5,...|        5|         1|
|(54,[0,1,2,3,4,5,...|        2|         1|
|(54,[0,1,2,3,4,5,...|        2|         1|
|(54,[0,1,2,3,4,5,...|        5|         1|
+--------------------+---------+----------+
```

As you can see, there do not seem to be many patterns that would differentiate the forest cover types. However, let's see whether our segmentation simply performs poorly and that this is why we are not finding any patterns, or whether we are finding patterns that are simply not really aligning with `CoverType`:

```
clustering_ev = ev.ClusteringEvaluator()
clustering_ev.evaluate(results)
```

`.ClusteringEvaluator(...)` is a new evaluator available since Spark 2.3 and is still experimental. It calculates the Silhouette metrics for the clustering results.

 To learn more about the silhouette metrics, check out `http://scikit-learn.org/stable/modules/generated/sklearn.metrics.silhouette_score.html`.

Here's what we got for our k-means model:

```
0.4999826131644061
```

As you can see, we got a decent model, as anything around 0.5 or more indicates well-separated clusters.

See also

- Check out `http://scikit-learn.org/stable/modules/clustering.html` for a comprehensive overview of the clustering models. Note that many of them are not available in Spark.

Tuning hyperparameters

Many models already mentioned in this chapter have multiple parameters that determine how the model will perform. Selecting some is relatively straightforward, but there are many that we simply cannot set intuitively. That's where hyperparameters-tuning comes to play. The hyperparameters-tuning methods help us select the best (or close to) set of parameters that maximizes some metric we defined.

In this recipe, we will show you two approaches for hyperparameter-tuning.

Getting ready

To execute this recipe, you will need a working Spark environment and you would have already loaded the data into the `forest` DataFrame. You would also have gone through all the previous recipes as we assume you have a working knowledge of Transformers, Estimators, Pipelines, and some of the regression models.

No other prerequisites are required.

How to do it...

We start with grid search. It is a brute-force method that simply loops through specific values of parameters, building new models and comparing their performance given some objective evaluator:

```
import pyspark.ml.tuning as tune

vectorAssembler = feat.VectorAssembler(
    inputCols=forest.columns[0:-1]
    , outputCol='features')

selector = feat.ChiSqSelector(
    labelCol='CoverType'
    , numTopFeatures=5
    , outputCol='selected')

logReg_obj = cl.LogisticRegression(
    labelCol='CoverType'
    , featuresCol=selector.getOutputCol()
    , family='multinomial'
)

logReg_grid = (
    tune.ParamGridBuilder()
    .addGrid(logReg_obj.regParam
            , [0.01, 0.1]
        )
    .addGrid(logReg_obj.elasticNetParam
            , [1.0, 0.5]
        )
    .build()
)

logReg_ev = ev.MulticlassClassificationEvaluator(
    predictionCol='prediction'
```

```
    , labelCol='CoverType')

cross_v = tune.CrossValidator(
    estimator=logReg_obj
    , estimatorParamMaps=logReg_grid
    , evaluator=logReg_ev
)

pipeline = Pipeline(stages=[vectorAssembler, selector])
data_trans = pipeline.fit(forest_train)

logReg_modelTest = cross_v.fit(
    data_trans.transform(forest_train)
)
```

How it works...

There's a lot happening here, so let's unpack it step-by-step.

We already know the .VectorAssembler(...), .ChiSqSelector(...), and .LogisticRegression(...) classes, so we will not be repeating ourselves here.

> Check out previous recipes if you are not familiar with the preceding concepts.

The core of this recipe starts with the logReg_grid object. This is the .ParamGridBuilder() class, which allows us to add elements to the grid that the algorithm will loop through and estimate the models with all the combinations of all the parameters and the specified values.

> A word of caution: the more parameters you include and the more levels you specify, the more models you will have to estimate. The number of models grows exponentially in both the number of parameters and in the number of levels you specify for these parameters. Beware!

In this example, we loop through two parameters: regParam and elasticNetParam. For each of the parameters, we specify two levels, thus we will need to build four models.

As an evaluator, we once again use `.MulticlassClassificationEvaluator(...)`.

Next, we specify the `.CrossValidator(...)` object, which binds all these things together: our `estimator` will be `logReg_obj`, `estimatorParamMaps` will be equal to the built `logReg_grid`, and `evaluator` is going to be `logReg_ev`.

The `.CrossValidator(...)` object splits the training data into a set of folds (by default, 3) and these are used as separate training and test datasets to fit the models. Therefore, we not only need to fit four models based on the parameters grid we want to traverse, but also for each of those four models we build three models with different training and validation datasets.

Note that we first build the Pipeline that is purely data-transformative, that is, it only collates the features into the full features vector and then selects the top five features with the most predictive power; we do not fit `logReg_obj` at this stage.

The model-fitting starts when we use the `cross_v` object to fit the transformed data. Only then will Spark estimate four distinct models and select the one that performs best.

Having now estimated the models and selected the best performing one, let's see whether the selected model performs better than the one we estimated in the *Predicting forest coverage types* recipe:

```
data_trans_test = data_trans.transform(forest_test)
results = logReg_modelTest.transform(data_trans_test)

print(logReg_ev.evaluate(results, {logReg_ev.metricName:
'weightedPrecision'}))
print(logReg_ev.evaluate(results, {logReg_ev.metricName:
'weightedRecall'}))
print(logReg_ev.evaluate(results, {logReg_ev.metricName: 'accuracy'}))
```

With the help of the preceding code, we get the following results:

```
0.6024281861281453
0.6602048575905612
0.6602048575905614
```

As you can see, we do slightly worse than the previous model, but this is most likely due to the fact that we only selected the top 5 (versus 10 before) features with our selector.

There's more...

Another approach that aims at finding the best performing model is called **train-validation split**. This method performs a split of the training data into two smaller subsets: one that is use to train the model, and another one that is used to validate whether the model is not overfitting. The split is only performed once, thus in contrast to cross-validation, it is less expensive:

```
train_v = tune.TrainValidationSplit(
    estimator=logReg_obj
    , estimatorParamMaps=logReg_grid
    , evaluator=logReg_ev
    , parallelism=4
)

logReg_modelTrainV = (
    train_v
    .fit(data_trans.transform(forest_train))
)

results = logReg_modelTrainV.transform(data_trans_test)

print(logReg_ev.evaluate(results, {logReg_ev.metricName:
'weightedPrecision'}))
print(logReg_ev.evaluate(results, {logReg_ev.metricName:
'weightedRecall'}))
print(logReg_ev.evaluate(results, {logReg_ev.metricName: 'accuracy'}))
```

The preceding code is not that dissimilar from what we saw with `.CrossValidator(...)`. The only additional parameter we specify for the `.TrainValidationSplit(...)` method is the level of parallelism that controls how many threads are spun up when you select the best model.

Using the `.TrainValidationSplit(...)` method produces the same results as the `.CrossValidator(...)` approach:

```
0.6024281861281453
0.6602048575905612
0.6602048575905614
```

Extracting features from text

Often, data scientists need to deal with unstructured data such as free-flow text: companies receive feedback or recommendations (among other things) from customers that can be a gold mine for predicting a customer's next move or their sentiment toward a brand.

In this recipe, we will learn how to extract features from text.

Getting ready

To execute this recipe, you will need a working Spark environment.

No other prerequisites are required.

How to do it...

A general process that aims to extract data from text and convert it into something a machine learning model can use starts with the free-flow text. The first step is to take each sentence of the text and split it on the space character (most often). Next, all the stop words are removed. Finally, simply counting distinct words in the text or using a hashing trick takes us into the realm of numerical representations of free-flow text.

Here's how to achieve this with Spark's ML module:

```
some_text = spark.createDataFrame([
    ['''
    Apache Spark achieves high performance for both batch
    and streaming data, using a state-of-the-art DAG scheduler,
    a query optimizer, and a physical execution engine.
    ''']
    , ['''
    Apache Spark is a fast and general-purpose cluster computing
    system. It provides high-level APIs in Java, Scala, Python
    and R, and an optimized engine that supports general execution
    graphs. It also supports a rich set of higher-level tools including
    Spark SQL for SQL and structured data processing, MLlib for machine
    learning, GraphX for graph processing, and Spark Streaming.
    ''']
    , ['''
    Machine learning is a field of computer science that often uses
    statistical techniques to give computers the ability to "learn"
    (i.e., progressively improve performance on a specific task)
    with data, without being explicitly programmed.
```

```
        ''']
], ['text'])

splitter = feat.RegexTokenizer(
    inputCol='text'
    , outputCol='text_split'
    , pattern='\s+|[,.\"]'
)

sw_remover = feat.StopWordsRemover(
    inputCol=splitter.getOutputCol()
    , outputCol='no_stopWords'
)

hasher = feat.HashingTF(
    inputCol=sw_remover.getOutputCol()
    , outputCol='hashed'
    , numFeatures=20
)

idf = feat.IDF(
    inputCol=hasher.getOutputCol()
    , outputCol='features'
)

pipeline = Pipeline(stages=[splitter, sw_remover, hasher, idf])

pipelineModel = pipeline.fit(some_text)
```

How it works...

As mentioned earlier, we start with some text. In our example, we use some extracts from Spark's documentation.

`.RegexTokenizer(...)` is the text tokenizer that uses regular expressions to split the sentence. In our example, we split the sentences on a minimum of one (or more) space—that's the \s+ expression. However, our pattern also splits on either a comma, period, or the quotation marks—that's the [, .\"] part. The pipe, |, means split on either the spaces or the punctuation marks. The text, after passing through `.RegexTokenizer(...)`, will look as follows:

```
[Row(text_split=['apache', 'spark', 'achieves', 'high', 'performance', 'for', 'both', 'batch', 'and', 'streaming', 'da
ta', 'using', 'a', 'state-of-the-art', 'dag', 'scheduler', 'a', 'query', 'optimizer', 'and', 'a', 'physical', 'executi
on', 'engine'])]
```

Next, we use the `.StopWordsRemover(...)` method to remove the stop words, as the name suggests.

 Check out NLTK's list of the most common stop words: `https://gist.github.com/sebleier/554280`.

`.StopWordsRemover(...)` simply scans the tokenized text and discards any stop word it encounters. After removing the stop words, our text will look as follows:

```
[Row(no_stopWords=['apache', 'spark', 'achieves', 'high', 'performance', 'batch', 'streaming', 'data', 'using', 'state
-of-the-art', 'dag', 'scheduler', 'query', 'optimizer', 'physical', 'execution', 'engine'])]
```

As you can see, what is left is an essential meaning of the sentence; a human can read these words and somewhat make sense of it.

A hashing trick (or feature hashing) is a method that transforms an arbitrary list of features into indices in a vector form. It is a space-efficient way of tokenizing text and, at the same time, turning text into a numerical representation. The hashing trick uses a hashing function to convert from one representation into another. A hashing function is essentially any mapping function that transforms one representation into another. Normally, it is a lossy and one-way mapping (or conversion); different input can be hashed into the same hash (a term called a **collision**) and, once hashed, it is almost always prohibitively difficult to reconstruct the input. The `.HashingTF(...)` method takes the input column from the `sq_remover` object and transforms (or encodes) the tokenized text into a vector of 20 features. Here's what our text will look like after it has been hashed:

```
[Row(features=SparseVector(20, {2: 0.0, 3: 0.0, 4: 0.0, 5: 0.863, 8: 0.2877, 9: 0.0, 15: 0.0, 16: 0.6931, 18: 0.2877,
19: 0.0}))]
```

Now that we have the features hashed, we could potentially use these features to train a machine learning model. However, simply counting the occurrences of words might lead to misleading conclusions. A better measure is the **term frequency-inverse document frequency (TF-IDF)**. It is a metric that counts how many times a word occurs in the whole corpus and then calculates a proportion of the word's count in a sentence to its count in the whole corpus. This measure helps to evaluate how important a word is to a document in the whole collection of documents. In Spark, we use the `.IDF(...)` method, which does this for us.

Here's what our text would look like after passing the whole Pipeline:

```
[Row(text='\n    Apache Spark achieves high performance for both batch\n    and streaming data, using a state-of-the-a
rt DAG scheduler, \n    a query optimizer, and a physical execution engine.\n    ', features=SparseVector(20, {2: 0.0,
3: 0.0, 4: 0.0, 5: 0.863, 8: 0.2877, 9: 0.0, 15: 0.0, 16: 0.6931, 18: 0.2877, 19: 0.0}))]
```

So, effectively, we have encoded the passage from Spark's documentation into a vector of 20 elements that we could now use to train a machine learning model.

There's more...

Another way of encoding text into a numerical form is by using the Word2Vec algorithm. The algorithm computes a distributed representation of words with the advantage that similar words are placed close together in the vector space.

 Check out this tutorial to learn more about Word2Vec and the skip-gram model: `http://mccormickml.com/2016/04/19/word2vec-tutorial-the-skip-gram-model/`.

Here's how we do it in Spark:

```
w2v = feat.Word2Vec(
    vectorSize=5
    , minCount=2
    , inputCol=sw_remover.getOutputCol()
    , outputCol='vector'
)
```

We will get a vector of five elements from the `.Word2Vec(...)` method. Also, only words that occur at least twice in the corpus will be used to create the word-embedding. Here's what the resulting vector will look like:

```
[Row(vector=DenseVector([0.0187, -0.0121, -0.0208, -0.0028, 0.002]))]
```

See also

- To learn more about text-feature engineering, check out this position from Packt: `http://bit.ly/2IZ7ZZA`

Discretizing continuous variables

Sometimes, it is actually useful to have a discrete representation of a continuous variable.

In this recipe, we will learn how to discretize a numerical feature with an example drawn from the Fourier series.

Getting ready

To execute this recipe, you will need a working Spark environment.

No other prerequisites are required.

How to do it...

In this recipe, we will use a small dataset that is located in the `data` folder, namely, `fourier_signal.csv`:

```
signal_df = spark.read.csv(
    '../data/fourier_signal.csv'
    , header=True
    , inferSchema=True
)

steps = feat.QuantileDiscretizer(
        numBuckets=10,
        inputCol='signal',
        outputCol='discretized')

transformed = (
    steps
    .fit(signal_df)
    .transform(signal_df)
)
```

How it works...

First, we read the data into `signal_df`. The `fourier_signal.csv` contains a single column called `signal`.

Next, we use the `.QuantileDiscretizer(...)` method to discretize the signal into 10 buckets. The bin ranges are chosen based on quantiles, that is, each bin will have the same number of observations.

Here's what the original signal looks like (the black line), and what its discretized representation looks like:

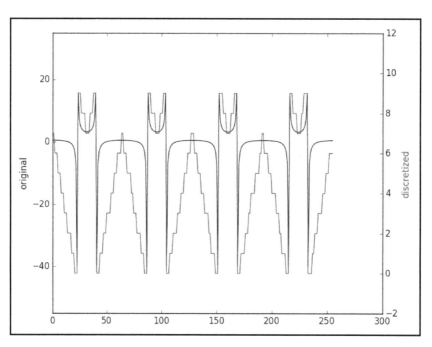

Standardizing continuous variables

Building a machine learning model using features that have significantly different ranges and resolutions (such as age and salary) might pose not only computational problems, but also model-convergence and coefficient-interpretability problems.

In this recipe, we will learn how to standardize continuous variables so they have a mean of 0 and a standard deviation of 1.

Getting ready

To execute this recipe, you will need a working Spark environment. You will also have to have executed the previous recipe.

No other prerequisites are required.

How to do it...

To standardize the `signal` column we introduced in the previous recipe, we will use the `.StandardScaler(...)` method:

```
vec = feat.VectorAssembler(
    inputCols=['signal']
    , outputCol='signal_vec'
)

norm = feat.StandardScaler(
    inputCol=vec.getOutputCol()
    , outputCol='signal_norm'
    , withMean=True
    , withStd=True
)

norm_pipeline = Pipeline(stages=[vec, norm])
signal_norm = (
    norm_pipeline
    .fit(signal_df)
    .transform(signal_df)
)
```

How it works...

First, we need to transform the single feature into a vector representation, as the `.StandardScaler(...)` method accepts only vectorized features.

Next, we instantiate the `.StandardScaler(...)` object. The `withMean` parameter instructs the method to center the data with the mean, while the `withStd` parameter scales to a standard deviation equal to 1.

Here's what the standardized representation of our signal look like. Note the different scales for the two lines:

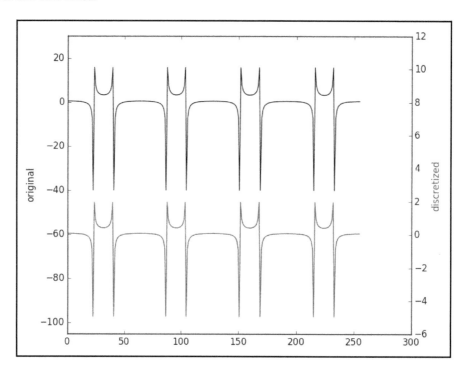

Topic mining

Sometimes, it is necessary to cluster text documents into buckets based on their content.

In this recipe, we will walk through an example of assigning a topic to a set of short paragraphs extracted from Wikipedia.

Getting ready

To execute this recipe, you will need a working Spark environment.

No other prerequisites are required.

How to do it...

In order to cluster the documents, we first need to extract the features from our articles. Note that the following text is abbreviated for space considerations—refer to the GitHub repository for the full code:

```
articles = spark.createDataFrame([
    ('''
        The Andromeda Galaxy, named after the mythological
        Princess Andromeda, also known as Messier 31, M31,
        or NGC 224, is a spiral galaxy approximately 780
        kiloparsecs (2.5 million light-years) from Earth,
        and the nearest major galaxy to the Milky Way.
        Its name stems from the area of the sky in which it
        appears, the constellation of Andromeda. The 2006
        observations by the Spitzer Space Telescope revealed
        that the Andromeda Galaxy contains approximately one
        trillion stars, more than twice the number of the
        Milky Way's estimated 200-400 billion stars. The
        Andromeda Galaxy, spanning approximately 220,000 light
        years, is the largest galaxy in our Local Group,
        which is also home to the Triangulum Galaxy and
        other minor galaxies. The Andromeda Galaxy's mass is
        estimated to be around 1.76 times that of the Milky
        Way Galaxy (~0.8-1.5×1012 solar masses vs the Milky
        Way's 8.5×1011 solar masses).
    ''','Galaxy', 'Andromeda')
    (...)
    , ('''
        Washington, officially the State of Washington, is a state in the
Pacific
        Northwest region of the United States. Named after George
Washington,
        the first president of the United States, the state was made out of
the
        western part of the Washington Territory, which was ceded by
Britain in
        1846 in accordance with the Oregon Treaty in the settlement of the
        Oregon boundary dispute. It was admitted to the Union as the 42nd
state
        in 1889. Olympia is the state capital. Washington is sometimes
referred
        to as Washington State, to distinguish it from Washington, D.C.,
the
        capital of the United States, which is often shortened to
Washington.
    ''','Geography', 'Washington State')
```

```
], ['articles', 'Topic', 'Object'])

splitter = feat.RegexTokenizer(
    inputCol='articles'
    , outputCol='articles_split'
    , pattern='\s+|[,.\"]'
)

sw_remover = feat.StopWordsRemover(
    inputCol=splitter.getOutputCol()
    , outputCol='no_stopWords'
)

count_vec = feat.CountVectorizer(
    inputCol=sw_remover.getOutputCol()
    , outputCol='vector'
)

lda_clusters = clust.LDA(
    k=3
    , optimizer='online'
    , featuresCol=count_vec.getOutputCol()
)

topic_pipeline = Pipeline(
    stages=[
        splitter
        , sw_remover
        , count_vec
        , lda_clusters
    ]
)
```

How it works...

First, we create a DataFrame with our articles.

Next, we go through pretty much the same steps as we went through in the *Extracting features from text* recipe:

1. We split the sentences using `.RegexTokenizer(...)`
2. We remove the stop words using `.StopWordsRemover(...)`
3. We count each word's occurrence using `.CountVectorizer(...)`

To find the clusters in our data, we will use the **Latent Dirichlet Allocation** (**LDA**) model. In our case, we know that we expect to have three clusters, but if you do not know how many clusters you might have, you can use one of the techniques we introduced in the *Tuning hyperparameters* recipe earlier in this chapter.

Finally, we put everything in the Pipeline for our convenience.

Once the model is estimated, let's see how it performs. Here's a piece of code that will help us do that; note the NumPy's .argmax(...) method that helps us find the index of the highest value:

```
for topic in (
            topic_pipeline
            .fit(articles)
            .transform(articles)
            .select('Topic','Object','topicDistribution')
            .take(10)
):
    print(
        topic.Topic
        , topic.Object
        , np.argmax(topic.topicDistribution)
        , topic.topicDistribution
    )
```

Here's what we get back:

```
Galaxy Andromeda 2 [0.003053456550444906,0.0033317477861422363,0.9936147956634129]
Galaxy Milky Way 2 [0.004752646858051239,0.0050467276024757125,0.9902006255394731]
Geography Australia 1 [0.00632938201257351,0.9877519489900843,0.005918668997342191]
Geography USA 1 [0.002525770470526258,0.9951088020926291,0.002365427436844653]
Geography China 1 [0.005154138170494813,0.6008937537867546,0.3939521080427506]
Geography Poland 1 [0.006814345676648856,0.986849415140345,0.006336239183006135]
Animal Dog 0 [0.9901640623662747,0.005226762717124236,0.004609174916600995]
Animal Dog 0 [0.9926300349445092,0.003938103061207765,0.0034318619942831073]
Geography Washington State 1 [0.005261811808175384,0.9898606664191076,0.004877521772717041]
```

As you can see, with proper processing, we can properly extract topics from the articles; the articles about galaxies are grouped in cluster 2, geographies are in cluster 1, and animals are in 0 cluster.

7
Structured Streaming with PySpark

In this chapter, we will cover how to work with Apache Spark Structured Streaming within PySpark. You will learn the following recipes:

- Understanding DStreams
- Understanding global aggregations
- Continuous aggregations with structured streaming

Introduction

With the prevalence of machine-generated *real-time data*, including but not limited to IoT sensors, devices, and beacons, it is increasingly important to gain insight into this fire hose of data as quickly as it is being created. Whether you are detecting fraudulent transactions, real-time detection of sensor anomalies, or sentiment analysis of the next cat video, streaming analytics is an increasingly important differentiator and business advantage.

As we progress through these recipes, we will be combining the constructs of *batch* and *real-time* processing for the creation of continuous applications. With Apache Spark, data scientists and data engineers can analyze their data using Spark SQL in batch and in real time, train machine learning models with MLlib, and score these models via Spark Streaming.

An important reason for the rapid adoption of Apache Spark is that it unifies all of these disparate data processing paradigms (machine learning via ML and MLlib, Spark SQL, and streaming). As note, in *Spark Streaming: What is It and Who's Using it* (`https://www.datanami.com/2015/11/30/spark-streaming-what-is-it-and-whos-using-it/`), companies such as Uber, Netflix, and Pinterest often showcase their uses case through Spark Streaming:

- *How Uber Uses Spark and Hadoop to Optimize Customer Experience* at `https://www.datanami.com/2015/10/05/how-uber-uses-spark-and-hadoop-to-optimize-customer-experience/`
- Spark and Spark Streaming at Netflix at `https://spark-summit.org/2015/events/spark-and-spark-streaming-at-netflix/`
- Can Spark Streaming survive Chaos Monkey? at `http://techblog.netflix.com/2015/03/can-spark-streaming-survive-chaos-monkey.html`
- Real-time analytics at Pinterest at `https://engineering.pinterest.com/blog/real-time-analytics-pinterest`

Understanding Spark Streaming

For real-time processing in Apache Spark, the current focus is on structured streaming, which is built on top of the DataFrame/dataset infrastructure. The use of DataFrame abstraction allows streaming, machine learning, and Spark SQL to be optimized in the Spark SQL Engine Catalyst Optimizer and its regular improvements (for example, Project Tungsten). Nevertheless, to more easily understand Spark Streaming, it is worthwhile to understand the fundamentals of its Spark Streaming predecessor. The following diagram represents a Spark Streaming application data flow involving the Spark driver, workers, streaming sources, and streaming targets:

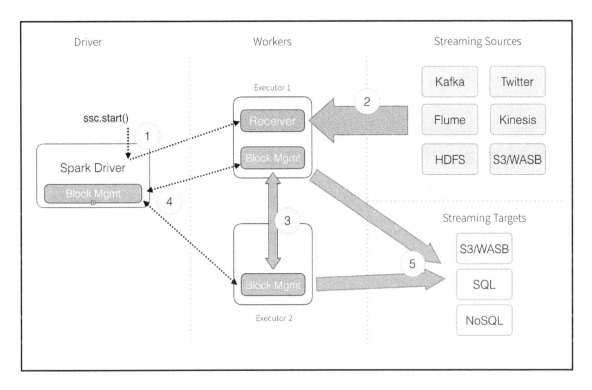

The description of the preceding diagram is as follows:

1. Starting with the **Spark Streaming Context** (**SSC**), the driver will execute long-running tasks on the executors (that is, the Spark workers).
2. The code defined within the driver (starting `ssc.start()`), the **Receiver** on the executors (**Executor 1** in this diagram) receives a data stream from the **Streaming Sources**. Spark Streaming can receive **Kafka** or **Twitter**, and/or you can build your own custom receiver. With the incoming data stream, the receiver divides the stream into blocks and keeps these blocks in memory.
3. These data blocks are replicated to another executor for high availability.
4. The block ID information is transmitted to the block manager master on the driver, thus ensuring that each block of data in memory is tracked and accounted for.
5. For every batch interval configured within SSC (commonly, this is every 1 second), the driver will launch Spark tasks to process the blocks. Those blocks are then persisted to any number of target data stores, including cloud storage (for example, S3, WASB), relational data stores (for example, MySQL, PostgreSQL, and so on), and NoSQL stores.

In the following sections, we will review recipes with **Discretized Streams** or **DStreams** (the fundamental streaming building block) and then perform global aggregations by performing stateful calculations on DStreams. We will then simplify our streaming application by using structured streaming while at the same time gaining performance optimizations.

Understanding DStreams

Before we dive into structured streaming, let's start by talking about DStreams. DStreams are built on top of RDDs and represent a stream of data divided into small chunks. The following figure represents these data chunks in micro-batches of milliseconds to seconds. In this example, the lines of DStream is micro-batched into seconds where each square represents a micro-batch of events that occurred within that second window:

- At time interval 1 second, there were five occurrences of the event **blue** and three occurrences of the event **green**
- At time interval 2 seconds, there is a single occurrence of **gohawks**
- At time interval 4 seconds, there are two occurrences of the event **green**

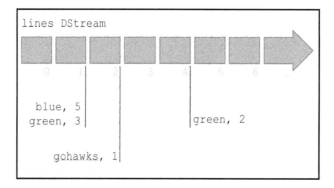

Because DStreams are built on top of RDDs, Apache Spark's core data abstraction, this allows Spark Streaming to easily integrate with other Spark components such as MLlib and Spark SQL.

Getting ready

For these Apache Spark Streaming examples, we will be creating and executing a console application via the bash terminal. To make things easier, you will want to have two terminal windows open.

How to do it...

As noted in the previous section, we will use two terminal windows:

- One terminal window to transmit an event
- Another terminal to receive those events

Note that the source code for this can be found in the Apache Spark 1.6 Streaming Programming Guide at: `https://spark.apache.org/docs/1.6.0/streaming-programming-guide.html`.

Terminal 1 – Netcat window

For the first window, we will use Netcat (or nc) to manually send events such as blue, green, and gohawks. To start Netcat, use the following command; we will direct our events to port `9999`, where our Spark Streaming job will detect:

```
nc -lk 9999
```

To match the previous diagram, we will type in our events so that the console screen looks like this:

```
$nc -lk 9999
blue blue blue blue blue green green green
gohawks
green green
```

Terminal 2 – Spark Streaming window

We will create a simple PySpark Streaming application using the following code called `streaming_word_count.py`:

```
#
# streaming_word_count.py
```

```
#

# Import the necessary classes and create a local SparkContext and
Streaming Contexts
from pyspark import SparkContext
from pyspark.streaming import StreamingContext

# Create Spark Context with two working threads (note, `local[2]`)
sc = SparkContext("local[2]", "NetworkWordCount")

# Create local StreamingContextwith batch interval of 1 second
ssc = StreamingContext(sc, 1)

# Create DStream that will connect to the stream of input lines from
connection to localhost:9999
lines = ssc.socketTextStream("localhost", 9999)

# Split lines into words
words = lines.flatMap(lambda line: line.split(" "))

# Count each word in each batch
pairs = words.map(lambda word: (word, 1))
wordCounts = pairs.reduceByKey(lambda x, y: x + y)

# Print the first ten elements of each RDD generated in this DStream to the
console
wordCounts.pprint()

# Start the computation
ssc.start()

# Wait for the computation to terminate
ssc.awaitTermination()
```

To run this PySpark Streaming application, execute the following command from your `$SPARK_HOME` folder:

```
./bin/spark-submit streaming_word_count.py localhost 9999
```

In terms of how you time this, you should:

1. First start with `nc -lk 9999`.
2. Then, start your PySpark Streaming application: `/bin/spark-submit streaming_word_count.py localhost 9999`.

3. Then, start typing your events, for example:

    1. For the first second, type `blue blue blue blue blue green green green`

    2. For the second second, type `gohawks`

    3. Wait a second; for the fourth second, type `green green`

The console output from your PySpark streaming application will look something similar to this:

```
$ ./bin/spark-submit streaming_word_count.py localhost 9999
-------------------------------------------------
Time: 2018-06-21 23:00:30
-------------------------------------------------
(u'blue', 5)
(u'green', 3)
-------------------------------------------------
Time: 2018-06-21 23:00:31
-------------------------------------------------
(u'gohawks', 1)
-------------------------------------------------
Time: 2018-06-21 23:00:32
-------------------------------------------------

-------------------------------------------------
Time: 2018-06-21 23:00:33
-------------------------------------------------
(u'green', 2)
-------------------------------------------------
```

To end the streaming application (and the `nc` window, for that matter), execute a termination command (for example, *Ctrl + C*).

How it works...

As noted in the previous subsections, this recipe is comprised of one terminal window transmitting event data using `nc`. The second window runs our Spark Streaming application, reading from the port that the first window is transmitting to.

The important call outs for this code are noted here:

- We're creating a Spark context using two working threads, hence the use of `local[2]`.
- As noted in the Netcat window, we're using `ssc.socketTextStream` to listen to the local socket of the `localhost`, port `9999`.
- Recall that for each 1-second batch, we're not only reading a single line (for example, `blue blue blue blue blue green green green`), but also splitting it up into individual `words` via `split`.
- We're using a Python `lambda` function and PySpark `map` and `reduceByKey` functions to quickly count the occurrences of words within the 1-second batch. For example, in the case of `blue blue blue blue blue green green green`, there are five blue and three green events, as reported at *2018-06-21 23:00:30* of our streaming application.
- `ssc.start()` is in reference to the application starting the Spark Streaming context.
- `ssc.awaitTermination()` is waiting for a termination command to stop the streaming application (for example, *Ctrl + C*); otherwise, the application will continue to run.

There's more...

When using the PySpark console, often there are a lot of messages that are sent out to the console that can make it difficult to read the streaming output. To make it easier to read, ensure that you have created and modified the `log4j.properties` file within the `$SPARK_HOME/conf` folder. To do this, follow these steps:

1. Go to the `$SPARK_HOME/conf` folder.
2. By default, there is a `log4j.properties.template` file. Copy it with the same name, removing the `.template`, that is:

   ```
   cp log4j.properties.template log4j.properties
   ```

3. Edit the `log4j.properties` in your favorite editor (for example, sublime, vi, and so on). In line 19 of the file, change this line:

   ```
   log4j.rootCategory=INFO, console
   ```

To this:

```
log4j.rootCategory=ERROR, console
```

This way, instead of all log information (that is, `INFO`) being directed to the console, only errors (that is, `ERROR`) will be directed to the console.

Understanding global aggregations

In the previous section, our recipe provided a snapshot count of events. That is, it provided the count of events at the point in time. But what if you want to understand a sum of events for some time window? This is the concept of global aggregations:

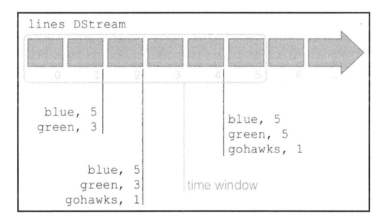

If we wanted global aggregations, the same example as before (Time 1: 5 blue, 3 green, Time 2: 1 gohawks, Time 4: 2 greens) would be calculated as:

- Time 1: 5 blue, 3 green
- Time 2: 5 blue, 3 green, 1 gohawks
- Time 4: 5 blue, 5 green, 1 gohawks

Within the traditional batch calculations, this would be similar to a `groupbykey` or `GROUP BY` statement. But in the case of streaming applications, this calculation needs to be done within milliseconds, which is typically too short of a time window to perform a `GROUP BY` calculation. However, with Spark Streaming global aggregations, this calculation can be completed quickly by performing a stateful streaming calculation. That is, using the Spark Streaming framework, all of the information to perform the aggregation is kept in memory (that is, keeping the data in *state*) so that it can be calculated in its small time window.

Getting ready

For these Apache Spark Streaming examples, we will be creating and executing a console application via the bash terminal. To make things easier, you will want to have two terminal windows open.

How to do it...

As noted in the previous section, we will use two terminal windows:

- One terminal window to transmit an event
- Another terminal to receive those events

The source code for this can be found in the Apache Spark 1.6 Streaming Programming Guide at: https://spark.apache.org/docs/1.6.0/streaming-programming-guide.html.

Terminal 1 – Netcat window

For the first window, we will use Netcat (or nc) to manually send events such as blue, green, and gohawks. To start Netcat, use the following command; we will direct our events to port 9999 where our Spark Streaming job will detect:

```
nc -lk 9999
```

To match the previous diagram, we will type in our events so that the console screen looks like this:

```
$nc -lk 9999
blue blue blue blue blue green green green
gohawks
green green
```

Terminal 2 – Spark Streaming window

We will create a simple PySpark Streaming application using the following code called streaming_word_count.py:

```
#
# stateful_streaming_word_count.py
#
```

```
# Import the necessary classes and create a local SparkContext and
Streaming Contexts
from pyspark import SparkContext
from pyspark.streaming import StreamingContext

# Create Spark Context with two working threads (note, `local[2]`)
sc = SparkContext("local[2]", "StatefulNetworkWordCount")

# Create local StreamingContextwith batch interval of 1 second
ssc = StreamingContext(sc, 1)

# Create checkpoint for local StreamingContext
ssc.checkpoint("checkpoint")

# Define updateFunc: sum of the (key, value) pairs
def updateFunc(new_values, last_sum):
    return sum(new_values) + (last_sum or 0)

# Create DStream that will connect to the stream of input lines from
connection to localhost:9999
lines = ssc.socketTextStream("localhost", 9999)

# Calculate running counts
# Line 1: Split lines in to words
# Line 2: count each word in each batch
# Line 3: Run `updateStateByKey` to running count
running_counts = lines.flatMap(lambda line: line.split(" "))\
        .map(lambda word: (word, 1))\
        .updateStateByKey(updateFunc)

# Print the first ten elements of each RDD generated in this stateful
DStream to the console
running_counts.pprint()

# Start the computation
ssc.start()

# Wait for the computation to terminate
ssc.awaitTermination()
```

To run this PySpark Streaming application, execute the following command from your $SPARK_HOME folder:

```
./bin/spark-submit stateful_streaming_word_count.py localhost 9999
```

In terms of how you time this, you should:

1. First start with `nc -lk 9999`.
2. Then, start your PySpark Streaming application: `./bin/spark-submit stateful_streaming_word_count.py localhost 9999`.
3. Then, start typing your events, for example:
   1. For the first second, type `blue blue blue blue blue green green green`
   2. For the second second, type `gohawks`
   3. Wait a second; for the fourth second, type `green green`

The console output from your PySpark streaming application will look something similar to the following output:

```
$ ./bin/spark-submit stateful_streaming_word_count.py localhost 9999
-------------------------------------------
Time: 2018-06-21 23:00:30
-------------------------------------------
(u'blue', 5)
(u'green', 3)
-------------------------------------------
Time: 2018-06-21 23:00:31
-------------------------------------------
(u'blue', 5)
(u'green', 3)
(u'gohawks', 1)
-------------------------------------------
Time: 2018-06-21 23:00:32
-------------------------------------------
-------------------------------------------
Time: 2018-06-21 23:00:33
-------------------------------------------
(u'blue', 5)
(u'green', 5)
(u'gohawks', 1)
-------------------------------------------
```

To end the streaming application (and the `nc` window, for that matter), execute a termination command (for example, *Ctrl + C*).

How it works...

As noted in the previous subsections, this recipe is comprised of one terminal window transmitting event data using `nc`. The second window runs our Spark Streaming application reading from the port that the first window is transmitting to.

The important call outs for this code are noted here:

- We're creating a Spark context using two working threads, hence the use of `local[2]`.
- As noted in the Netcat window, we're using `ssc.socketTextStream` to listen to the local socket of the `localhost`, port `9999`.
- We have created a `updateFunc`, which performs the task of aggregating the previous value with the currently aggregated value.
- Recall that for each 1-second batch, we're not only reading a single line (for example, `blue blue blue blue blue green green green`) but also splitting it up into individual `words` via `split`.
- We're using a Python `lambda` function and PySpark `map` and `reduceByKey` functions to quickly count the occurrences of words within the 1-second batch. For example, in the case of `blue blue blue blue blue green green green`, there are 5 blue and 3 green events, as reported at *2018-06-21 23:00:30* of our streaming application.
- The difference between the previous streaming application vs. the current stateful version is that we're calculating running counts (`running_counts`) with the current aggregation (for example, five blue and three green events) with `updateStateByKey`. This allows Spark Streaming to keep the state of the current aggregation within the context of the previously defined `updateFunc`.
- `ssc.start()` is in reference to the application starting the Spark Streaming context.
- `ssc.awaitTermination()` is waiting for a termination command to stop the streaming application (for example, *Ctrl + C*); otherwise, the application will continue to run.

Continuous aggregation with structured streaming

As noted in earlier chapters, the execution of Spark SQL or DataFrame queries revolves around building a logical plan, choosing a physical plan (of the many generated physical plans) based on its cost optimizer, and then generating the code (that is, code gen) via the Spark SQL Engine Catalyst Optimizer. What structured streaming introduces is the concept of an *incremental* execution plan. That is, structured streaming repeatedly applies the execution plan for every new block of data it receives. This way, the Spark SQL engine can take advantage of the optimizations included within Spark DataFrames and apply them to an incoming data stream. Because structured streaming is built on top of Spark DataFrames, this means it will also be easier to integrate other DataFrame-optimized components, including MLlib, GraphFrames, TensorFrames, and so on:

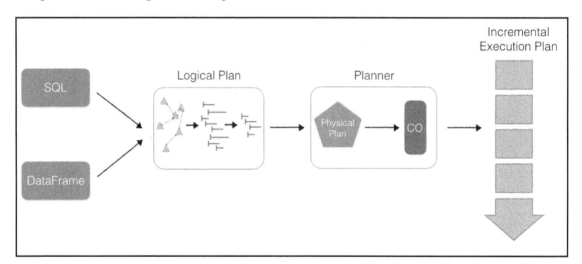

Getting ready

For these Apache Spark Streaming examples, we will be creating and executing a console application via the bash terminal. To make things easier, you will want to have two terminal windows open.

How to do it...

As noted in the previous section, we will use two terminal windows:

- One terminal window to transmit an event
- Another terminal to receive those events

The source code for this can be found in the Apache Spark 2.3.1 Structured Streaming Programming Guide at: `https://spark.apache.org/docs/latest/structured-streaming-programming-guide.html`.

Terminal 1 – Netcat window

For the first window, we will use Netcat (or `nc`) to manually send events such as blue, green, and gohawks. To start Netcat, use this command; we will direct our events to port `9999`, where our Spark Streaming job will detect:

```
nc -lk 9999
```

To match the previous diagram, we will type in our events so that the console screen looks like this:

```
$nc -lk 9999
blue blue blue blue blue green green green
gohawks
green green
```

Terminal 2 – Spark Streaming window

We will create a simple PySpark Streaming application using the following code called `structured_streaming_word_count.py`:

```
#
# structured_streaming_word_count.py
#

# Import the necessary classes and create a local SparkSession
from pyspark.sql import SparkSession
from pyspark.sql.functions import explode
from pyspark.sql.functions import split

spark = SparkSession \
    .builder \
```

```
    .appName("StructuredNetworkWordCount") \
    .getOrCreate()


  # Create DataFrame representing the stream of input lines from connection
to localhost:9999
lines = spark\
  .readStream\
  .format('socket')\
  .option('host', 'localhost')\
  .option('port', 9999)\
  .load()

# Split the lines into words
words = lines.select(
  explode(
      split(lines.value, ' ')
  ).alias('word')
)

# Generate running word count
wordCounts = words.groupBy('word').count()


# Start running the query that prints the running counts to the console
query = wordCounts\
  .writeStream\
  .outputMode('complete')\
  .format('console')\
  .start()

# Await Spark Streaming termination
query.awaitTermination()
```

To run this PySpark Streaming application, execute the following command from your $SPARK_HOME folder:

```
./bin/spark-submit structured_streaming_word_count.py localhost 9999
```

In terms of how you time this, you should:

1. First start with nc -lk 9999.
2. Then, start your PySpark Streaming application: ./bin/spark-submit
   stateful_streaming_word_count.py localhost 9999.

3. Then, start typing your events, for example:
   1. For the first second, type `blue blue blue blue blue green green green`
   2. For the second second, type `gohawks`
   3. Wait a second; for the fourth second, type `green green`

The console output from your PySpark streaming application will look something similar to the following:

```
$ ./bin/spark-submit structured_streaming_word_count.py localhost 9999
-------------------------------------------
Batch: 0
-------------------------------------------
+-----+-----+
| word|count|
+-----+-----+
|green|    3|
| blue|    5|
+-----+-----+


-------------------------------------------
Batch: 1
-------------------------------------------
+-------+-----+
|   word|count|
+-------+-----+
|  green|    3|
|   blue|    5|
|gohawks|    1|
+-------+-----+


-------------------------------------------
Batch: 2
-------------------------------------------
+-------+-----+
|   word|count|
+-------+-----+
|  green|    5|
|   blue|    5|
|gohawks|    1|
+-------+-----+
```

To end the streaming application (and the `nc` window, for that matter), execute a termination command (for example, *Ctrl + C*).

 Similar to global aggregations with DStreams, with structured streaming, you can easily perform stateful global aggregations within the context of a DataFrame. Another optimization you'll notice with structured streaming is that the streaming aggregations will only appear whenever there are new events. Specifically notice how when we delayed between time = 2s and time = 4s, there is not an extra batch being reported to the console.

How it works...

As noted in the previous subsections, this recipe is comprised of one terminal window transmitting event data using `nc`. The second window runs our Spark Streaming application, reading from the port that the first window is transmitting to.

The important callouts for this code are noted here:

- Instead of creating a Spark context, we're creating a `SparkSession`
- With the SparkSession, we can use `readStream` to specify the `socket` *format* to specify that we're listening to `localhost` at port `9999`
- We use the PySpark SQL functions `split` and `explode` to take our `line` and break it down to `words`
- To generate our running word count, we need only to create `wordCounts` to run a `groupBy` statement and `count()` on `words`
- Finally, we will use `writeStream` to write out the `complete` set of `query` data to the `console` (as opposed to some other data sink)
- Because we're using a Spark session, the application is waiting for a termination command to stop the streaming application (for example, <Ctrl><C>) via `query.awaitTermination()`

Because structured streaming is using DataFrames, it is simpler and easier to read because we're using the familiar DataFrame abstraction while also gaining all the performance optimizations of DataFrames.

GraphFrames – Graph Theory with PySpark

In this chapter, we will cover how to work with GraphFrames for Apache Spark. You will learn the following recipes:

- A quick primer on graph theory and GraphFrames for Apache Spark
- Installing GraphFrames
- Preparing the data
- Building the graph
- Running queries against the graph
- Understanding the graph
- Using PageRank to determine airport ranks
- Finding the fewest number of connections
- Visualizing your graph

Introduction

Graphs enable solving certain data problems more easily and intuitively. At the core of a graph lies concepts of edges, nodes (or vertices), and their properties. For example, the following are two seemingly disconnected graphs. The left one represents a social network and the relationship (the *edges* of the graph) between friends (the *vertices* of the graph), while the right one is a graph that represents restaurant recommendations. Note that the vertices for our restaurant recommendations are not only the restaurants themselves but also the cuisine type (for example, Ramen) and location (for example, Vancouver, B.C., Canada); these are the properties of the vertices. This ability to assign nodes to virtually anything and use edges to define the relationship between these nodes is the greatest virtue of graphs, that is, their flexibility:

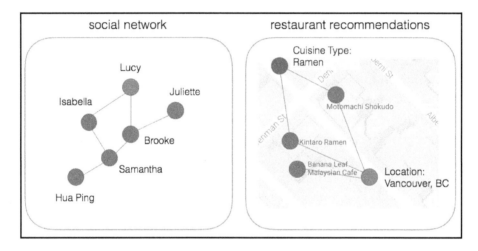

This flexibility allows us to conceptually connect these two seemingly disparate graphs into one common graph. In this case, we can join the social network with restaurant recommendations, in which the edges (that is, connections) between the friends and the restaurants are through their ratings:

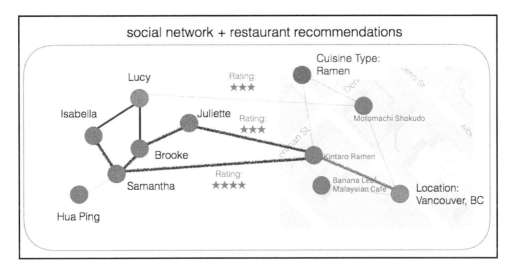

For example, if Isabella wants to find a great ramen restaurant (vertex: cuisine type) in Vancouver (vertex: location), then traversing her friends' reviews (edge: ratings), she will most likely choose Kintaro Ramen (vertex: restaurant) as both Samantha (vertex: friend) and Juliette (vertex: friend) have rated the restaurant favorably.

While graphs are intuitive and flexible, one of the key problems with a graph is that its traversal and computation of graph algorithms are often resource intensive and slow. With GraphFrames for Apache Spark, you are able to leverage the speed and performance of Apache Spark DataFrames to traverse and compute your graphs in a distributed and performant manner.

Installing GraphFrames

Under the hood of GraphFrames are two Spark DataFrames: one for the vertices and other one for the edges. GraphFrames might be thought of as the next generation of Spark's GraphX library, with some major improvements over the latter:

- GraphFrames leverages the performance optimizations and simplicity of the DataFrame API.
- By using the DataFrame API, GraphFrames can be interacted with through Python, Java, and Scala APIs. In contrast, GraphX was only available through the Scala interface.

You can find the latest information on GraphFrames within the GraphFrames overview at `https://graphframes.github.io/`.

Getting ready

We require a working installation of Spark. This means that you would have followed the steps outlined in `Chapter 1`, *Installing and Configuring Spark*. As a reminder, to start the PySpark shell for your local Spark cluster, you can run the following command:

```
./bin/pyspark --master local[n]
```

Where `n` is the number of cores.

How to do it...

If you are running your job from a Spark CLI (for example, `spark-shell`, `pyspark`, `spark-sql`, or `spark-submit`), you can use the `--packages` command, which will extract, compile, and execute the necessary code for you to use the GraphFrames package.

For example, to use the latest GraphFrames package (which, at the time of writing this book, is version 0.5) with Spark 2.1 and Scala 2.11 with `spark-shell`, the command is:

```
$SPARK_HOME/bin/pyspark --packages graphframes:graphframes:0.5.0-spark2.3-s_2.11
```

However, in order to use GraphFrames with Spark 2.3, you need to build the package from sources.

> Check out the steps outlined here: `https://github.com/graphframes/graphframes/issues/267`.

If you are using a service such as Databricks, you will need to create a library with GraphFrames. For more information, please refer to how to create a library in Databricks at `https://docs.databricks.com/user-guide/libraries.html`, and how to install a GraphFrames Spark package at `https://cdn2.hubspot.net/hubfs/438089/notebooks/help/Setup_graphframes_package.html`.

How it works...

You can install a package such as GraphFrames by building it off the GraphFrames GitHub repository at `https://github.com/graphframes/graphframes`, but an easier way is to utilize the GraphFrames Spark package which is available at `https://spark-packages.org/package/graphframes/graphframes`. Spark Packages is a repository that contains an index of third-party packages for Apache Spark. By using Spark packages, PySpark will download the latest version of the GraphFrames Spark package, compile it, and then execute it within the context of your Spark job.

When you include the GraphFrames package using the following command, notice the call `graphframes` console output, denoting that the package is being pulled in from the `spark-packages` repository for compilation:

```
$ ./bin/pyspark --master local --packages graphframes:graphframes:0.5.0-
spark2.1-s_2.11
...
graphframes#graphframes added as a dependency
:: resolving dependencies :: org.apache.spark#spark-submit-parent;1.0
  confs: [default]
  found graphframes#graphframes;0.5.0-spark2.1-s_2.11 in spark-packages
  found com.typesafe.scala-logging#scala-logging-api_2.11;2.1.2 in central
  found com.typesafe.scala-logging#scala-logging-slf4j_2.11;2.1.2 in
central
  found org.scala-lang#scala-reflect;2.11.0 in central
  found org.slf4j#slf4j-api;1.7.7 in central
downloading
http://dl.bintray.com/spark-packages/maven/graphframes/graphframes/0.5.0-sp
ark2.1-s_2.11/graphframes-0.5.0-spark2.1-s_2.11.jar ...
  [SUCCESSFUL ] graphframes#graphframes;0.5.0-spark2.1-
s_2.11!graphframes.jar (600ms)
:: resolution report :: resolve 1503ms :: artifacts dl 608ms
  :: modules in use:
  com.typesafe.scala-logging#scala-logging-api_2.11;2.1.2 from central in
[default]
  com.typesafe.scala-logging#scala-logging-slf4j_2.11;2.1.2 from central in
[default]
  graphframes#graphframes;0.5.0-spark2.1-s_2.11 from spark-packages in
[default]
  org.scala-lang#scala-reflect;2.11.0 from central in [default]
  org.slf4j#slf4j-api;1.7.7 from central in [default]
  ---------------------------------------------------------------------
  |  | modules || artifacts |
  | conf | number| search|dwnlded|evicted|| number|dwnlded|
```

```
-------------------------------------------------------------
| default | 5 | 1 | 1 | 0 || 5 | 1 |
-------------------------------------------------------------
:: retrieving :: org.apache.spark#spark-submit-parent
confs: [default]
1 artifacts copied, 4 already retrieved (323kB/9ms)
```

Preparing the data

The example scenario we will use for the cookbook is on-time flight performance data (that is, flights scenario) that will make use of two sets of data:

- Airline On-Time Performance and Causes of Flight Delays, available at http://bit.ly/2ccJPPM. These datasets contain information about scheduled and actual departure and arrival times of flights, and the delay causes. The data is represented as reported by US air carriers and is collected by the Office of Airline Information, **Bureau of Transportation Statistics** (**BTS**).
- OpenFlights, airport and airline data available at http://openflights.org/data.html. This dataset contains the list of US airport data, including the IATA code, airport name, and airport location.

We will create two DataFrames: one for the airports and one for the flights. The airports DataFrame will make up our vertices and the flights DataFrames will represent all the edges of our GraphFrame.

Getting ready

If you are running this locally, please copy the linked files to your local folder; for the purpose of this recipe, we'll call the location /data:

- Airline On-Time Performance and Causes at http://bit.ly/2xs0XLH
- OpenFlights—Airports and airline data at http://bit.ly/2J1CU7D

If you are using Databricks, the data is already loaded into the /databricks-datasets folder; the location of the files can be found at /databricks-datasets/flights/airport-codes-na.txt and /databricks-datasets/flights/departuredelays.csv for airports and flights data, respectively.

How to do it...

To prepare our data for our graph, we will initially clean up the data and include only the airport codes that exist within the available flight data. That is, we exclude any airports that do not exist in the `DepartureDelays.csv` dataset. The upcoming recipe executes the following:

1. Sets the file paths to the files you had downloaded
2. Creates the `apts` and `deptDelays` DataFrames by reading the CSV files and inferring the schema, configured with headers
3. The `iata` contains only the airport codes (the `IATA` column) that exist in the `deptDelays` DataFrame
4. Joins the `iata` and `apts` DataFrames to create the `apts_df` DataFrame

The reason we filter out the data to create the `airports` DataFrame is that when we create our GraphFrame in the following recipes, we will only have vertices with edges for our graph:

```
# Set File Paths
delays_fp = "/data/departuredelays.csv"
apts_fp = "/data/airport-codes-na.txt"

# Obtain airports dataset
apts = spark.read.csv(apts_fp, header='true', inferSchema='true', sep='\t')
apts.createOrReplaceTempView("apts")

# Obtain departure Delays data
deptsDelays = spark.read.csv(delays_fp, header='true', inferSchema='true')
deptsDelays.createOrReplaceTempView("deptsDelays")
deptsDelays.cache()

# Available IATA codes from the departuredelays sample dataset
iata = spark.sql("""
    select distinct iata
    from (
        select distinct origin as iata
        from deptsDelays
        union all
        select distinct destination as iata
        from deptsDelays
    ) as a
""")
iata.createOrReplaceTempView("iata")
```

```
# Only include airports with atleast one trip from the departureDelays
dataset
airports = sqlContext.sql("""
    select f.IATA
         , f.City
         , f.State
         , f.Country
    from apts as f
    join iata as t
        on t.IATA = f.IATA
""")
airports.registerTempTable("airports")
airports.cache()
```

How it works...

The two key concepts used for this code snippet are:

- `spark.read.csv`: This `SparkSession` method returns a `DataFrameReader` object that encompasses the classes and functions that will allow us to read CSV files from a filesystem
- `spark.sql`: This allows us to execute Spark SQL statements

For more information, please refer to the preceding chapters on Spark DataFrames, or refer to the PySpark master documentation of the `pyspark.sql` module at `http://spark.apache.org/docs/2.3.0/api/python/pyspark.sql.html`.

There's more...

Before we read the data into our GraphFrame, let's create one more DataFrame:

```
import pyspark.sql.functions as f
import pyspark.sql.types as t

@f.udf
def toDate(weirdDate):
    year = '2014-'
    month = weirdDate[0:2] + '-'
    day = weirdDate[2:4] + ' '
    hour = weirdDate[4:6] + ':'
    minute = weirdDate[6:8] + ':00'
```

```
        return year + month + day + hour + minute

deptsDelays = deptsDelays.withColumn('normalDate',
toDate(deptsDelays.date))
deptsDelays.createOrReplaceTempView("deptsDelays")

# Get key attributes of a flight
deptsDelays_GEO = spark.sql("""
    select cast(f.date as int) as tripid
        , cast(f.normalDate as timestamp) as `localdate`
        , cast(f.delay as int)
        , cast(f.distance as int)
        , f.origin as src
        , f.destination as dst
        , o.city as city_src
        , d.city as city_dst
        , o.state as state_src
        , d.state as state_dst
    from deptsDelays as f
    join airports as o
        on o.iata = f.origin
    join airports as d
        on d.iata = f.destination
""")

# Create Temp View
deptsDelays_GEO.createOrReplaceTempView("deptsDelays_GEO")

# Cache and Count
deptsDelays_GEO.cache()
deptsDelays_GEO.count()
```

The preceding code snippet packs some additional optimizations to create the
deptsDelays_GEO DataFrame:

- It creates a `tripid` column that allows us to uniquely identify each trip. Note
  that this is a bit of a hack as we had converted the date (each trip has a unique
  date in this dataset) into an int column.
- The `date` column isn't really a traditional date per se as it is in the format of
  MMYYHHmm. Therefore, we first apply a `udf` to convert it into a proper format (the
  `toDate(...)` method). We then convert it into an actual timestamp format.
- Re-casts the `delay` and `distance` columns into integer values as opposed to
  string.

- In the following sections, we will be using the airport codes (the `iata` column) as our vertex. To create the edges for our graph, we will need to specify the IATA codes for the source (originating airport) and destination (destination airport). The `join` statement and renaming of `f.origin` as `src` and `f.destination` as `dst` are in preparation for creating the GraphFrame to specify the edges (they are explicitly looking for the `src` and `dst` columns).

Building the graph

In the preceding sections, you installed GraphFrames and built the DataFrames required for the graph; now, you can start building the graph itself.

How to do it...

The first component of this recipe involves importing the necessary libraries, in this case, the PySpark SQL functions (`pyspark.sql.functions`) and GraphFrames (`graphframes`). In the previous recipe, we had created the `src` and `dst` columns as part of creating the `deptsDelays_geo` DataFrame. When creating edges within GraphFrames, it is specifically looking for the `src` and `dst` columns to create the edges as per `edges`. Similarly, GraphFrames is looking for the column `id` to represent the graph vertex (as well as join to the `src` and `dst` columns). Therefore, when creating the vertexes, `vertices`, we rename the IATA column to `id`:

```
from pyspark.sql.functions import *
from graphframes import *

# Create Vertices (airports) and Edges (flights)
vertices = airports.withColumnRenamed("IATA", "id").distinct()
edges = deptsDelays_geo.select("tripid", "delay", "src", "dst", "city_dst",
"state_dst")

# Cache Vertices and Edges
edges.cache()
vertices.cache()

# This GraphFrame builds up on the vertices and edges based on our trips
(flights)
graph = GraphFrame(vertices, edges)
```

Note that `edges` and `vertices` are DataFrames containing the edges and vertices of the graph, respectively. You can check this by viewing the data as noted in the following screenshots (in this case, we're using the `display` command within Databricks).

For example, the command `display(vertices)` shows the id (IATA code), `City`, `State`, and `Country` columns of the `vertices` DataFrame:

id	City	State	Country
STL	St. Louis	MO	USA
EKO	Elko	NV	USA
RAP	Rapid City	SD	USA
GRK	Killeen	TX	USA
ABQ	Albuquerque	NM	USA
LBB	Lubbock	TX	USA
SAT	San Antonio	TX	USA
BDL	Hartford	CT	USA

Meanwhile, the command `display(edges)` shows the `tripid`, `delay`, `src`, `dst`, `city_dst`, and `state_dst` of the `edges` DataFrame:

tripid	delay	src	dst	city_dst	state_dst
1011158	-5	SAN	IAH	Houston	TX
1011516	-8	SAN	IAH	Houston	TX
1010937	16	SAN	IAH	Houston	TX
1010702	1	SAN	IAH	Houston	TX
1010620	3	SAN	IAH	Houston	TX
1020620	1	SAN	IAH	Houston	TX
1021507	10	SAN	IAH	Houston	TX
1020814	-3	SAN	IAH	Houston	TX
1021158	0	SAN	IAH	Houston	TX

The final statement, `GraphFrame(vertices, edges)`, performs the task of merging the two DataFrames into our GraphFrame, `graph`.

How it works...

As noted in the previous section, when creating a GraphFrame, it specifically looks for the following columns:

- `id`: This identifies the vertex and will join to the `src` and `dst` columns. In our example, the IATA code `LAX` (representing **Los Angeles Airport**) is one of many airports that make up the vertices in our graph (`graph`).
- `src`: The source vertex of our graph's edges; for example, a flight from Los Angeles to New York has `src = LAX`.
- `dst`: The destination vertex of our graph's edges; for example, a flight from Los Angeles to New York has `dst - JFK`.

By creating the two DataFrames (`vertices` and `edges`) where the attributes follow the previously noted naming convention, we can invoke the GraphFrame to create our graph, utilizing the performance optimizations of the two DataFrames underneath.

Running queries against the graph

Now that you have created your graph, start off by creating and running some simple queries against your GraphFrame.

Getting ready

Ensure that you have created the `graph` GraphFrame (derived from the `vertices` and `edges` DataFrames) from the previous section.

How to do it...

Let's start with some simple count queries to determine the number of airports (nodes or vertices; remember?) and the number of flights (the edges), which can be determined by applying `count()`. The call to `count()` is similar to a DataFrame except that you also need to include whether you are counting `vertices` or `edges`:

```
print "Airport count: %d" % graph.vertices.count()
print "Trips count: %d" % graph.edges.count()
```

The output of these queries should be similar to the following output, denoting the 279 vertices (that is, airports) and more than 1.3 million edges (that is, flights):

```
Output:
  Airports count: 279
  Trips count: 1361141
```

Similar to DataFrames, you can also execute the `filter` and `groupBy` clauses to better understand the number of delayed flights. To understand the number of on-time or early flights, we use the filter where `delay <= 0`; the delayed flights, on the other hand, show `delay > 0`:

```
print "Early or on-time: %d" % graph.edges.filter("delay <= 0").count()
print "Delayed: %d" % graph.edges.filter("delay > 0").count()

# Output
Early or on-time: 780469
Delayed: 580672
```

Diving further, you can filter for delayed flights (`delay > 0`) departing from San Francisco (`src = 'SFO'`) grouped by the destination airports, sorting by average delay descending (`desc("avg(delay)")`):

```
display(
    graph
    .edges
    .filter("src = 'SFO' and delay > 0")
    .groupBy("src", "dst")
    .avg("delay")
    .sort(desc("avg(delay)"))
)
```

src	dst	avg(delay)
SFO	OKC	59.073170731707314
SFO	JAC	57.13333333333333
SFO	COS	53.976190476190474
SFO	OTH	48.09090909090909
SFO	SAT	47.625
SFO	MOD	46.80952380952381
SFO	SUN	46.723404255319146

If you are using the Databricks notebooks, you can visualize the GraphFrame queries. For example, we can determine the destination states with `delay > 100` minutes departing from Seattle using the following query:

```
# States with the longest cumulative delays (with individual delays > 100
minutes)
# origin: Seattle
display(graph.edges.filter("src = 'SEA' and delay > 100"))
```

The preceding code produces the following map. The darker the blue hue, the more the delay that the flights experienced. From the following graph, you can see that most of the delayed flights departing Seattle have their destination within the state of California:

How it works...

As noted in previous sections, GraphFrames are built on top of two DataFrames: one for vertices and one for edges. This simply means that GraphFrames take advantage of the same performance optimizations as DataFrames (unlike the older GraphX). Just as importantly, they also take on many components of the Spark SQL syntax.

Understanding the graph

To easily understand the complex relationship of city airports and the flights between each of them, we can use the concept of **motifs** to find patterns of airports connected by flights. The result is a DataFrame in which the column names are given by the motif keys.

Getting ready

To make it easier to view our data within the context of Motifs, let's first create a smaller version of the `graph` GraphFrame called `graphSmall`:

```
edgesSubset = deptsDelays_GEO.select("tripid", "delay", "src", "dst")
graphSmall = GraphFrame(vertices, edgesSubset)
```

How to do it...

To execute a Motif, execute the following command:

```
motifs = (
    graphSmall
    .find("(a)-[ab]->(b); (b)-[bc]->(c)")
    .filter("""
        (b.id = 'SFO')
        and (ab.delay > 500 or bc.delay > 500)
        and bc.tripid > ab.tripid
        and bc.tripid < ab.tripid + 10000
    """)
)
display(motifs)
```

The result of this query can be seen as follows:

Output of the motif query

How it works...

There is a lot to unpack with this example motif query, so let's start with the query itself. The first part of the query is to establish what our Motif is, which is to establish that we are looking for the relationships between vertices (a), (b), and (c). Specifically, we're concerned with the edges between the two sets of vertices, between (a) and (b), as represented by [ab], and between vertices (b) and (c) as represented by [bc]:

```
graphSmall.find("(a)-[ab]->(b); (b)-[bc]->(c)")
```

For example, we are trying to determine all the flights between two different cities where Los Angeles is the layover city (for example, Seattle - Los Angeles -> New York, Portland - Los Angeles -> Atlanta, and so on):

- (b): This represents the city of Los Angeles
- (a): This represent the originating cities, such as Seattle and Portland in this example
- [ab]: This represents the flights, such as Seattle - Los Angeles and Portland - Los Angeles in this example
- (c): This represents the destination cities, such as New York and Atlanta in this example
- [bc]: This represents the flights, such as Los Angeles -> New York and Los Angeles -> Atlanta in this example

Deviating from the preceding example, in our code snippet we have specified San Francisco as our layover point (b.id = 'SFO'). We're also specifying any trips (that is, graph edges) where the delay is greater than 500 minutes (ab.delay > 500 or bc.delay > 500). We have also specified that the second leg of the trip must occur after the first leg of the trip (bc.tripid > ab.tripid and bc.tripid < ab.tripid + 10000").

Note that this last statement is an oversimplification of flights because it isn't taking into account which flights are valid connector flights. Also, recall that tripid was generated based on time in the format of MMDDHHMM converted to an integer:

```
filter("(b.id = 'SFO') and (ab.delay > 500 or bc.delay > 500) and bc.tripid
> ab.tripid and bc.tripid < ab.tripid + 10000")
```

The output displayed in the preceding subsection denotes all the flights where the stopover was San Francisco and there were flight delays of greater than 500 minutes for either flights arriving or leaving SFO. Digging further into a single flight, let's review the output of the first row, though we have pivoted it to make it easier to review:

Vertices	Values
[ab]	• tripid: 2021900 • delay: 39 • src: STL • dst: SFO
(a)	• id: STL • City: St. Louis • State: MO • Country: USA
(b)	• id: SFO • City: San Francisco • State: CA • Country: USA
[bc]	• tripid: 2030906 • delay: 516 • src: SFO • dst: PHL
(c)	• id: PHL • City: Philadelphia • State: PA • Country: USA

As noted previously, [ab] and [bc] are the flights while [a], [b], and [c] are the airports. In this example, the flight departing from St. Louis (STL) to San Francisco had a delay of 39 minutes, but its potential connecting flight to Philadelphia (PHL) had a delay of 516 minutes. As you dig through the results, you can see a lot of different potential flight patterns between originating and final destination cities centered around San Francisco as the primary stop over. This query will become more complicated as you take on even larger hub cities such as Atlanta, Dallas, and Chicago.

Using PageRank to determine airport ranking

PageRank is an algorithm popularized by the Google Search Engine and created by Larry Page. Ian Rogers says (see http://www.cs.princeton.edu/~chazelle/courses/BIB/pagerank.htm):

> "(...)PageRank is a "vote", by all the other pages on the Web, about how important a page is. A link to a page counts as a vote of support. If there's no link there's no support (but it's an abstention from voting rather than a vote against the page)."

As you might imagine, this method can be applied to other problems and not only to ranking web pages. In our context, we can use it to determine airport ranking. To achieve this, we can use the number of flights and connections to and from various airports included that are in this departure delay dataset.

Getting ready

Ensure that you have created the `graph` GraphFrame from the preceding subsections.

How to do it...

Execute the following code snippet to determine the most important airport in our dataset via the PageRank algorithm:

```
# Determining Airport ranking of importance using `pageRank`
ranks = graph.pageRank(resetProbability=0.15, maxIter=5)
display(ranks.vertices.orderBy(ranks.vertices.pagerank.desc()).limit(20))
```

As you can see from the output in the following graph, Atlanta, Dallas, and Chicago are the top three most important cities (note that this dataset contains US data only):

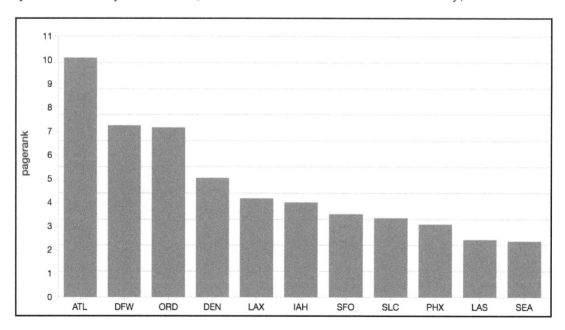

How it works...

At the time of writing this book,, the current version of GraphFrames is v0.5, which contains two implementations of PageRank:

- The one we are using utilizes the GraphFrame interface and runs PageRank for a fixed number of iterations by setting `maxIter`
- Another version uses the `org.apache.spark.graphx.Pregel` interface and runs PageRank until convergence by setting `tol`

For more information, please refer to the GraphFrames Scala documentation on PageRank at `https://graphframes.github.io/api/scala/index.html#org.graphframes.lib.PageRank`.

As noted previously, we are using the standalone GraphFrame version of PageRank by setting:

- `resetProbability`: This is currently set to the default value of `0.15`, which represents the probability of resetting to a random vertex. If the value is too high, it means that it will take longer to complete its calculation, but if the value is too low, the calculations may overshoot and not converge.

- `maxIter`: For this demo, we have set the value to 5; the higher the number, the higher the probability of a more precise calculation.

Finding the fewest number of connections

When you're flying to many cities, one of the recurring problems is to determine either the shortest path between two cities or the shortest time of travel. From the viewpoint of the airline traveler, the aim is to find the shortest set of flights between two cities. From the viewpoint of the airline, determining how to route their passengers between cities as efficiently as possible increases customer satisfaction and lowers prices (less fuel, wear and tear on equipment, ease for the flight crew, and so on). Within the context of GraphFrames and graph algorithms, one approach would be to use the **breadth first search** (**BFS**) algorithm to help us find the shortest path between these airports.

Getting ready

Ensure that you have created the `graph` GraphFrame from the preceding subsections.

How to do it...

Let's start using our BFS algorithm to determine whether there are any direct flights between SFO and SEA:

```
subsetOfPaths = graph.bfs(
    fromExpr = "id = 'SEA'",
    toExpr = "id = 'SFO'",
    maxPathLength = 1)

display(subsetOfPaths)
```

As you can tell from the output, there are many direct flights between Seattle (SEA) and San Francisco (SFO):

from	e0	to
▸ {"id":"SEA","City":"Seattle","State":"WA","Country":"USA"}	▸ {"tripid":1010710,"delay":31,"src":"SEA","dst":"SFO","city_dst":"San Francisco","state_dst":"CA"}	▸ {"id":"SFO","City":"San Francisco","State":"CA","Country":"USA"}
▸ {"id":"SEA","City":"Seattle","State":"WA","Country":"USA"}	▸ {"tripid":1012125,"delay":-4,"src":"SEA","dst":"SFO","city_dst":"San Francisco","state_dst":"CA"}	▸ {"id":"SFO","City":"San Francisco","State":"CA","Country":"USA"}
▸ {"id":"SEA","City":"Seattle","State":"WA","Country":"USA"}	▸ {"tripid":1011840,"delay":-5,"src":"SEA","dst":"SFO","city_dst":"San Francisco","state_dst":"CA"}	▸ {"id":"SFO","City":"San Francisco","State":"CA","Country":"USA"}
▸ {"id":"SEA","City":"Seattle","State":"WA","Country":"USA"}	▸ {"tripid":1010610,"delay":-4,"src":"SEA","dst":"SFO","city_dst":"San Francisco","state_dst":"CA"}	▸ {"id":"SFO","City":"San Francisco","State":"CA","Country":"USA"}
▸ {"id":"SEA","City":"Seattle","State":"WA","Country":"USA"}	▸ {"tripid":1011230,"delay":-2,"src":"SEA","dst":"SFO","city_dst":"San Francisco","state_dst":"CA"}	▸ {"id":"SFO","City":"San Francisco","State":"CA","Country":"USA"}
Showing the first 1000 rows.		

How it works...

When calling the BFS algorithm, the key parameters are `fromExpr`, `toExpr`, and `maxPathLength`. As our vertices contain the airports, to understand the number of direct flights from Seattle to San Francisco, we will specify:

```
fromExpr = "id = 'SEA'",
toExpr = "id = 'SFO'
```

The `maxPathLength` is the parameter used to specify the maximum number of edges between the two vertices. If `maxPathLength` = 1, it means that we have only one edge between the two vertices. That is, there is only one flight between the two airports or a direct flight between those two cities. Increasing this value means BFS will attempt to find multiple connections between your two cities. For example, if we were to specify `maxPathLength` = 2, this would mean two edges or two flights between Seattle and San Francisco. That indicates a layover city, for example, SEA - POR -> SFO, SEA - LAS -> SFO, SEA - DEN -> SFO, and so on.

There's more...

What if you want to find connections between two cities that typically do not have direct flights? For example, let's find out the possible routes between San Francisco and Buffalo:

```
subsetOfPaths = graph.bfs(
    fromExpr = "id = 'SFO'",
    toExpr = "id = 'BUF'",
    maxPathLength = 1)

display(subsetOfPaths)

Output:
    OK
```

The `OK` in this case indicates that there are no direct flights between San Francisco and Buffalo as we could not retrieve a single edge (at least from this dataset). But to find out whether there are any layover flights, just change `maxPathLength` = 2 (to indicate a single stopover city):

```
subsetOfPaths = graph.bfs(
    fromExpr = "id = 'SFO'",
    toExpr = "id = 'BUF'",
    maxPathLength = 2)

display(subsetOfPaths)
```

As you can see here, there are many flights with a single stopover connecting San Francisco and Buffalo:

See also

But what is the most common layover between San Francisco and Buffalo? Looking at the preceding results, it seems like Minneapolis, but looks can be deceiving. Instead, run the following query:

```
display(subsetOfPaths.groupBy("v1.id",
"v1.City").count().orderBy(desc("count")).limit(10))
```

As you can see from the following graph, JFK is the most common transfer point between these two cities:

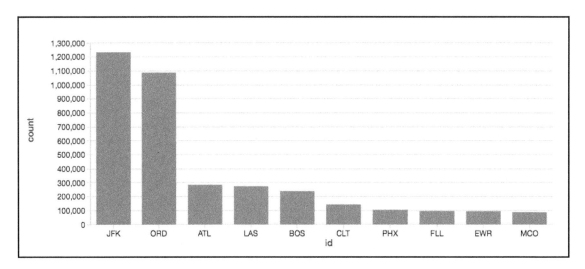

Visualizing the graph

In the preceding recipes, we have been visualizing our flights using Databrick notebook's native visualizations (for example, bar chart, line chart, maps, and so on). But we have not yet visualized our graph as a graph. In this section, we will leverage Mike Bostock's Airports D3.js visualization (`https://mbostock.github.io/d3/talk/20111116/airports.html`) within our Databricks notebook.

Getting ready

Ensure that you have created the `graph` GraphFrame and the source `deptsDelays_GEO` DataFrame from the preceding subsections.

How to do it...

We will be leveraging our Python Databricks notebook, but we will include the following Scala cell. At the top level here's the flow of the code:

```scala
%scala
package d3a

import org.apache.spark.sql._
import
com.databricks.backend.daemon.driver.EnhancedRDDFunctions.displayHTML

case class Edge(src: String, dest: String, count: Long)
case class Node(name: String)
case class Link(source: Int, target: Int, value: Long)
case class Graph(nodes: Seq[Node], links: Seq[Link])

object graphs {
val sqlContext =
SQLContext.getOrCreate(org.apache.spark.SparkContext.getOrCreate())
import sqlContext.implicits._

def force(clicks: Dataset[Edge], height: Int = 100, width: Int = 960): Unit
= {
  val data = clicks.collect()
  val nodes = (data.map(_.src) ++ data.map(_.dest)).map(_.replaceAll("_", "
")).toSet.toSeq.map(Node)
  val links = data.map { t =>
    Link(nodes.indexWhere(_.name == t.src.replaceAll("_", " ")),
```

```
nodes.indexWhere(_.name == t.dest.replaceAll("_", " ")), t.count / 20 + 1)
  }
  showGraph(height, width, Seq(Graph(nodes, links)).toDF().toJSON.first())
}

/**
 * Displays a force directed graph using d3
 * input: {"nodes": [{"name": "..."}], "links": [{"source": 1, "target": 2,
"value": 0}]}
 */
def showGraph(height: Int, width: Int, graph: String): Unit = {

displayHTML(s"""<!DOCTYPE html>
<html>
  <head>
    <link type="text/css" rel="stylesheet"
href="https://mbostock.github.io/d3/talk/20111116/style.css"/>
    <style type="text/css">
      #states path {
        fill: #ccc;
        stroke: #fff;
      }

      path.arc {
        pointer-events: none;
        fill: none;
        stroke: #000;
        display: none;
      }

      path.cell {
        fill: none;
        pointer-events: all;
      }

      circle {
        fill: steelblue;
        fill-opacity: .8;
        stroke: #fff;
      }

      #cells.voronoi path.cell {
        stroke: brown;
      }

      #cells g:hover path.arc {
        display: inherit;
      }
```

```
    </style>
  </head>
  <body>
    <script
src="https://mbostock.github.io/d3/talk/20111116/d3/d3.js"></script>
    <script
src="https://mbostock.github.io/d3/talk/20111116/d3/d3.csv.js"></script>
    <script
src="https://mbostock.github.io/d3/talk/20111116/d3/d3.geo.js"></script>
    <script
src="https://mbostock.github.io/d3/talk/20111116/d3/d3.geom.js"></script>
    <script>
      var graph = $graph;
      var w = $width;
      var h = $height;

      var linksByOrigin = {};
      var countByAirport = {};
      var locationByAirport = {};
      var positions = [];

      var projection = d3.geo.azimuthal()
          .mode("equidistant")
          .origin([-98, 38])
          .scale(1400)
          .translate([640, 360]);

      var path = d3.geo.path()
          .projection(projection);

      var svg = d3.select("body")
          .insert("svg:svg", "h2")
          .attr("width", w)
          .attr("height", h);

      var states = svg.append("svg:g")
          .attr("id", "states");

      var circles = svg.append("svg:g")
          .attr("id", "circles");

      var cells = svg.append("svg:g")
          .attr("id", "cells");

      var arc = d3.geo.greatArc()
          .source(function(d) { return locationByAirport[d.source]; })
          .target(function(d) { return locationByAirport[d.target]; });
```

```
d3.select("input[type=checkbox]").on("change", function() {
  cells.classed("voronoi", this.checked);
});

// Draw US map.
d3.json("https://mbostock.github.io/d3/talk/20111116/us-states.json",
function(collection) {
    states.selectAll("path")
      .data(collection.features)
      .enter().append("svg:path")
      .attr("d", path);
});

// Parse links
graph.links.forEach(function(link) {
  var origin = graph.nodes[link.source].name;
  var destination = graph.nodes[link.target].name;

  var links = linksByOrigin[origin] || (linksByOrigin[origin] = []);
  links.push({ source: origin, target: destination });

  countByAirport[origin] = (countByAirport[origin] || 0) + 1;
  countByAirport[destination] = (countByAirport[destination] || 0) +
1;
});

d3.csv("https://mbostock.github.io/d3/talk/20111116/airports.csv",
function(data) {

// Build list of airports.
var airports = graph.nodes.map(function(node) {
  return data.find(function(airport) {
    if (airport.iata === node.name) {
      var location = [+airport.longitude, +airport.latitude];
      locationByAirport[airport.iata] = location;
      positions.push(projection(location));

      return true;
    } else {
      return false;
    }
  });
});

// Compute the Voronoi diagram of airports' projected positions.
var polygons = d3.geom.voronoi(positions);

var g = cells.selectAll("g")
```

```
          .data(airports)
          .enter().append("svg:g");

      g.append("svg:path")
        .attr("class", "cell")
        .attr("d", function(d, i) { return "M" + polygons[i].join("L") +
"Z"; })
        .on("mouseover", function(d, i) { d3.select("h2
span").text(d.name); });

      g.selectAll("path.arc")
        .data(function(d) { return linksByOrigin[d.iata] || []; })
        .enter().append("svg:path")
        .attr("class", "arc")
        .attr("d", function(d) { return path(arc(d)); });

      circles.selectAll("circle")
        .data(airports)
        .enter().append("svg:circle")
        .attr("cx", function(d, i) { return positions[i][0]; })
        .attr("cy", function(d, i) { return positions[i][1]; })
        .attr("r", function(d, i) { return
Math.sqrt(countByAirport[d.iata]); })
        .sort(function(a, b) { return countByAirport[b.iata] -
countByAirport[a.iata]; });
      });
    </script>
  </body>
</html>""")
  }

  def help() = {
displayHTML("""
<p>
Produces a force-directed graph given a collection of edges of the
following form:</br>
<tt><font color="#a71d5d">case class</font> <font
color="#795da3">Edge</font>(<font color="#ed6a43">src</font>: <font
color="#a71d5d">String</font>, <font color="#ed6a43">dest</font>: <font
color="#a71d5d">String</font>, <font color="#ed6a43">count</font>: <font
color="#a71d5d">Long</font>)</tt>
</p>
<p>Usage:<br/>
<tt>%scala</tt></br>
<tt><font color="#a71d5d">import</font> <font
color="#ed6a43">d3._</font></tt><br/>
<tt><font color="#795da3">graphs.force</font>(</br>
  <font color="#ed6a43">height</font> = <font
```

```
color="#795da3">500</font>,<br/>
  <font color="#ed6a43">width</font> = <font
color="#795da3">500</font>,<br/>
  <font color="#ed6a43">clicks</font>: <font
color="#795da3">Dataset</font>[<font color="#795da3">Edge</font>])</tt>
</p>""")
  }
}
```

In the next cell, you will call the following Scala cell:

```scala
%scala
// On-time and Early Arrivals
import d3a._
graphs.force(
 height = 800,
 width = 1200,
 clicks = sql("""select src, dst as dest, count(1) as count from
deptsDelays_GEO where delay <= 0 group by src, dst""").as[Edge])
```

Which results in the following visualization:

How it works...

As we're using a Databricks notebook, even though its default language is Python, we can specify Scala by using %scala as the first line within a cell. The first code snippet refers to package d3a, which specifies the JavaScript calls that define our airport visualization. As you dive into the code, you'll notice that this is a force-directed graph (def force) visualization that shows a graph (show graph) that builds up the map of the US and location of the airports (blue bubbles).

The force function has the following definition:

```
def force(clicks: Dataset[Edge], height: Int = 100, width: Int = 960): Unit
= {
  ...
  showGraph(height, width, Seq(Graph(nodes, links)).toDF().toJSON.first())
}
```

Recall that we call this function in the next cell using the following code snippet:

```
%scala
// On-time and Early Arrivals
import d3a._
graphs.force(
  height = 800,
  width = 1200,
  clicks = sql("""select src, dst as dest, count(1) as count from
deptsDelays_GEO where delay <= 0 group by src, dst""").as[Edge])
```

The height and width are readily apparent, but the key call out is that we use a Spark SQL query against the deptsDelays_GEO DataFrame to define the edges (that is, the source and destination IATA codes). As the IATA codes are already defined within the calls within showGraph, we already have the vertices of our visualization. Note that as we had already created the DataFrame deptsDelays_GEO, even though it was created using PySpark, it is accessible by Scala within the same Databricks notebook.

Index

R

R
  installing 15
  reference 15
random forest classifier
  forest coverage types, predicting 232, 233, 235,
  236
random forest regression model
  forest elevation, estimating 236, 237, 238, 239
RDD actions
  .collect() action 82
  .count() action 83
  .reduce(...) action 82
  .saveAsTextFile(...) action 83
  .take(...) action 81
  implementing 84, 85, 86, 87
  overview 80, 81
RDD transformations
  .distinct() transformation 69
  .filter(...) transformation 68
  .flatMap(...) transformation 69
  .join(...) transformation 70
  .map(...) transformation 68
  .mapPartitionsWithIndex(...) transformation 75
  .reduceByKey(...) transformation 72
  .repartition(...) transformation 71
  .sample(...) transformation 70
  .sortByKey(...) transformation 73
  .union(...) transformation 74
  .zipWithIndex() transformation 71
  implementing 76, 77, 78, 79
  overview 66, 67
  reference 67
Receiver Operating Characteristics (ROC) 207
redirection pipes
  reference 34
reflection
  schema, inferring 110, 111, 112
regression metrics
  reference 238
regression
  about 185
  AFTSurvivalRegression 219
  DecisionTreeRegressor 219

GBTRegressor 219
GeneralizedLinearRegression 219
IsotonicRegression 219
LinearRegression 219
RandomForestRegressor 219
Resilient Distributed Datasets (RDDs)
  .take(...) method 60
  about 57
  accessing 103, 104, 105
  creating 58, 59
  creating, for training 194, 196, 197
  for classification 195
  for regression 195
  pitfalls 88, 89, 91, 92, 94
  Spark context parallelize method 59

S

Scala
  installing 15
schema
  inferring, with reflection 110, 111, 112
  reference 112, 115
  specifying, programmatically 113, 114, 115
silhouette metrics
  reference 242
skip-gram model
  reference 250
Spark DataFrame 98
Spark Streaming Context (SSC) 261
Spark Streaming
  about 260, 261
  console application, creating 265, 267
  Netcat window, using 263
  PySpark Streaming application, creating 263,
  265
  reference 263
Spark
  about 7
  features 8
  installing, from binaries 24, 25
  installing, from sources 17, 18, 19, 20, 21, 22,
  23
  Java, installing 14
  local instance, configuring 27, 29
  Maven, installing 16

CPSIA information can be obtained
at www.ICGtesting.com
Printed in the USA
LVHW040002041218
599174LV00007B/38/P

9 781788 835367